SECOND OPINION

8 DEADLY DISEASES

WESTERN MEDICINE | EASTERN MEDICINE | YOU POWER

TOGETHER THEY COULD SAVE YOUR LIFE

SECOND OPINION

8 DEADLY DISEASES

WESTERN MEDICINE | EASTERN MEDICINE | YOU POWER

TOGETHER THEY COULD SAVE YOUR LIFE

RADHA GOPALAN, MD

CARDIOLOGIST | ACUPUNCTURIST | CERTIFIED YOGA INSTRUCTOR

PLATA®
PUBLISHING

Published by Plata Publishing LLC
The H-I Triangle and You Power are registered trademarks of Healthy Human LLC.

Plata Publishing LLC
4330 N. Civic Center Plaza
Suite 100
Scottsdale, AZ 85251
480-998-6971

Visit our Web sites:
        PlataPublishing.com
        HealthyHuman.us
        CuraPersonalis.us

Printed in the United States of America

First Edition: January 2016

ISBN: 978-1-612680-23-1

012016

DEDICATION

This book is dedicated to
everyone who strives for improved health.

Who Should Read this Book — and Why

And why this book was written

This book was written to help you navigate the often complex and confusing world of health care, medicine, and human interactions within this world and to empower you in a lifelong journey of good health and avoidance of disease.

It offers not only a contextual framework that is essential to understanding where we, as humans—equipped with the most amazing and resilient bodies—fit into the big picture of health, wellness, disease, and health care. This book chronicles my observations and experiences over 30 years in the medical field as a doctor, patient, and fellow human being.

As with most good books, there's a story behind this book...

Why this book was written

Thirty years in the field of medicine has allowed me to witness tremendous advances in medicine. Organ transplants are providing patients with a second chance at life. Mechanical devices such as total artificial hearts and heart-assist devices are helping people to live longer and enjoy an enhanced quality of life. Technology—from high-tech imaging devices to the da Vinci® robotic Surgery System—has created a new normal for how we assess and address disease. Improvements in treatment options for cancer are progressing at a rapid pace. Stem cell research is making tremendous strides.

One could easily claim that the most significant medical advancements have been made in the field of cardiology. Yet, heart disease is still the #1 killer in the world.

Something is still not right. Despite all the therapies and treatments that we have to offer patients, they still struggle with illness and disease. The negative aspects of the burden of disease continue to far outweigh the positive outcomes that patients experience. Patients and healthy people alike continue to be frustrated, unhappy, and confused as they struggle with issues related to health and where to turn for answers, advice, and guidance.

This dilemma has prompted me to ask myself the same questions over and over again: *Are we focusing on the wrong aspects of our health and wellness resources to accomplish our goals of improved health, quality of life, and long life?* And *What are we missing…?*

Here are a few of my personal observations that I believe that individual patients—you and me—need to be made aware of and empowered to address:

- Western medicine alone did not make anyone healthy.
- Eastern medicine alone did not make anyone healthy.
- Patients made themselves healthy or unhealthy.
- Disease did not start at the physical level. It started at a level deeper than the physical level, but manifested at the physical level.
- Patients did not have any control over their care when they became ill or got admitted to the hospital.
- What is best for the patient is not the interest of the collective health care system.
- Patients kept coming back for treatment for the same illnesses—even when they were receiving the best available treatment.
- Physicians did not heal patients…patients healed themselves.
- When patients became powerless, they lost their life.

There are only three players in this game. The patients, the physicians, and the framework of the system under which the care is provided. Physicians and the health care system are working hard to enhance their outcomes. Patients, on the other hand, are simply relying on "the system" for their health. Isn't it time that patients and healthy people concerned with maintaining their health and wellness get empowered?

Who should read this book

This book was written for healthy people—as well as those who are struggling with illness or disease. It is a guide for people who are not ill and who want to maintain their good health.

Over the past three decades, I have observed three groups of people in the field of health, disease, and medicine. The first group is made up of those who are healthy, and who want to proactively maintain a healthy status. The second group consists of those who are ill but are helped, to some extent, by Western medicine. This group continues to struggle and is not optimizing all the resources that are available to them to improve their quality of life, both physically and mentally. The third group consists of those who are ill and for whom Western medicine is unable to offer robust therapy.

Whether you are among those who are proactively making health a priority in their lives or fighting the battle of your life against cancer or heart disease, this book was written for you. It is my intention to make readers aware of the multitude of choices we humans have in how we address heath, wellness, and disease and empower them to make well-informed choices in their lives.

Why you should read this book

Schools do not teach us much about health or disease. Nor are we taught much about it at home, from parents or grandparents who may have faced health challenges or fought illness or disease because *they* were never taught about health. And doctors do not really teach us about health and disease. Doctors simply tell us what to do and most often that doesn't happen until we're faced with disease or illness.

We learn to navigate health and disease as we go along without a proper understanding of the entire landscape...and we hope for the best. The experiences shared in this book as second opinions will assist you in building a framework within which you can successfully take control of your own health.

This book is not a prescription. It is not written for Western medical practitioners or Eastern medical practitioners. It is written for you... someone who is interested in taking control of his or her own health to live a rich, healthy, and happy life.

"A wise man should consider that health is the greatest of human blessings, and learn how by his own thought to derive benefit from his illnesses."

—Hippocrates

The Rich Life Series of Books and The Rich Dad Company

because a **Rich Life**
is about **More than Money**

"Like those whom I teach, I am learning and growing,
too. I recognize that finding true happiness means
expanding beyond a mission of financial well-being to a
mission of complete well-being: in health and wellness,
spiritual awakening, philanthropy, and purpose.
In essence, a Rich Life."

– Robert Kiyosaki, author of
Rich Dad Poor Dad
in an excerpt from
I Am The Rich Dad Company

Acknowledgments

No task is ever accomplished by a single person. This book would not have been possible without the convergence of energy of several people at different points in my life. Numerous people have contributed to the accumulation of knowledge that has resulted in this book, and all of them deserve acknowledgment. While I am grateful to all of those who contributed to my base of knowledge, I have limited these acknowledgments to the people who had a direct connection to the successful completion of this book. The following expressions of appreciation are stated in chronological order.

I am very grateful to all of my patients who taught me lessons on life and death, and the relationship of health and disease related to Western medicine, Eastern medicine, and personality. I acknowledge and thank my parents for allowing me the independence to learn life freely without constraints of religion, culture, ethnicity or citizenship, and for accepting me for who I am—at every point in my life—without judgment. To my late brother, and my sister for their continued support. To my Yoga master in Sri Lanka for the lessons on the Yogic way of life. To my late Acupuncture Professor, Dr. Anton Jayasooriya for introducing me to the dualism of Acupuncture philosophy and for teaching me to look at both sides of a coin before taking action. To the late Mr. Narayana Panikar for the countless hours of extensive discussion on Yoga and meditation during my medical school training in Sri Lanka. To my good friend Dr. Ravi Ponniah for the many hours we spent in hotel lounges in London discussing health, disease, constitutional make-up, and complementary medicines over more than a few cups of tea.

To my friend, colleague, and Professor, Dr. Jagat Narula for guiding me to train in heart transplant which enabled the priceless observations of hundreds of patients from whom the insightful information in this book was drawn. To Diane Kasper and Carol Bachtel, two seasoned and gifted transplant coordinators, for sharing their personal experiences on the matters of life, death, health, and disease.

This book would not have come to fruition without the guidance and support of my good friends Robert and Kim Kiyosaki. Their confidence in me has fueled my relentless pursuit of this book to its completion.

I am forever indebted to Nicole Srednicki, FNP, for her enthusiasm, encouragement, and support and for her unwavering belief in me throughout the entire process of this book. From the early development stages through the celebration of its release, she has been steadfast in her editorial support and in working through the book's revisions. My thanks to Julie and Michael Srednicki for their input on the flow of the book's chapters and messages. To Virginia Marshall for believing in me and for the positive encouragement she offered. To Karen Strickland for her input on the importance, relevance, flow of material, and contents of the book. To each and every member of the Rich Dad Advisors for their time and effort in reading this book and for providing candid feedback on its structure and content.

I am grateful to Plata Publishing and Mona Gambetta for helping to transition this material from my desktop computer to the hands of readers around the world.

Finally, I am very appreciative of my two wonderful children, Spencer and Brooke, for graciously allowing me to use some of our time together for writing this book.

Table of Contents

Foreword

by Robert Kiyosaki

A Second Opinion

My mom was a registered nurse. She had rheumatic fever while I was in her womb. One of the doctors went so far as to suggest an abortion, to save her life. They did not think her heart was strong enough to carry me through childbirth. I'm thankful that mom and dad refused.

I came into the world with a congenital birth defect, a murmur in my heart, due to my mom's rheumatic fever. The doctors suggested my mom and dad keep me out of strenuous sports. I'm glad my mom did not listen to our doctor's advice.

Although I was a bit weak, I began playing football and baseball at the age of seven and played through college. I captained my football team in high school and my rowing team at the Merchant Marine Academy. I also played rugby internationally, until in my mid 30s.

While I was in high school, I received two Congressional nominations, one to the U.S. Naval Academy at Annapolis in Maryland, and another to the U.S. Merchant Marine Academy, at Kings Point in New York.

Once again, I was told not to get my hopes up too high. My family doctor said, "If the medical examiner detects your heart defect, you won't get into either Academy."

I was flown from my little town of Hilo, Hawaii to Honolulu, and went through a three-day battery of tests at Tripler Army Hospital. Somehow, I got through the medical exams and was awarded an appointment to Kings Point. At the Academy, I continued to row and play varsity football, both extremely strenuous sports.

Upon graduation, in 1969, I volunteered for the U.S. Marine Corps and applied for pilot training. Again, I went through an intense round of medical exams and stress tests—the whole time expecting to be told that my heart defect would disqualify me. Although I crashed my helicopter three times while in Vietnam, my heart kept ticking, functioning perfectly, even under horrific fear, terror, and stress.

I returned to the states in 1973 and became an entrepreneur, another very stressful profession.

By 2005, I knew something was wrong. I could not fool myself, or the doctors, any longer. I was breathing okay, but my heart was struggling. I was 58 years old and all my weak points were becoming more evident.

Every cardiologist I consulted said the same thing: My heart was oversized. I had pushed it too hard. Something had to be done—and soon.

The problem was I did not like any of the cardiologists.

Eventually, I went to the "most respected, big-name" cardiologist in Phoenix. He was the worst. It was, by far, one of the worst medical experiences of my life. My wife Kim and I went into the waiting room at 8 a.m. and I did not see him until 6 p.m. It was a cold, inhumane 10 hours as I went through test after test, not talking with anyone. No one wanted to answer our questions. They were too busy.

Finally, the world famous doctor saw me for about 10 minutes. With Kim sitting next to me, and without a "hello" or a handshake, he said, "You are in trouble. Do not go home. I suggest you check yourself in tonight and I will operate in the morning."

When Kim asked why, his message was simple and direct: "Your heart cannot take anymore stress. You are critical. You could collapse walking out the door."

We felt like we were in the office of a used car salesman and his sales manager, pressuring us to "buy now."

Assuming he had made the sale, the world-renowned cardiologist left the office and "the closer," the business manager, came in. Again, without a "hello" or a handshake, this "closer" began by saying, "May I have your insurance card?"

While "the closer" was busy filling out the paperwork, Kim and I stepped out of the room and went home, never to return.

For about six months, I went from cardiologist to cardiologist, looking for someone I could talk to. While most were pleasant and (I assumed) competent, I found that most were cold, sterile, and too busy to give me much time. I went through test after test, racking up huge expenses, but not learning much.

Finally, I gave up and randomly chose a cardiologist who lived in San Francisco. I made my decision by looking at his pictures on his website. By this time, I did not care who did the surgery. I just wanted to get it over with.

As luck would have it, a friend from Pennsylvania who is a chiropractor was in Phoenix. When I told him of my decision, he got a bit hysterical. He could not believe I would let someone I did not know, did not trust, (and possibly would not like) operate on me. He kept mumbling about the importance of the relationship between patient and doctor. He kept saying, "You must be aligned spiritually and philosophically with your doctor."

I had no idea what he was talking about. I asked him, "Why would I need to be spiritually and philosophically aligned to my doctor?"

Looking at me in disbelief, he said, "Because that is where healing takes place. Healing is not physical. Healing is spiritual—because health is spiritual. Health is life and God gives you life. Not doctors." He went on to say: "You must give your spirit a chance to heal you. Your doctor may be a good person, but if he is not aligned with you spiritually, he could kill you."

"Cancel San Francisco," he demanded. "Give me some time to find a cardiologist who is aligned with you—spiritually, philosophically, and physically." His search for the perfect cardiologist began.

This gave me time to reflect upon my mom and dad and their beliefs about doctors. I thought about their spiritual and philosophical beliefs about life, health, and healing.

My mom was a registered nurse, a surgical nurse, who spent most of her time in operating rooms. She grew to be distrustful of doctors. The longer she was a nurse, the more she searched for other answers, for second opinions outside of traditional medicine. Her search led her into alternative practices, chiropractors, naturopathic doctors, as well as spiritual healers. Obviously, she had to keep her personal beliefs to herself when she was on duty at the hospital.

My Second Opinion

As I waited for my chiropractor friend to find the perfect cardiologist for me, I had the time to examine my beliefs on health, medicine, life, and spirituality. The more I thought about it, the more I realized my friend was correct. We are all different. We all have different beliefs and it's important to find doctors who are in alignment with our beliefs. That is where health and healing begins.

Finally my chiropractor friend called and said, "I've found him."

"Where is he?" I asked.

"You won't believe this," he said. "I called my friend in London and asked for his recommendation on the best cardiologist in the world. I told him that you would go anywhere. My friend in London laughed and said, "You won't believe this. The best cardiologist in the world trained with me in London—and just moved to Phoenix."

And that's how I met Dr. Radha Gopalan.

I walked into his office in Phoenix and the bond was instantaneous. It was like old souls meeting. And I knew I had found my doctor.

Radha has become a great friend and advisor on more than health. His views on the spirit, healing, and vital energy have changed my life for the better. When we talk, we start with spiritual health, long before we discuss physical health.

He is an advisor to my Rich Dad Advisors, often speaking to us about the power of spirit, life...and then health. He is our advisor because health and wealth are closely related. Both are spiritual.

My mom passed away in 1971. Her heart finally gave out. She was only 48 years old.

I know her greatest joy, her greatest happiness came from giving her children life. I have three younger brothers and sisters, all healthy, and all thankful for our lives knowing that she risked hers for us.

This may sound corny to some people, but I believe it was her spirit that guided me to Radha, a healer who would save my life, spiritually as well as physically.

Who is Dr. Radha Gopalan?

It was not until after my surgery and recovery that I got to know Radha. We became very good friends as he began teaching me the Eastern medicine side of health. Although I am Asian and of Japanese ancestry, the learning process has not been easy. Being fourth generation American, much of my Asian culture has been lost.

Radha succeeded in teaching me to meditate. It was not easy. I have a hard time meditating. My mind won't shut off. Teaching me Yoga was also difficult. My body is no longer Asian. I grew up playing football. I was a six-foot-tall, 235-pound lineman in high school. My body is not flexible. I have no "moves." I only know how to block and run—so holding Yoga poses was more painful than playing football.

As Radha worked with me as a teacher and as I learned more about him as a person, I began to realize he was no ordinary doctor. He has come a very long way from a tiny village in Sri Lanka, a journey he describes in this book.

Today, Radha's position as a heart transplant cardiologist puts him in a unique position amongst other doctors. Whenever a patient requires organ transplant surgery—be it a heart, liver, kidney, lungs, or bone marrow transplant—the patient's doctor comes to Dr. Gopalan for a second opinion. It is up to Radha to decide if the other doctor's patient is a viable candidate for organ transplant surgery. In other words: Is the patient worthy of such a gift, a viable candidate for a miracle of modern medicine? It is much like lawyers, going before a judge, seeking the judge's opinion on behalf of their client.

From his unique position, Radha has viewed the world of medicine, doctors, patients, disease, and health...all filtered through a mind trained in the disciplines of both Eastern and Western medical philosophies. It is his opinion—as a *second opinion*—that often determines the life or death of another doctor's patient.

After getting to know Dr. Gopalan, first as a doctor and then as a friend, I encouraged him to write this book and tell us what he sees, what he knows, what he thinks about when he counsels and treats patients and consults with other doctors—as both an Eastern and Western doctor—before he offers his second opinion. I wanted him to share with you, as he has with me, his experience and insights and his belief that we—ourselves—have power to influence our health and wellness.

This book is not for Western or Eastern doctors. This book is for people like you and me, ordinary people who simply want to enjoy the blessings of better health.

Preface

Second Opinion is the first of several books I will write, books that are a result of a lifetime of experiences—as a human being, a doctor, *and* a patient. My study of medicine, both Eastern and Western, has taken me to cities around the world in pursuit of experience, education, and a deeper understanding of the human condition related to health, wellness, and disease.

As a cardiologist and medical consultant who evaluates transplant candidates for every type of organ transplant surgery imaginable, I have been exposed to many and varied medical situations. Situations in which a person's life hangs in the balance. And while medicine, both Eastern and Western, plays a role in how a person's life unfolds, I have become more and more certain with each passing year that our You Power, the power that each of us possesses that enables us to direct and impact every facet of our lives, is an untapped resource. And, quite possibly, our most powerful resource in winning the game of good health and long life.

My story began in Sri Lanka, a small island country off the southern coast of India, and my early exposure to various traditions and philosophies shaped not only the man I became, but challenged my inquisitive mind and triggered a lifelong search for knowledge and answers.

My Story

Sri Lanka

When I was growing up in Sri Lanka, every Saturday was a day of the oil bath. It was also a day for a special meal. Like any child, after five days of school, I always looked forward to the weekend. But my exhilaration at the prospect of the special meal was diminished by the dislike I had for the oil bath.

Going through the process for the oil bath was unpleasant. The entire oil bath process took about two to three hours to complete. In addition, there was a waiting period of one to two hours after the oil was applied and before the bath was taken. There was nothing to do during this time, other than wait patiently for the time to pass. Fortunately, the oil bath carried another aspect that I grew to love—even thought I did not like it at that time. It was massage as part of the process of applying the oil. Even today, massage is a part of my wellness regimen.

I grew up on a tiny island off of the northern tip of Sri Lanka in the tradition of Ayurveda, as it was practiced at that time. Ayurveda is a system of traditional Hindu medicine native to the Indian subcontinent and many of the Ayurveda traditions are the foundations for alternative medicine. And while my thinking and lifestyle changed as I moved West, my experience with the Ayurveda teaching and practices provided the foundation for my understanding of the Eastern medical philosophy. Growing up in Ayurvedic tradition provided the depth of understanding to recognize significant differences between Eastern and Western medicine and would color, forever, how I would view health, wellness, and health care.

My first memory of the Saturday rituals goes back to age six. A local medicine man, we called him "Konnun" (not a medical doctor, although there were medical doctors in the village), came to our house once a week on Saturdays for the sole purpose of giving me an olive oil massage. That was the most pleasant part of the day. The massage was followed by the application of sesame oil to my head, waiting for an hour or two for the oils to soak into my body, and then exfoliating my skin. A drop of sesame oil was also applied to each eye, which resulted in profound tearing—a process my mother called cleansing of the eyes and tear ducts to ensure eye health and proper vision. Traditional soap, although available, was not used for cleansing the skin of the oils.

By the time the bath was finished, our freshly cooked lunch would be ready. We were non-vegetarians. Fresh seafood delivered daily in the island village was a staple at mealtime. But Saturdays and Sundays were different, with either chicken or lamb prepared as a special meal. This special Saturday meal of chicken or lamb was the second pleasant event of the day and one that I always looked forward to. The meal was followed by a short afternoon siesta and then play time with friends in the village.

I was, however, prohibited from playing strenuous games, as proper rest to rebalance my body's energy was emphasized after the massage and oil bath. The siesta and play was the third pleasant event of the day. The day would end with dinner and early bedtime.

Almost every month, one weekend was reserved for bowel cleansing. An Ayurvedic concoction that was so bitter (I used to throw up most of the time!) was ingested in the morning on an empty stomach. The rest of the day was spent fasting and only hot, black tea was consumed. The concoction induced diarrhea or bowel purging throughout the day. The lost fluid was replaced with only hot tea and water. No solid food was allowed that day until the diarrhea had subsided, which was usually close to dinnertime.

In another cleaning ritual, hydrogen peroxide was used to clean both ears every few weeks. This was a very pleasant activity as the peroxide bubbled up in the ear, and created a nice tingling sensation that I looked forward to. A Neti pot—a ceramic or plastic pot that looks like a cross between a small teapot and Aladdin's magic lamp and invokes the Ayurvedic traditions—is used to clean the nostrils and open the sinuses. I never used a Neti pot as a child because I hated the thought of putting water up my nostrils.

Although I was introduced to Yoga at the age of nine, I did not begin regular practice until I was 17 years old. As a child I was more involved in athletics and sports like track and field, soccer, and cricket. At 17, I was introduced to the autobiography of Mahatma Gandhi. His self experiments with regard to health, wellness, non-violence, and the Yogic way of life inspired me to take up Yoga again. Yoga and Yogic breathing are meant to invigorate the lungs and the musculoskeletal system. But, more importantly, it's useful as a way to unite the body and mind. I joined an Ashram to learn Hatha Yoga and meditation. During the process, I was exposed to mindfulness, Hinduism, and Ayurvedic life in great depth and detail. Yoga and meditation became part of my life and in 2001 I became a certified Yoga teacher. Through the practice and study of Yoga, I was able to develop a method that I call "dynamic stillness." It is a two-step process. First is an ability to quiet the mind while everything else around you is chaotic. In other words, you are internally still in dynamic world surroundings. Taking this further in a second step, you maintain this stillness of your mind even when you, yourself, are actively involved in doing some task like cleaning, walking, running, or eating.

Life in Sri Lanka was simple and close to nature. Our family raised cows, goats, and chickens in the backyard. All the milk that was consumed by our family came from our own animals that fed on green grass and hay. The chicken (for Saturdays!) and the daily eggs came from our own free-range flock of chickens. Fruit was abundant. There were fruit trees everywhere! Orange, lime, banana, mango, papaya, pomegranate, and coconut trees flourished in our backyard and provided a wide variety of fresh fruit for the family. Other vegetables and fruits were bought from other villagers who raised them. Rice, our staple food, came from our own paddy fields where the grain was harvested, chemical-free, twice a year. My grandparents lived with us and were cared for by the family. I grew up with a comforting sense of community, where everyone shared food and essential household items and practiced faith on a regular basis.

Wholesome organic foods, regular exercise in the form of daily activity, eating smaller quantities of meat, eating less in general, reveling in a sense of community and belonging, afternoon siestas, and taking care of parents and grandparents were all part of the way of life during my early years in Sri Lanka.

At the first sign of illness, or even when someone was just feeling "under the weather," we were ordered to rest. Resting was a way to conserve vital energy and concentrate the energy on overcoming the offending energy or agent—even if the "offender" is unknown. Even a fever was treated with rest, plenty of warm fluids, and fasting or consumption of only light foods. The overarching idea, in this case, was to avoid spending vital energy on digesting heavy food. Only when the illness persisted was medical advice sought.

Persistence is interpreted as the offending energy or agent being either equally powerful or more powerful than the body's internal healing vital energy and its ability to overcome the offending energy or agent.

My parents relied upon their judgment in recognizing and treating the state of transition from health to ill health.

I played a lot of soccer as a child, and I played barefoot. Every time I sprained my ankle playing soccer, Konnun would come to the house and I would get an Ayurvedic paste applied around my ankle that would immobilize the joint and absorb the swelling. I'm sure I sprained my ankles at least 15 times during my childhood! And not a single time did I go to the hospital for treatment.

On the other hand, I did go to the hospital for other serious febrile illnesses that did *not* get better with the traditional efforts. It was as if people inherently knew what modality, what type of treatment, to seek. The important point is that my parents never ignored symptoms or the transition from health to ill health. They recognized the subtle changes and sought medical advice—either from a traditional practitioner if the changes were subtle or a medical doctor when they felt the vital energy was being overwhelmed by the adverse energy. They knew how to combine Eastern and Western medical therapies either through explicit knowledge or intuition.

Which brings me to an interesting point...

In my current practice, patients and colleagues alike constantly ask me: Is it possible to combine East and West medicines?

There is a notion that Eastern and Western medicines are mutually exclusive. They are not.

They simply target *different aspects* of the same problem. They are like two sides of a same coin. This book will explore in detail innovative and key aspects of health and wellness from both philosophies.

It was a staggering realization to learn that people in developed countries have paid as much as $4,000 (U.S.) to spend a weekend learning the principles of the way of life that I just described —and lived...for the first 27 years of my life. In an underdeveloped country like Sri Lanka, these principles are lived daily and the traditions and practices are handed down from generation to generation. The villagers are happy to teach anyone their traditions—even strangers, free of charge. And while I have moved on from the ways of life of my childhood and rural Sri Lanka, I have preserved and utilized most of these principles as alternative points of view.

At that young age, I admired Konnun and wondered how he preformed the magic of making me feel better...how he knew what would "do the trick" related to treatment and healing. The reason was simple: I wanted to know it myself. Whenever I got the chance I would spend time at his practice and watch him treat people. Little did I know at that time that he did not make anybody feel better. It was their own bodies—those magical, miraculous healing machines—that had the capacity to heal themselves. Later, at age nine, the idea of wanting to become a physician had galvanized in my mind after meeting my uncle who was an ear, nose, and throat (ENT) surgeon in Singapore. Since then, my intention was steadily focused on becoming a physician. I continued with the traditional, Ayurvedic wellness-oriented way of living until my attention was forced to focus on the *science of disease*...and that happened when I entered medical school.

My medical education in Sri Lanka, started in 1984, but was abruptly cut short after three years when the universities closed due to the civil unrest. When that door closed, another door opened: I was given an opportunity to spend the next two years at an Acupuncture institute to become an Acupuncturist. I first learned the Chinese philosophy and techniques of Acupuncture and then taught Acupuncture as an instructor at that institute.

In January of 1990, I left Sri Lanka to complete my medical education and over the next three years I studied in London, New York, and Grenada in the West Indies. By that time, I had spent nine years as a medical student in four different countries and had been exposed to not only Western medicine but also to Ayurveda, Homeopathy, Spinal Manipulation, Herbal Remedies, and Acupuncture. And although born into the Hindu religion, during these nine years, I also had the opportunity to learn about Buddhism, Buddhist meditation, and Christianity as part of CCC's (Campus Crusade for Christianity) Bible study group with one of my closest friends.

As a result of these experiences and exposure I began to see a disturbing pattern emerge. It did not matter whether I was in the Far East (Sri Lanka), Europe and the United Kingdom (London), the West Indies (Grenada), or North America (New York)—nor did it matter whether Eastern or Western medicine was prescribed to a patient...the pattern I saw was consistent. ***Almost all patients kept coming back to the hospitals or to the practitioners with the same, recurrent problems.*** Age, race, religious faith... made no difference. It seemed as though this was a universal "truth" and I struggled with how this could happen—and why.

If medicine worked, I told myself, patients should *not* keep coming back for treatment of recurrent problems. And these experiences pointed to a problem that transcended religion, race, culture, geographic location—and medicine.

There are only two groups of players in this game: The patients and the physicians who use medicine as the tool. Either the medicine did not do something right or the patient did not do something right.

It had to be one or the other. This thought, this conundrum, nagged at me throughout my training and motivated me to keenly observe my patients throughout my career.

The United Kingdom

London is where I was able to build a bridge between what I understood about wellness from Eastern philosophies and what I understood about diseases from Western medical school. While in medical school, I chose to do part of my clinical rotations in the United Kingdom and part in the United States. After completing these clinical rotations, I had six months left before my graduation. I went back to London.

My intention of spending a few months in London extended into a total of two years of internship with my good friend Dr. Ravi Ponniah, an alternative medicine practitioner. I had met Ravi in Sri Lanka at the Acupuncture university where he visited each year to lecture on the subjects of Iridology (analysis of the iris to identify weaknesses related to one's health) and homeopathy. He practiced Iridology, Acupuncture, Homeopathy, Herbal medicine, and Osteopathic manipulation.

While working as an acupuncturist at Ravi's clinic, I was exposed to two groups of patients. Both groups of patients were frustrated with the health system in the UK. The first group of patients was frustrated with the absence of natural treatments to maintain health in their health system. These patients had no disease but wanted to proactively maintain their health and wellness. The second group was frustrated with the absence of treatments to cure their diseases in their health system. This second group of patients was told by Western medical practitioners that there was no cure, in Western medicine, for their illness.

As I watched the second group of patients go through the treatments, I noticed changes in them and an evolution—not only with regard to their illnesses, but also who they were. I saw that they were becoming happier people. Their illness got better, even though it may not have been cured completely. They became more adept at managing and finding a new equilibrium in their lives. The first group of people (those who had no disease) articulated that they were able to better manage their life stressors and maintain their equilibrium and happiness. This proactive effort, they told me, helped them to achieve the best performance they could in their daily life. Most of the patients in the first group were professionals, artists, performance artists, musicians, and dancers.

The notion of equilibrium as the cornerstone of health—a concept I learned from Acupuncture philosophy—became a living reality in those patients. Both groups of patients referred to improved equilibrium: The first group related to better maintenance of the equilibrium they had already achieved with Eastern modalities and the second group in finding a new equilibrium during an illness with the use of Eastern modalities.

I inherently knew that there was *another* group of patients—a group in between the two sets I just described. I had just finished observing this third group of patients in the hospitals during my training as a medical student. This third group of patients had diseases for which Western medicine was able to offer a treatment to help with the symptoms of their illness, prescribe medications, and give recommendations to prevent recurrence. Western medicine helped this third group of patients to get rid of the symptoms by treating the disease, but did not help to establish or strengthen their equilibrium by treating them as people. Finally, I understood that Eastern and Western modalities were *not* opposed...but were simply two sides of the same coin.

Both Eastern and Western disciplines help people move to a state of equilibrium. Western medicine by suppressing the disease, and Eastern medicine by enhancing the body's natural ability to expel the disease. What Western medicine lacks, Eastern medicine offers, and what is lacking in Eastern medicine is completed by Western medicine.

The first group of patients, like my parents, knew what modality (Eastern or Western) to use and when. The second group of patients had no choice but to seek alternative forms of therapy, since Western medicine did not offer any answers. The third group—those in the middle who had an illness or disease and were helped by the Western medicine— continued to suffer from illness because they were not given the tools to find equilibrium.

Ravi suggested that I stay in London and establish a practice in alternative and complementary medicine. His suggestion did not align with my plans and I proceeded to United States to complete the residency training in medicine. At that time I did not fully understand why I wanted to continue my training in Western medicine. Later I came to realize that I was puzzled by the three sets of patients and what my work with them taught me.

I particularly wanted to explore that third group of patients, the group that the Western medicine treatments were able to help. I later realized my reason for this: These patients kept coming back to the physicians with recurrence or continued worsening of their illness. I knew, instinctively, that there was a reason for this.

The United States

I went on to finish my residency in Internal Medicine in New Jersey, followed by a sub-specialty fellowship in Cardiology and two additional sub-sub specialty fellowships in Philadelphia, one in cardiac electrophysiology (heart rhythm disorders) and the other in advanced heart failure and heart transplant. I would practice medicine as a heart transplant cardiologist.

In 2005, I became the director of a heart transplant program and was feeling on top of the world. I had finally reached the pinnacle of my career. That feeling lasted only about 18 months. One fine morning, at the age of 44, I had a heart attack.

A heart attack! How could that be? I grew up in Ayurvedic tradition, exercised regularly, practiced Yoga, followed the same healthy and nutrient-rich diet that I advise to my patients, and had taken homeopathic treatments and Acupuncture treatments for general well-being. I knew what there was to know—about health, wellness, and medicine. And did what needed to be done to prevent an event like a heart attack. I was the specialist in heart attacks and knew virtually everything there was to know about the heart. Yet, I failed miserably—related to *my own* health—while diligently practicing the very things I recommend to my patients.

This triggered a troubling thought: If practicing what I advise my patients did not help me, it probably would not help them either. Why did none of this knowledge and education and experience help *me*? What went wrong?

This life-changing event and my search for answers led me to a fundamental realization: **Having the knowledge and medical experience does not appear to be enough to prevent the development of disease or its recurrence.**

Reflecting on these facts—while laying in a hospital bed in 2006, post-heart attack—revealed the last piece of the puzzle. I finally had some answers to why patients kept coming back with recurrent illness despite being diagnosed and treated with excellent medical therapies. It was at that point that I learned a very important lesson with regard to health and illness.

All along I had concentrated on what I have to do to prevent illness and that was what I advised my patients on a daily basis. But *doing* is not the answer. There is, I discovered, an additional layer to this spectrum:

We become ill not because of what we do or don't do, but because of who we are.

That day I told myself, *It is not what I must do, it is who I must be.*

Years later, I came to the realization that this principle not only applies to health. It can also be applied to success in any aspect of life—career, sports, finances, relationships, and spirituality. This revelation created a new problem: understanding ourselves.

It is difficult to change our self—our being—without understanding the matrix and components of what, precisely, we want to change. I spent the next few years observing and analyzing the components of internal and external human interaction to construct a simplified version of a human interaction matrix that can be easily adapted by anyone.

Five years after I embarked on this path, in 2012, I was introduced to Dr. Robert S. Eliott's work by two of my transplant coordinators. My discussions with them about human health and illness made them think of Dr. Eliott, whom they had worked with in Phoenix, Arizona. As I became more aware of Dr. Eliott's work and read his book, *Is It Worth Dying For?*, I was relieved to find that my independent revelation after my heart attack was not far from his research-based conclusions. The extensive research he had done related to stress and cardiovascular disease lead him to a conclusion similar to mine. In the Introduction of *Is It Worth Dying For?* he writes: "I know now that it's not what you do but *how you do* that counts."

I personally believe that this concept should be taken to the next level and the active emphasis should be placed on *being* rather than on *doing*. In fact, it is expressed in a simplified manner by my good friend Robert Kiyosaki in his financial books as "Be–Do–Have." *Being* leads to *doing* the right things and how you do them, which in turn leads to *having* what you intended to have. So... if the intention is to have a disease, then the same Be–Do–Have pathway will lead to having disease.

It is my belief that we are responsible for—and create or perpetuate—our own illness.

At a time when we can claim tremendous advances in medical technology, availability of new treatments, and improved health care delivery systems the burden of disease continues to increase. Breakthroughs and advances in medicine and technology have definitely impacted the horizon in making people with diseases live longer lives. However, it appears that these outside interventions have not improved the incidence or burden of disease. Despite the wide availability of medical tools and treatments, patients are not only getting ill more frequently but they are also suffering recurrences of either the same illness or developing a new illness.

This compels us to take a look at the person who is afflicted by the disease. As Hippocrates stated centuries ago: *"I would rather know what sort of person has disease than know what sort of disease a person has."*

What follows in this book does just that. It explores ways to understand the *person* in addition to understanding the disease and ways to combine both aspects to achieve better results in maintaining wellness.

This book is titled *Second Opinion*—and it is precisely that. *Second Opinion* represents an additional layer of insights based on patient observations, personal experience, and knowledge of both Eastern and Western health principles.

This book is not a prescription. The information provided will give a framework for understanding and adopting easy-to-understand principles that can enhance your health if you are already healthy or minimize the impact of ill health if you are already ill. This book combines both Eastern and Western medical principles seamlessly, and can be understood and applied whether your feet are firmly planted on the side of East or West... or somewhere in between. More importantly, it provides the contextual framework that is required for you to embark on the journey of who you have to be to achieve health, rather than continually focusing on what you must do.

Take heart: *The fundamental change that occurs when you alter your being will invariably lead to the doing that is required.*

Introduction

Every one of us knows that *disease* is bad and *being healthy* is good. We also know that disease inflicts pain—physically or emotionally— and reduces our chance of a long life. Without exception, all the patients I have seen during my 30 years as a doctor are afraid of dying. They were afraid because their chances of living a little bit longer were rapidly diminishing.

Are you not afraid of dying? Most of us are. And none of us think about dying until a disease is upon us and threatens our very existence.

When we *think* we are healthy, we don't think about the fact that disease may be just around the corner. Disease is something that happens to someone else—but not to us.

Patients who told me that they were not afraid of dying were not being true to themselves; they were in denial that death was imminent. What they were subliminally expressing was that they were either tired of fighting disease or didn't know how to fight it. They felt powerless over disease. They did not feel that the medical world—of which I am part— helped them. They just did not have the energy for the fight. **They had given up on living, because the desire to live is what gives the energy for the fight.**

You fail when you give up or hand over the power over health and disease to someone else. In the process of living and dying, you fail when you hand over the entire power over your life to physicians. I lost my brother to kidney disease because he had given over all of his power to the world of Western medicine—and then gave up on his life when Western medicine did not help him.

Many of you may be thinking, *How can he make these statements? He's a doctor, not a patient, or someone on the brink of death.* Let me tell you my real story.

By the year 2006, at age 44, I had reached a very significant milestone in my career. I was the director of a heart transplant program at a well-respected medical facility. I was feeling on top of the world. Until October 11, 2006, that is. On that eventful day my life changed.

It was 7:00 in the morning, and I was running on a treadmill. I felt a slight discomfort in my chest. I stopped and thought for a few minutes about what it could be. Being a cardiologist, I was aware that discomfort from the heart—called *angina pectoris*—is usually brought on by exertion and is relieved by rest. It is also exacerbated by more exercise. I decided to test this...and continued to exercise. The discomfort went away. The first occurrence of angina is labeled *unstable angina,* indicating that it can progress to a heart attack. It can also wax and wane. Likewise, continued angina without exertion for more than 20 to 30 minutes is also called *unstable angina,* since this can also indicate a possible heart attack. The discomfort came back when I was taking a shower and continued at a relatively low intensity—about a 2 on a scale of 1 to 10, with 0 representing no pain and 10 as the worst pain one has ever experienced.

Since there was no change in the intensity of pain with exertion, I decided to go to work and test myself at the office. This seemed reasonable, since my "office" was a hospital.

The first order of business was to rule out a heart attack. After four hours of continued chest pain, I did an ECG, an Electrocardiogram, which captures the electrical activity of the heart and enables biomedical doctors to diagnose a heart attack or insufficient blood supply to the heart. I also did a blood test to determine if I was, in fact, having a heart attack.

Both tests turned out to be negative. I continued to work through the day with pain that stayed at an intensity of 2 to 3 out of 10.

It wasn't long before fear set in. Not wanting to go home without a diagnosis, I went down to the Emergency Room at about 4:00 pm and talked to the physician about my symptoms. He and I agreed that it did not appear to be angina. We also wanted to rule out acid reflux. I swallowed viscous Lidocaine and waited in the Emergency Room to learn the results. If my condition was acid reflux, then the viscous Lidocaine should have relieved the pain within minutes of swallowing it. But the pain remained!

I admitted myself to the Emergency Room. The tests were repeated and the results were positive for a small heart attack. The on-call cardiologist (a colleague of mine) was not convinced that it was a true heart attack, considering my age. I was 44. He was also factoring in my physical capacity, endurance, and lack of significant predisposing factors. He wanted to monitor the situation until the next morning to see how the condition evolved without any aggressive intervention.

I insisted on an immediate cardiac catheterization, an invasive procedure involving catheters that are placed through a main artery in the groin and advanced to the heart where dye is injected into the blood vessels that supply blood to my heart, to see if there is a blockage. A blocked artery means a heart attack.

The catheterization revealed that one of the three blood vessels to my heart was completely blocked, cutting off the blood supply to the bottom part of my heart. The blood vessel was reopened and two metal tubes were placed inside to hold it open.

I learned a very important lesson that day on life and death, and health and disease...all within a 60-second period while I was in the Emergency Room. As I was lying in bed in the ER, I started having hiccups. I looked up at the heart monitor above my head and saw my heart beating abnormally. It was what I, in my job as a cardiologist, would call an abnormal rhythm. *An abnormal rhythm that precedes sudden death.* It started as a single beat and progressed to two to three beats at a time. Then it became five to seven beats, continuously. As a cardiologist, I knew what was next. This situation was an impending cardiac arrest. And that meant running a code (advanced cardiac support efforts) to resuscitate a dying person.

I have run advanced cardiac life support efforts on patients during my professional life. An irrefutable fact about advanced cardiac life support efforts is that no matter how hard you try, some patients die. There are no guarantees.

At that moment, I realized that I was staring at possible death—with no guarantee of a positive outcome of even the most valiant and skilled efforts that the Emergency Room personnel would perform on me.

My meditative mind transcended to a level where I realized that, at that moment, I was alone. And that *I alone* could guarantee the outcome of this situation. My future—my *life*—was up to me. I knew, with absolute certainty, that I could not turn my life over to the Emergency Room personnel.

I closed my eyes, ignored the outside world, went into a meditative state, focused on my heart, and started a silent communication with my deeper being. I channeled all my being to my heart and flooded the heart with it. I transcended to an unknown plane and allowed my *vital energy* (the energy of my true being) to take over the situation. As I was meditating through this process, my hiccups began to reduce in frequency and then slowly disappeared. I gently came out of my meditative state and looked up at the heart monitor. With few exceptions, the abnormal heartbeats had ceased. I was humbled.

I am an expert in heart attacks. I am a Western medical physician. I am also an Eastern medical physician and already knew about both medicines. I have been a practitioner of Yoga and meditation since the age of 17. I have practiced what Western medicine taught me, what Eastern medicine taught me—and yet I had a heart attack at a young age.

What came to my rescue while I was staring at death was my *true being*, the unknown level within myself. I realized that nothing and no one, except *me*, could alter the course of my life. And the ability to reach out to my true being at the unknown level was possible through skills I learned from the Eastern tradition of Yoga.

Doing what is recommended by either of the medical disciplines did not help me stop a heart attack. However, the ability to transcend to a deeper level within myself through meditation did help me to avert a potential cardiac arrest.

My colleagues will argue that this conclusion is not statistically sound. I am not aware of any statistics that guarantee—100 percent—a successful outcome. Through this process, I came to know that **in health and disease, it is not what we *do*, but who we must *be*.**

Every single day since then, after a day's work of interacting with patients at the hospital, I walk home heavy-hearted and dissatisfied. Deep down I know that I have not helped any of my patients to the extent to which I *could* help. I have only suggested interventions from the Western medical world, which is only 30 percent of the story—and by no means the complete story. I know that Eastern medical thoughts and disciplines are effective in treating patients, but I am not at liberty to recommend these modalities. Even if I was able to do that, Eastern medicine adds only another 30 percent to the story. The other 30 percent comes from you—you yourself and your 'being'. It is what I call You Power. The last 10 percent is left to chance...the unknown. This percentage is my personal formulation and is hypothetical, based upon my observations, intended to provide a degree of clarity with regard to the contribution of Eastern medicine, Western medicine, and our You Power in our health.

My efforts during the past few years in trying to combine Eastern and Western medicine into the current health care system have been less successful than I had hoped, because Western medicine is either not interested in it or afraid of it. But one thing I know: The unwillingness or inability to combine Eastern and Western disciplines is actually hurting us.

So I have decided to bring what I know directly to you, the health care consumer—because YOU are the most important person in this game. This book is the first in a series of books in which I will share what I know about health, disease, Western medicine, and Eastern medicine. I hope these books will allow you to take your health and your life to a higher level and enjoy control over your health—and your life—that you may never have imagined possible.

Friend or Foe?

Understanding the players and the playing field
in the game of health and disease.

Lying in the bed in the ER that day—nine years ago—and watching the abnormal beats of my heart made me re-evaluate the entire field of medicine from a patient's perspective. I had just had one of my cardiology colleagues tell me that my symptoms did not look like a heart attack, and suggest that we observe my situation and wait until morning to decide if I needed to undergo a cardiac catheterization. My cardiologist then left the ER for the evening after promising to come back early in the morning.

My abnormal heartbeats started after he had given me a recommendation and left. The erratic heartbeats were telling me that my heart was getting irritable. Common sense begged the question of why the heart—if tests showed that nothing was going on with my heart—would be getting irritable? As a cardiologist, I recognized the difference between the two recommendations and decided that I should have the catheterization right away. I am glad I did!

Today, my heart functions normally. I have no exercise limitations. I run three miles a day, four or five days a week, and take part in other vigorous activities along with daily Yoga and meditation. In other words, my awareness was heightened and I started living life mindfully.

The event on October 11, 2006 reminded me how dead (living mindlessly) I was in my own life, by being distracted by all the other external factors of life such as work, career, power, and money. Today I feel better than I felt in my twenties. My heart attack made me realize both the friends and the foes of health and disease. More importantly, I realized the importance of self—our true being—and what I call You Power.

But what if I was just your average person faced with chest pain? What if I wasn't a cardiologist? Would another person have had the same outcome I did? Or did I have an unfair advantage?

As an insider, I'll be the first to admit that I played the game differently. I was able to understand and make sound decisions knowing the positives and negatives of the entire system and how it functions. What if you're not an insider? You would be forced to play the game without knowing all of the rules. You would have to play the game on a field that you are not familiar with and team up with players that you do not really know—or know if they're on your side. In other words, you trust and hand over your power, like my brother did.

The playing field

All around the world, health and disease is played out within a system called the "health care system." Different countries have their own structures for this playing field. The structure falls primarily into two broad categories: a national health care system like that in Canada or England, or a private health care system like what exists in the United States. However, in reality, we find a mixture of the two concepts in most countries.

Although we call it a *health care system*, it is not really a "health" care system. It is actually a "disease" care system. In other words, you need to be sick with a disease before you can receive care in this system. Therefore, it is actually a "sick care system." Lately, as I watch the field of health and disease and see changes and challenges, I am convinced that it is not even a sick care system anymore.

One afternoon, I saw a patient in consultation in my subspecialty clinic for heart transplant. After the interview was over and a few tests were done to evaluate his symptoms, I formulated a plan of action. This included two prescription medications for the patient, one for his heart failure and one to replace testosterone because his testosterone level was too low. The prescription I gave him was not approved by the insurance company, and the pharmacy refused to fill the prescription.

The patient called me the next day and said that these medications had been denied. When the insurance company was contacted by my team, we learned that the insurance company felt that the patient should be prescribed different medications, rather than the ones that I had decided (based on my extensive training and years of experience) would benefit the patient most. I asked for the rationale for the denial. They said that the medications they recommend have to be tried first and a failure to respond to those medications needed to be documented. Then the medications that I had originally recommended, could be prescribed again. I pressed further and asked why they were recommending their choice of medications over mine. The answer was that those were generic medications and should be tried first before using brand name medications.

I was astounded! I was being told what medications to prescribe for MY patient and, by extension, how to really treat a patient's illness. I was being told how to manage illness by a non-medical entity.

This scenario tells us two things. First, your best interest is not the same as the interests of insurance carriers—even though you are the one paying the premiums that line their pockets. Second, an expert opinion on the best choice of medications does not matter.

This brings us to another very important question: What *does* really matter? I believe it is money.

I appealed to the insurance company, explaining my rationale for choosing the medications that I had prescribed. I was asked to talk to the medical director of the insurance company. When the medical director

9

came on the line, I asked him if he was a heart transplant specialist. He said, "I am a lung specialist." *Great,* I thought, *a lung specialist is going to give a verdict on how a heart specialist should treat a patient with a heart condition! Could this really be happening?* It was the equivalent of asking the pizza delivery guy what type of Chinese food you should order.

We are living in a Wealth care system world—that should be a *Health* care system world. This realization—that it is not even a sick care system— was devastating to me. It should be to you as well.

Taking the financial aspects of medical care into consideration when providing the best services to benefit the patient is acceptable, but it is unacceptable when financial considerations interfere with the provision of services that take care of a patient's best interests.

This is obviously a simple example of what goes on in the health care world on a daily basis. I frequently deal with more serious examples of this nature. It therefore becomes more important for you to be aware of the system in which you are trying to survive when a disease strikes you. I would therefore submit to you that not all the players of the system have your best interest in mind.

The other players on the field, in addition to insurance companies, are the various hospital systems, urgent care systems, and ambulatory care (doctor's office) systems that deliver the care. Figure 1 below shows an example of care delivery systems that can affect the outcome of your game. Each of these systems views your health in a different light and from a different point of view. Yet when you reach out to these entities, your view is always the same: get better from illness and restore health.

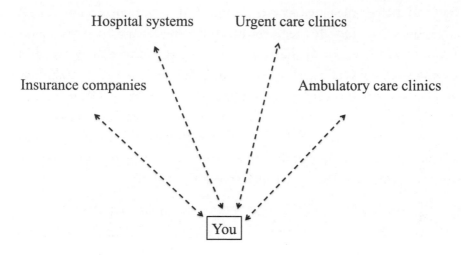

Figure 1: Different health care systems that interact with us.

These players, the care providers, have the power to make decisions that will determine a life-or-death outcome when you have a health problem.

Between the years 1990 and 2012, I was intimately involved with the Canadian medical system because of my brother, who had lived there for many years. He had multiple medical problems, the most important of which was kidney failure. He was on dialysis three times a week. He had a port in his chest under the clavicle for the purpose of accessing his blood to perform dialysis. During those years, I was frustrated with the delivery of care in that country for many reasons. Most notable, perhaps, were the facts that I was a physician from another care-delivery system and country, and that the person being affected was my sibling.

My frustration with how the system functioned became intense when things happened that were blatantly out of order. Because I realized that it was not about how the system functioned, but about life and death.

One early morning in April 2012, I received a call from my niece in Toronto, Canada. She told me that my brother was shaking and complaining of feeling cold. I asked a few questions and learned that he had had dialysis the previous evening and had come home feeling fine. At my request, she took his temperature and it revealed a fever. His blood pressure was low and his heart rate was high. I immediately asked my brother—who was talking to me through all of this—to call an ambulance and be taken to the nearest Emergency Room (ER). He was showing signs of a blood stream infection that could be deadly in a patient with a chronic disease such as kidney failure. He was at high risk of contracting a blood stream infection because of the catheter that was sitting in his blood vessel and was being accessed three times a week for dialysis.

My brother did as he was told. The ambulance arrived within a few minutes of being called, and he was taken to the ER immediately. His family accompanied him to the ER and I got a verbal report from them when he got to the hospital. Apparently, the ambulance had called ahead to inform the ER doctor about my brother and his condition. He was promptly transferred to an ER bed and was told that his blood pressure was low and that he was in critical condition. Yet, unbelievably, he was left in his ER bed for three hours before a physician came to see and care for him.

By that time his blood pressure was so low that they could not even get an intravenous (IV) line in him. He was losing consciousness and all hell broke loose in the ER. They had to insert an IV line into his groin and transfer him immediately to ICU, the Intensive Care Unit. I was appalled to hear this account of the delivery of care in a developed country such as Canada. After three days of care in the ICU, my brother died of overwhelming infection.

During the three days preceding his death, my efforts to contact any one of the physicians, including his primary kidney doctor and intensive care doctors on various shifts, was unsuccessful—even after communicating that I was not only the brother of the patient, but a physician. Not one of the doctors returned any of my multiple phone calls. So much for "physician courtesy."

I could not immediately fly to Toronto, as I was on call at my own facility and all my colleagues were out of the country at a weekend conference at the time. There was absolutely no one to cover for me so that I could get to my brother.

Finally, I called my nephew's cell phone and had him walk to the nursing station to find the intensive care physician and get him on the phone with me. The physician simply informed me that my brother's condition was hopeless. My brother passed that afternoon.

To this day, I cannot imagine a three-hour delay in caring for a critically-ill patient in an ER of a developed country. When dealing with a critically-ill patient, three hours can mean life or death. It was obvious to me that this delay resulted in his demise.

Who was responsible for the circumstances that resulted in my brother's death? Who was responsible for the outcome? I ask that you be the judge. If you put yourself in his shoes—or mine, or his children's—what would your verdict be?

The so-called health care system is composed primarily of Western medical practices. Eastern medical practices are not built into the main framework of this system. If you choose to obtain Eastern medical services for your illness, in most instances you will need to pay out-of-pocket for those services.

Additionally—if you aren't already aware of this—there is a war going on between Western medical practitioners and Eastern medical practitioners as to whose services and treatments are better for your health.

Western medical practitioners claim that Eastern medicine is quackery. The Eastern medical practitioners, on the other hand, claim that the Western medicines not only do not really help (except in the case of emergencies), but will actually harm you.

As both an Eastern and Western medical practitioner—and based upon the opposing opinions related to Eastern and Western medicine—I guess I could be considered a quack who harms my patients.

But it is you, as a patient, who is caught in the middle. You who must make decisions related to your health and wellness. And this brings us to the other players in the game.

The players in the game of health and disease

If you are truly concerned about health and disease, it is wise to try to understand what resources are available to you and how these resources can enhance your chance of winning.

You have a choice between using Western medicine or Eastern medicine to help you. Alternatively, you may choose to use the best of what both Eastern and Western systems can offer—in combination. My recommendation is the combined use of the best of both worlds. When you choose to use both medicines to your advantage, your teammates in the game are Western medical practitioners *and* Eastern medical practitioners...a diverse team with depth and perspective that allows them to see both sides of the coin as it relates to your health.

But the most important player in this game is still YOU. It's your life! And you, more than anyone else, have the power to impact your health and your future.

So the big question I pose to you is this: Do you want to let the medical practitioners play the game for you and watch—from the sidelines—the unfolding outcomes that can impact your life, or do you want to be an active participant in the game? In the end, it is up to you to decide which teammates you want on your side when you are sick or fighting disease. You can choose to play with one teammate or more. And this may be a case of when more... really *is* more.

That decision is in your hands. But if you do want to play the health game actively, you first need to understand the differences in how Eastern and Western medical practitioners play the game.

The operative structure of Western medicine

I have a good friend who recently went to the doctor for a check up because she wanted to make sure she was "healthy." She didn't have any specific complaints and when she explained this to the doctor, he said, "Well then, what do you want me to do?" This response exemplifies how Western medicine recognizes and treats health and disease. Unless there is a specific complaint, Western medicine does nothing for a person in search of optimal health—except for a yearly physical and screening tests to detect already-existing or early-stage disease.

Let me be very clear: I am not suggesting that this is wrong. Rather, it is incomplete. It does not take you, the patient, into consideration.

Western medicine's main focus is on disease. If you happen to lose your health by developing a disease, then the system will help restore your heath or minimize the effect of disease. That is what happened in my case in 2006. The system views health, quite simply, as the elimination of or control of diseases. This concept is illustrated in Figure 2 below.

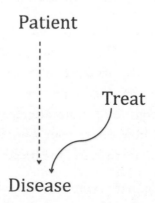

Figure 2: What a Western medical practitioner addresses when you have a symptom.

A Western practitioner, therefore, focuses only on disease when you come to them for help...as Figure 2 illustrates. You think they are focusing on you. They are not.

They are focused—solely—on determining the presence or absence of disease in you. A Western practitioner's patient history assessment and physical examination are geared toward identifying a disease state in you. That's it.

They require a *symptom* to begin this process. If you have no symptom, a Western practitioner is paralyzed. The story of my friend I just shared underscores that.

Do you remember the doctor's response? If there were no symptoms to diagnose (as was the case with my friend) then this is a Western medical practitioner's response:

"What do you want me to do?"

If they have a symptom to diagnose, they will finish the history and physical exam and do blood tests and other imaging tests to detect abnormalities to confirm their suspicion of disease. That is the process in Western medicine. The reason for tests is to identify evidence of **biochemical changes** in your body. Biochemical changes are the underlying mechanisms by which Western medicine explains disease.

Anyone who has been in an ER seeking help will understand what focusing on disease means. When several people arrive at an ER at once, the way the staff determines who gets seen first by a doctor is determined by a system called *triaging*. A practitioner or a nurse in the ER will ask basic questions about your complaints (after first asking for your insurance card!) and determine how severe your symptoms are and if there is a potential for an immediate threat to life based on your symptoms.

If you, for example, have symptoms that suggest a heart attack or a stroke (a *brain attack*) you will move to the front of the line and be seen first. Others are lined up behind you, in order of the initial "threat to life" assessment. This determination does not take into account who you are or how long you have suffered with the pain or symptom. It is all about your symptom and disease.

Western medicine excels in controlling or eliminating disease. What Western medicine does not do is make you healthy.

Western medicine puts you on the path to restoring health—*if* you have a disease.

All of us need more than Western medical help to become healthy. And this is where Eastern medicine excels: in making you healthy. To win the battle over disease, Western medicine uses either pharmaceutical medications or surgery as its main tools. Physical therapy and rehabilitation are its main adjuncts, or supporting modalities.

The operative structure of Eastern medicine

Understanding health from an Eastern perspective is simple. It is based on a state of *BALANCE*...not on the presence or absence of disease. There is no consideration of the existence of disease in these traditions. A healthy state requires a BALANCED state, or EQUILIBRIUM. Departure from balance to imbalance is considered an unhealthy state, which can lead to disease.

The first question that usually arises when a person is exploring Eastern medical philosophies and the balanced state they advocate is: What, specifically, needs to be in equilibrium? **Eastern disciplines propose equilibrium of what they call *vital energy* of a person.** The concept of vital energy has been around for thousands of years. And although no clear explanation exits as to what *vital energy* is... **most people are inherently able to feel its presence within themselves.**

Several terms are used to describe this vital energy by different civilizations, cultures, religions, and philosophies. Perhaps the most commonly used and most easily understood term is *spirit*. The term *spiritus* was coined in European traditions that were trying to understand this concept of *spirit* and its origins in China and India.

Experiments to understand the spirit in Western medicine have failed and, therefore, there is **no clear concept of sprit that exists in Western medical practice.** As it stands today, our understanding of the *spirit* is confined to our belief that death occurs when the spirit leaves the body. The Ayurvedic tradition—a system of traditional Hindu medicine native to the Indian subcontinent and what many believe to be the foundation for alternative medicine—referred to this energy as *Prana*...energy that flows through the body and is stored in centers called *chakras*. Traditional Chinese medicine referred to this energy as *Qi* (pronounced *chi*), energy that flows through distinct Acupuncture channels. The Greeks called it *Pneuma*. Luigi Galvani, an Italian physician, physicist, biologist, and philosopher, called it *animal electricity*. Paracelsus, a Swiss German Renaissance physician, botanist, alchemist, and astrologer, called it *quintessence*. In Homeopathy, it is called *vital force*. And, in Anthropology and Theosophy, it is called the *health aura*.

For our purposes, let us call this force *vital energy*. Just as Western medicine explains disease by identifying biochemical changes in the body, Eastern medicine explains and understands imbalance in terms of vital energy.

In Eastern medical perspectives, the abnormalities of vital energy are thought to underlie even the biochemical changes that Western medicine relies on. Therefore, Eastern medicine attempts to explain human health and disease at a level deeper than just physical health. Eastern medicine encompasses physical, emotional, and spiritual levels of a human being. Eastern medicine concerns itself with treating the *person*—and not the disease.

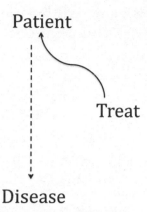

Patient

Treat

Disease

Figure 3: Where an Eastern medical practitioner looks when you have a symptom.

The concept of treating the person—versus the disease—speaks to the equilibrium of the person. And the equilibrium of the person depends upon the equilibrium of his or her vital energy.

In 1987, when I first entered the free Acupuncture clinic at the University of Complementary and Alternative Medicine in Sri Lanka, my singular mental focus was to find out how they were cheating the hundreds and hundreds of innocent and unsuspecting folks (aka: patients) who came in for Acupuncture treatments. As a young, third-year medical student who had just passed the first part of the 3rd MBBS (Bachelor of Medicine and Bachelor of Science) exam, I was full of confidence in my understanding of the human body from the anatomical (a body's normal structure), physiological (a body's normal function), and pathophysiological (a body's abnormal function) perspectives. Alternative medicine did not make sense from where I was standing—at the time. Little did I know that, years later, it would make perfect sense.

Growing up in Ayurvedic tradition and mastering Yoga practice has helped me keep an open mind toward exploring other traditions that made no sense to me at the beginning of my career in medicine. The fact that the master Acupuncturist at the clinic was trained in Western medicine in the specialty of rheumatic diseases (Rheumatology) and had subsequently given up the Western medical practice to provide Acupuncture, also caught my interest. Hundreds of patients (sometimes as many as 300!) visited the Acupuncture clinic each day. All received free treatments. Ten young clinical instructors (including myself) provided the treatments, directed by the master Acupuncturist. The clinic hosted 10 to 15 students of Acupuncture on a monthly basis from various countries around the world, giving them the opportunity to learn and serve. Most of them were from European countries and Australia.

It was an open-air clinic and the set up was nothing like what I had become used to at medical school. But, then, the treatment philosophy of treating the patient—not the disease—wasn't the same either. In fact, it was the complete opposite.

In medical school, the emphasis is on identifying, diagnosing, and treating a disease. It seemed to me, at the time, that the two philosophies were diametrically opposed, as Figure 4 below illustrates.

Western Concept of Treatment   Eastern Concept of Treatment

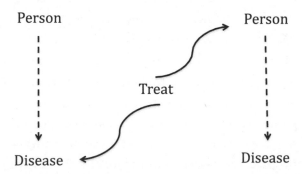

Figure 4: Seemingly opposed view of Western and Eastern medicines.

Treat the Patient—not the Disease

My initial motivation (of wanting to find out how innocent folks were being cheated) turned into a more curious thought: *All these patients, collectively, couldn't be following something that makes no sense.* I became even more intrigued when I realized that approximately 60 percent of the patients were helped by the acupuncture treatments. Recovery ranged from results as simple as relief from chronic arthritic pain to as extreme as paralyzed limbs moving again and bedridden patients with multiple vertebral fractures being able to walk. I can't tell you how many times I asked myself: *How can a needle inserted into specific points in the body help a body heal?*

Acupuncture balances your energy. That's what I was told. And my response to this was very Western in nature: "I cannot document the transformation." This triggered a conflict in me, since I was taught that although you may not see or document the results, *you feel the change.* Balancing the body's energy allows the body to utilize its own power to heal itself, I was told. I couldn't fathom, at the time, how one could administer a treatment program in which neither a change could be documented immediately, nor the mechanism of action actually known.

I was used to getting immediate results in Western medical practice. For example, if I prescribed antibiotics for an infection, I could document the results of the antibiotics—the patient's fever would subside, he or she would confirm that they were feeling better, and blood tests would confirm that white blood cell counts were improving. I also understood how the drug worked from a pharmacological perspective.

At that time, I did not fully understand that I was being introduced to a level of human functioning that is beyond the physical and mental level of sensory perception. A level of human functioning that was, perhaps, metaphysical.

From that point forward, I started looking at health and disease from both sides—the Eastern perspective *and* the Western perspective—and as my studies progressed, I was introduced to an even deeper understanding of these philosophies.

In short, what I am trying to say is this: Western medicine begins when symptoms begin. Eastern medicine begins before symptoms begin. Western medicine helps **restore** your health. Eastern medicine helps you to **acquire and maintain** health.

Take note: If you don't acquire it, you don't have it; if you don't restore it, you don't have it either. And if you don't maintain it, you will lose it. Acquiring, restoring and maintaining are all essential for long-lasting well-being.

Understanding this, do you now think it is useful to have members from both sides on your team? I certainly think so. I certainly *use* both. But wait, there is even more. There is your You Power that ensures how much benefit you are going to obtain from these two team members.

In the chapters that follow, I share how I look at a patient—from both Western and Eastern medical perspectives—when they present with health complaints. Eight of the most daunting and deadly diseases that are currently killing us have been selected to illustrate how to play the game of health and disease with both Western *and* Eastern practitioners as your teammates. This is revolutionary thinking that could change forever how we think about health and wellness. It can give new meaning to taking control of our health and the healing power of our bodies. It merges East and West...and You Power.

And equally, if not more importantly, I want you to be able to recognize when one of your friendly teammates (or the seemingly friendly playing field) can turn into a foe. That is when you lose. Remember how cutting-edge Western medicine turned into a foe in my brother's case by delaying treatment for his critical condition? Keep in mind that it is not only the field you are playing on and who you choose as teammates to win the game—but also how you navigate the entire game. How YOU navigate the entire game of life.

"Each patient carries his own doctor inside him. They come to us not knowing this truth."

"We are at our best when they give the doctor who resides in each patient a chance to go to work."

—Albert Schweitzer, MD

Chapter One

Heart

The Sudden Killer

I am not loved enough.

In the medical world, a heart attack is known as *myocardial infarction*. *Myocardium* means the muscle cells of the heart itself and *infarction* means cell death from lack of blood supply; together it means heart muscle cell death. This happens when the blood supply to the heart is abruptly cut off by a clot that forms in any one of the blood vessels that supplies blood to the heart. The clot forms in a blood vessel as a result of the rupture of cholesterol plaques that have developed over time in these vessels.

The problem with a heart attack is that one out of every two people who have a heart attack in the United States does not get to the Emergency Room alive. This means about 50 percent of people who have a heart attack do not get a chance to tell their story because they die suddenly and outside of the hospital[1]. This is true for people in most countries.

Let me illustrate this. A young man in his early fifties suddenly collapsed at work. Fortunately, people around him immediately recognized this as a heart attack, initiated cardiopulmonary resuscitation (CPR) and called emergency medical services (911). When emergency medical personnel arrived, they found the man to be in what we call *ventricular fibrillation*, an abnormal rhythm of the heart where the blood-pumping chambers quiver at a very rapid rate without effectively pumping the blood. This condition usually results in sudden death.

The man was shocked with a defibrillator several times to restore his normal rhythm and was taken to the hospital. He was shocked again on the way to the hospital and in the emergency room because his heart kept going back into an abnormal rhythm. In other words: This man was, repeatedly, trying to die.

Prompt interventions in the hospital kept him alive and the next day a cardiac catheterization revealed that one of the three main blood vessels that supply the heart was completely blocked. He had a heart attack—just like mine. The hospital staff learned that he did not feel any chest symptoms, such as chest pain, prior to collapsing. He told me that he felt fatigued in the days preceding the cardiac event, but apart from feeling tired he had no other symptoms. If there had been no one around when he collapsed, he would have experienced what we call *sudden death*—and would not have lived to tell his story.

This brings us to the 50:50:50 Rule in my specialty of cardiology. Approximately 50 percent of patients who suffer a heart attack die suddenly. We do not know if those who died felt any prior symptoms. In the other half of the patients, 50 percent of them (like our patient in the previous example) did not feel the typical symptoms of a heart attack. This other half of the patients present to the doctor's office or emergency room with what we call *atypical symptoms of a heart attack*. Patients with atypical symptoms tend to ignore the symptoms, simply because they're not typically associated with a heart problem.

Who are these people who tend to have atypical symptoms and are at risk of not recognizing a heart attack when it happens? They are the elderly (older than 65 years of age), people with diabetes, and women. They run the risk of missing an early diagnosis and therefore may end up having serious consequences.

It is important to recognize that most of the research on heart attacks in the modern world comes from less than half of the people who survived a heart attack or a sudden death.

Sudden death occurs when the heart goes into what we call an *abnormal rhythm* that is lethal enough to kill someone. What *lethal rhythm* means is that the heart becomes irritable and starts quivering, rather than beating in a slow, rhythmic fashion. When the heart quivers, it does not effectively pump enough blood to the rest of the body and if the quivering lasts long enough, the person dies. One of the most common causes of lethal rhythm resulting in death is a heart attack.

It is important to remember that the heart can go into this quivering lethal rhythm due to intense emotional insult, or stress, without having a heart attack. In other words, a heart attack makes you vulnerable to abnormal heart rhythms and, therefore, sudden death. But not all cardiac sudden death will be preceded by a heart attack.

Here is what we know about heart attacks from the stories of survivors. Cardiovascular disease is the leading cause of death in the United States[1]. The second leading cause of death is cancer, followed by lung disease, stroke, and, fifth on the list, accidents[1]. One in every three deaths in the United States[2] is attributed to heart disease. Every one minute and 23 seconds someone in America dies from a heart attack[2]. Every 34 seconds a man or woman in the United States has a cardiac event[2]. Every seven minutes a Canadian has a heart attack[3]. Every seven minutes a British citizen dies of heart attack in the United Kingdom[4]. Every 10 minutes an Australian has a heart attack and every 53 minutes an Australian dies of a heart attack[5].

These are all developed countries. Despite advances in medical technology and health (and health care) delivery, we continue to carry an overwhelming burden of disease—often resulting in death. The efforts of the health care systems are not resulting in the desired impact in reducing or minimizing the burden of illness on you and me. This raises questions as to whether looking at external factors alone—factors like high blood pressure and high cholesterol—are enough to minimize the impact of disease on human beings.

Western side of the heart coin

When a patient presents for consultation regarding a cardiac condition or an abnormality, one of the first things we Western doctors do is to look for causes of the abnormality. Part of evaluating the causes includes what we call *predisposing factors*. The more predisposing factors one has, the more potential there is for developing heart disease. This information is gathered during the first interview with the patient by compiling what we call a past medical history. It helps us learn other medical problems the patient has, his or her family history (to look for genetic or inheritance factors), social history (to look for abnormal behavior as well as drug use, excessive drinking, or smoking), and so on. Sometimes my patients get frustrated from answering the same questions over and over again with different physicians. Oftentimes even I wonder why I need to elicit the same information, over and over again, rather than accepting what another physician has already learned and documented. What I discovered is that different physicians, with different styles and slightly different questions, can elicit different information or clues that may change the entire course of treatment or management of that patient.

I've seen it happen time and time again and it makes the case for why a second opinion—or even a third—is a smart idea.

Overall, a Western physician looks for predisposing factors for heart disease in patients and then looks for the presence or absence of disease by inquiring about symptoms, doing a physical exam, laboratory tests, and other investigations as seen fit by the physician. Blood tests are performed to identify abnormal **biochemical reactions** (physiology) and imaging studies are done to look for structural (anatomical) abnormalities. Once all the information and test results are collected, treatment is tailored as follows:

- Give recommendations to correct or modify the disease, if present.
- Give recommendations to correct or modify the causes of the disease.
- Give recommendations to follow up with the patient to monitor their progress.

By now you have probably realized that evaluation of a medical problem by a Western physician has two components:

- First is making a diagnosis by taking a history, doing a physical exam, and doing tests to confirm the presence of a disease.
- Second is to formulate a plan of treatment and then decide on follow up visits to see how the disease is responding to treatment.

The pre-existing factors that are associated with heart disease are detailed below:

- High blood pressure
- High cholesterol level
- Presence of diabetes or pre-diabetic status
- Smoking
- Being overweight or obese
- Physical inactivity
- Family history of heart attacks at a young age or heart disease
- History of high blood pressure during pregnancy
- Poor or unhealthy dietary habits
- Age (older than 55 for women)

The presence of these risk factors leads to the development of heart disease by altering the biological mechanisms within our bodies that result in organic changes in the heart itself that later manifest as coronary artery disease, heart attack, or heart muscle dysfunction referred to as heart failure. The prevailing concept in Western medicine is that if you have these risk factors, you have a high potential to develop heart disease in your lifetime.

As a result, Western medicine focuses on minimizing the effect of these risk factors before and after heart disease is diagnosed. Several thousands of studies have researched these risk factors and their influence in the development, progression, and contribution to heart attacks. Based on these studies, Western medicine has developed guidelines as to how to treat and manage patients who are at risk for developing heart disease and patients who already have heart disease.

While these guidelines serve as a road map, one aspect of them that is unsatisfactory is that they were derived from studying people as a group.

If you are not represented in a group that's been studied, the guideline-based strategies recommended for you may *not* be optimal for *you*. It is up to your physician to determine the best that Western medicine can offer you. But consider this: The worst decision you can make regarding your health is to think that you have become healthy because a disease has been addressed by Western medicine. This is only part of the story of your illness.

The Eastern side of the heart coin

In Eastern medicine, as will be repeated again and again in this book, organ systems are defined by functions (physiology), rather than by anatomy (structure) and physiology together as it is in Western medicine. It is no different when it comes to the heart.

The functions described in Eastern medicine have **energy flow** as the underlying component, whereas, in Western medicine, the fundamental component of function is **biochemical reactions**. Therefore, the diagnostic methods for finding abnormalities of fundamental components in each of these medicines are different.

In Western medicine, functional abnormalities are detected by doing laboratory blood tests to determine abnormal results. Once it's determined that abnormal biochemical results are present—and indicate an organ's inability to perform normal functions—a diagnosis of abnormal organ function is made. Western medicine then looks for structural (or anatomical) changes in those organs to see if we can fix them. For example, a doctor may perform coronary *angiography*, or the placement of a stent to open a narrowing blood vessel that supplies blood to your heart—like the procedure I had done after my heart attack. In Eastern medicine, the functions described are not related to any test. They are, instead, related to how the person behaves, feels, eats, and conducts him or herself.

An Eastern medical practitioner makes a diagnosis by examining the patient with regard to energy flow in the body, which is identified by pulse diagnosis, tongue diagnosis, sleep patterns, change in dietary habits, mood level or changes in mood, and changes in color, texture and appearance of face, tongue, and skin, as well as a tendency to like certain colors or tastes. Eastern medicine does not concern itself with identifying biochemical abnormalities, as Western medical practitioners do. **This is because Eastern medicine believes that abnormal energy flow patterns influence the biochemical reactions at a subtle and deeper level in the body.** Eastern medicine views the energy of every person as unique and individual to that person only. Eastern medical evaluation processes, therefore, become very specific to each person and individualized.

In Acupuncture philosophy, the heart is considered to be an extremely vital system. It has been described as the "emperor" of the human body[6], master of the body and emperor of the organ networks[7], ruler of the human body[8]. Interestingly, Acupuncture philosophy concedes that the heart also stores the spirit and is considered to be the seat of consciousness and mental functioning. Acupuncture philosophy describes a very close association between the heart, lungs, liver, kidney, and blood. Parallels can be drawn in Western medicine with regard to this association. When a patient develops heart failure, the lungs and kidneys fail, the liver gets congested, and the patient has a low blood count (called *anemia*). These associations are recognized in Western medicine as well, but Western medicine does not place equal importance on these associations, as Eastern medicine does.

What is important to recognize is that Eastern medicines recognize internal factors such as individuality, energetic influence, and emotional contribution to the development of disease—in addition to external factors. This is in stark contrast to the current and primary focus of Western medical practice. Western medicine looks outside of an individual to identify causative factors, whereas Eastern medicine looks inside the individual.

You Power • The third side of the heart coin

As a cardiologist who is well versed in both Western and Eastern medicine, I have met and treated thousands of patients with heart disease—including, ironically, myself. I have had the opportunity to watch and observe those who did well with treatment and those who did not do well.

My most profound educational experiences have come from my work as a heart transplant cardiologist. I have had the opportunity to interact with, communicate with, and care for patients who are, essentially, dying. At times of extreme illness—when faced with a very real threat that our life will be cut short—the primal being in all of us is revealed and our personalities evolve and express themselves in their most naked form. I have watched people whose health had deteriorated to a point of impending death and needed a heart transplant, as well as those who successfully avoided transplant. There are those who changed their lives and lived as long as 29 years after the transplant and others who did not fare as well, perishing within five years after a transplant. I have seen young recipients who survived many years as well as patients who required multiple transplants, sometimes as many as three heart transplants in their lifetime.

Likewise, among older recipients of heart transplants, I have seen many who lived a long time after transplant surgery—and just as many who did not. My observations of these patients established a pattern as to who these people, these patients, were. The patterns I saw were tied to characteristics these patients exhibited—characteristics that, I came to realize, could be determining factors for life or death.

Age, I learned, did not matter much. And certainly not as much as the psychological characteristics (or personality traits) that patients possessed. These observed psychological characteristics tended to be similar among most of the patients regardless of whether the patient utilized Western medicine or Eastern medicine. Unfortunately, neither the current practices of Western medicine nor Eastern medicine are paying much attention to addressing these characteristics.

The characteristics I observed in my patients included:

- They were caring and loving people, but tended to feel that they did not receive the degree of love they longed for from others and did not exhibit a high degree of love for themselves.

- Their very first reaction to anything tended to be negative, or resistant in nature, resulting in the rejection of recommendations or in modifying recommendations that were made. These were people who wanted to be in control—and who tended to develop heart disease when they felt that they had lost control.

- They shared a tendency to suppress anger and discontent, and behaved as if those emotions did not exist in them.

- They tended to be more givers than takers.

Whether the anger and negativity arose from their internal sense of not receiving adequate love, recognition, and caring from others, or if it arose from their constitutional make up (or what we call personality) is a matter of debate.

One day, when I was on call for cardiology service, another hospital wanted to transfer a young man to our facility because that man's heart was failing to the point of needing support by a mechanical device. He was on a breathing machine and was transferred to our hospital. He had the typical characteristics of a heart attack with severe dysfunction of his heart resulting in very low blood supply to the rest of his body. When we looked at the blood vessels that supplied his heart (called coronary arteries), there were no clots in any of them. Blood clots in the blood vessels are normally found when a person experiences a heart attack. There were no cholesterol plaques in the coronary arteries either. He did not, in fact, have a heart attack—but Western medicine was fooled by his symptoms and the laboratory tests indicated (by its standards) that he did have a heart attack.

An astounding story was elicited from the patient in the days that followed, when he was able to talk. On the day he first experienced the heart-related symptoms that led to the hospitalization, he had gone to work as usual. Then, everything changed when he was told that he was fired from his job. He suddenly developed shortness of breath and chest pain that led to his admission to a hospital and treatment for a heart attack. In our hospital, once we determined that he had *not* had a heart attack, we were back to square one with regard to the answer to the critical question. *What is causing his heart to suddenly fail?* In this case, it was a condition called *broken heart syndrome.*

For many centuries, the heart organ has been considered the seat of the soul. It was also the organ associated with emotions such as love, caring, joy, and (to some degree) anger and fear.

People are inherently aware that emotions are not only felt, physically, but that they can affect one's heart. The folklore of "broken heart syndrome" has been around for years. Only recently have we started to understand the mechanism underlying this folklore. A study published in the *New England Journal of Medicine* in February of 2005 confirmed the mechanisms (biochemical reactions) underlying the broken heart syndrome. In this article, the authors confirm an association between sudden emotional stress and the weakening of the heart muscle, leading to what we call heart failure[9]. This finding aligns with the Acupuncture explanation of how shock leads to the scattering of the heart energy and causes weakness. The good news is that the heart function frequently recovers. However, I have seen patients who develop irreversible heart failure after undergoing extreme and shocking emotional experiences, such as the loss of a loved one. These patients present late, often a year or so after the traumatic event, with evident heart failure, but such association is not readily identified by the diagnosing physician.

What this patient illustrated was that intense emotions can alter biochemical or structural changes in the body that Western medicine relies on to make diagnoses. It also gives credibility to Eastern medicine's claim that energy imbalances precede biological and structural changes. In this case, we were able to identify the effect of emotions on the man's heart. What we do not know is what effect these intense emotions have on other organs in the body, such as the liver, kidney, and lungs—and how these other organs react to intense emotions. I believe that all organs are affected by emotions but, at this time, we are only able to easily identify how emotions affect the heart.

This is testament to the fact that emotion can influence our health. As Eastern medicine emphasizes, changes to the energy in and around us can be the underlying influence causing abnormalities, without apparent biochemical or structural changes. Emotion is energy in motion. Why, then, have we not advanced in recognizing or treating these aspects in Western medicine? I venture to say that it's because there is no financial benefit for the players in this game—doctors, hospitals, insurance companies, Big Pharma, government agencies, or health care systems—to do so.

To further complicate this issue, the energy and emotions of a person are very unique to that person. Eastern medicine can significantly help develop this energetic aspect of you, but the emotional aspect of health needs to be dealt with by you.

When I had further discussion with the patient whose job loss led to cardiac failure, he admitted that he had always been a nervous type of person and reacted intensely, within himself, to negative events in life. What he was describing to me at the time is what I call You Power—our personality and the way we handle stressors in our lives.

From an Eastern perspective, the ancient Acupuncture did attribute psychological characteristics to the heart. In Acupuncture, the heart is said to be associated with emotional characteristics, primarily joy, sadness or grief, anger, and worry[10]. Joy is manifested as happiness and is derived from love, therefore these emotions are also associated with the organ heart. Other psychological characteristics associated with the heart are irritability, passion, fear, inhibition, apprehensiveness, and fluctuations in willpower, motivation, and self-discipline.

Although the heart shares several emotions, the predominant emotions are **joy and love**. Acupuncture philosophy ascertains certain emotions to have predominant association with particular organ functions as described below[10]:

- Anger affects the liver
- Joy and shock affect the heart
- Sadness affects the lungs and heart
- Worry affects the lungs and spleen
- Pensiveness affects the spleen
- Fear affects the kidneys

As such, if there is an overlap of emotional manifestation, this overlap is exerted through the abnormal function of the other organs that are associated with those predominant emotions. In other words, if you identify a mixture of emotions, consider the possibility that other organs may also be affected—even if you do not feel symptoms associated with those other organs. This is because Acupuncture philosophy considers all organs to be interdependent on each other with regard to the development of ill health. Therefore, in Eastern medicine, the imbalance of one organ may cause the imbalance of another. Emotional associations or the influence of emotions are not considered in Western medical philosophy.

Ayurveda considers the heart an important vital organ for sustaining life. The heart is considered critical to the structural integrity of the body, like a central pillar or the load-bearing walls that support a building or a house[11]. Ayurveda also explains the abnormalities in terms of energy imbalance in one's body. Instead of describing it as energy, as it's described in Acupuncture, Ayurveda calls it an imbalance of the three Humors that underlie the vitality of the person. These Humors (called Vata, Pita, and Kapa) indicate the three predominant forces that influence health. Ayurveda describes lifestyle factors such as a balanced diet, regular exercise, balanced thoughts and actions, maintenance of neutrality, and better social status as requirements for heart health or health in general. These recommendations are not far from what is recommended by Western medicine for the prevention of heart disease.

Our personality influences our emotions and how we handle emotions. Not only in Acupuncture, but in Western medicine as well, emotions and personality are considered to be strongly associated with heart disease. The only problem is that, despite having enough information, psychological counseling, or ways to improve coping mechanisms, are not recommended by either Western practitioners or Eastern practitioners to patients with heart disease. Several studies of personality have been conducted with regard to heart disease. Collectively, they seem to point to the personality characteristics of the individual—what I call your You Power—as game changers.

What can you do?

First: Understand that there are three sides that need to be considered. These are Western medicine, Eastern medicine, and your You Power.

Western medicine is helpful only 30 percent of the time. When you receive treatment for an illness from a hospital and go home, only one-third of your problem is taken care of. If you want to address another 30 percent, another one-third, of your being, then you need to utilize the Eastern medicines. However, if you want to be successful in accomplishing your goal of good health and long life—and reap the very best benefits of both Western and Eastern medicines—you need to pay attention to another 30 percent of you by understanding your You Power. The other 10 percent, as I stated in the Introduction, is left to chance. Remember, no one is ever 100 percent in control of anything in life.

Your success or failure in either overcoming a disease or maintaining health depends in large part on how well *you* influence your You Power. Every day I go home from the hospital frustrated and dissatisfied because I am only able to offer a "one-third solution"—only a 30-percent help to a patient's health problems as a Western practitioner due to the constraints of the system.

What can Western medicine offer you?

There are several avenues that Western medicine supports:

Medications
A Western medical practitioner will prescribe medications based on your cardiac problems. These medications are designed to alter the biochemical reactions that lead to heart disease and will be

specific to heart-related conditions. It is important to take these medications, even if you don't like pharmaceutical pills. It makes no sense to resist or fight taking medications once a major disease has developed in you. It makes more sense to resist or fight before a disease develops. These medications will help put out the fire immediately and allow you to take charge again and catch your breath. At that point, if you want to consider going off of the medications with alternative efforts, talk to your doctor to devise a plan of action. This would most likely require the consultation of Eastern medical practitioners, especially if health optimization is your goal. If you are concerned about side effects and the effects of chemicals in your body, there are ways to cleanse your body of these effects.

Diet

Diet is a major contributor to abnormal cardiac health. The most important aspect of adopting a special diet program is that it helps you reduce weight and cholesterol. These are two factors that are strongly associated with heart disease. You should make a commitment to extensive change with regard to your dietary habits. I cannot emphasize enough the importance of diet. The general recommendation is a low-fat, low-cholesterol cardiac diet. A consultation with a nutritionist will get you on the right track.

Exercise

Regular moderate exercise is one of the best ways to improve your cardiovascular health. In fact, it improves overall health and aids in daily stress management. People who engage in moderate exercise regularly tend to live longer. More importantly, regular exercise makes you feel better. Let me share with you the importance of regular exercise.

When I had my heart attack, it was not a typical scenario. Neither my cardiologist nor I believed that I was having a major heart attack. We cardiologists were right, based on the degree of pain I had during the attack, and wrong because I did have an entirely blocked artery. During the entire cardiac event, my chest pain was only 2 to 3 on a scale of 1 to 10. Usually patients feel as if an elephant is sitting on their chest and, typically, the degree of pain ranges from 5 to 10, unless they belong to one of the atypical population I mentioned earlier in this chapter. The other outlier is that I had no heart muscle damage as a result of the heart attack— even though one of the blood vessels was completely blocked.

These findings exemplify the benefits of exercise. Prior to my heart attack, I had exercised regularly. As the blood vessels were filling up with cholesterol plaque and narrowing, new small blood vessels were forming from the other two unblocked arteries toward the area of heart that was supplied by this narrowing blood vessel. And the reason this was happening—and what might have saved my life—was my regular exercise regimen. Therefore, even though the culprit vessel was completely blocked during the heart attack, there was still some blood supply from the other side through these small vessels (called *collaterals*) which prevented extensive damage to the heart muscle. If I had not had these little vessels— which had developed as a result of my exercise habits prior to the heart attack—I could have joined the line of those waiting for a heart transplant due to extensive heart muscle damage that leads to heart failure.

I want you to understand how a behavior deflected a major adverse outcome in the face of an acute illness. This relates not just to the heart, but to any disease or organ. Your lifestyle has a lot to do with where you will stand after a major insult, via disease or accident, in life.

Stop smoking…if you are a smoker
Smoking makes coronary artery disease worse and also leads to the

narrowing of the blood vessels throughout the body, especially in your legs and the head (like the carotid arteries in our neck). An important but often unwelcome piece of advice: Stop smoking. Immediately.

I have had patients who continued to smoke, even after a heart attack. And many come back, with recurrent heart attacks, because they continue to smoke. Smoking is a habit, just like drinking coffee is a habit. I hear my patients say that they are trying to quit smoking. After a heart attack, there is no such thing as *trying* to quit. When someone says that they are trying, it means they do not really want to stop. You either smoke or don't smoke. It is a habit that we pick up along the way in life, for whatever reason, and then find ourselves addicted to it. I have seen patients who were able to stop cold turkey. It often comes down to the value they put on themselves—and their life.

What can Eastern medicine offer you?

There are a myriad of Eastern medical disciplines that one can choose to use either alone or in combination to help you continue to address your disease...or simply to maintain a healthy state.

Acupuncture

An Acupuncturist is a great asset to your health team. Acupuncture, like most Eastern medicines, aims to balance the energy of the person. Needles are inserted at certain points in the body along what are called Acupuncture channels. The energy is said to flow in the space between muscles and tendons throughout the entire body. Acupuncture not only balances the overall energy of the person, but can also be directed to influence the cardiovascular system or, for that matter, any other organ system in the body. There are several studies being conducted to find out how

Acupuncture can help treat cardiac conditions.

I want to emphasize one important point: Acupuncture does not treat specific diseases, but it does treat specific imbalances. If an Acupuncturist claims that they can treat specific diseases, they are not being true to the philosophy of Acupuncture. With Acupuncture, the concept of treating the disease—rather than treating the person—has no power behind it. If there is no power, the treatment will not be successful. Acupuncture treats the person to balance the energy, and it is expected that this balancing will then influence the person to eradicate the disease. As a result, the effects of Acupuncture are slow to manifest. Most often, when I suggest to my patients that Acupuncture's effect may be slow to manifest, they lose heart. That is unfortunate, because a little patience could go along way...and Acupuncture could be a component of a multi-faceted approach to health and disease control that could deliver positive results.

When I was practicing Acupuncture in London at Ravi's clinic, several executives, musicians, and well-known performance artists used to come weekly for a session of Acupuncture just as a general balancing therapy. They did not have any health problems. They claimed that Acupuncture offered them such a balanced state that their performances were better. My experience was the same in New York in the 1990s when I treated several professionals and performing artists in the city.

So to treat imbalances related to cardiac health, the Acupuncturist may use points to influence the sympathetic and parasympathetic (fight or flight) system to influence your blood vessels and heart. This could, in turn, potentially aid in cardiac health. The Acupuncturist can also influence internal inflammation by stimulating certain Acupuncture points. Minimizing internal inflammation can also play a role in cardiac health. The Acupuncturist cannot specifically prevent a heart attack (or any specific disease), but by balancing different energies and associated imbalances that can cause symptoms that play a role in cardiac disease, the Acupuncturist can achieve some indirect influence.

Massage

Massage is one of my favorite modalities because I grew up using it. And it's one that so many people can benefit from. How often have you felt tension building up in your muscles? If you're like most of us, in this fast-paced and high-stress world, it could be something you deal with daily.

Therapies like deep tissue massage help get rid of muscular tensions and energy blockages in our body and facilitate better energy flow. Some massage therapists can also use massage to stimulate Acupuncture points that are specifically related to the heart organ and its associated organs. Massage is especially useful in children for whom the thought of needles or Acupuncture would not fare favorably. In today's world, regular massage therapy is not only a welcome break, but a very therapeutic tool from a mind-body perspective. It calms the nerves, relaxes the body, and helps eliminate toxins. Make sure to drink plenty of water before and after massage therapy.

Massage helps the body by modifying and enhancing our ability to handle stress and, as a result, it reduces the harmful effects of stress on our system. Additionally, massage enhances the function of the muscles and aligns these functions with those of the rest of the body. As discussed earlier, the stressed personality type (Type-A personality) is at higher risk for cardiac disease. Massage is a great complement to other stress management techniques.

Homeopathy

Homeopathy is a discipline that aims to treat what is called the *constitutional make-up* of a person. In other words, it treats your core and fundamental structure. The mainstay of this modality is the use of substances that occur naturally in nature. The goal of Homeopathic treatment is that your ability to ward off disease or resist disease is improved. It improves your resistance to developing disease and, if you have a disease already, it strengthens your ability to fight it. Homeopathy is an energy medicine. Most Homeopathic remedies do not have the molecular structure of a medical substance in them. What the remedy captures and delivers is the energy of the substance. Therefore, there is no chance of feeling a side effect. The philosophy of Homeopathy is referred to as "like cures like." For example, we normally drink mega doses of coffee to stay awake. The treatment in Homeopathy for insomnia (the inability to fall asleep) is actually coffee—but in a very minute dose. What causes insomnia in a high dose is what, in a very small dose, cures insomnia...like cures like. When I was in London, I witnessed significant improvement in patients' conditions with Homeopathy as a result of those principles enhancing the patient's chance of fighting a disease...either with Western medicine or by itself.

Chiropractic Care

A chiropractic physician aims to influence your nervous system. Nerves supply all organs and tissues in the body. The heart is no different. A chiropractor will manipulate the vertebral column to release the tension on the nerves that exit from the spinal column at different levels of the vertebrae on their way to supply the various organs and tissues. By releasing the tension of the nerves that build up over time through our daily living, a chiropractor will help reset the vitality of the nerves to the organs which in turn enhance their ability to function better. Specific to cardiac, the chiropractor may pay more attention to the vertebrae at the neck and chest level to optimize the nerves that exit at this level to get to the heart. Additionally, chiropractors may have extra training in Acupuncture, herbs and so on, therefore they may provide some of the therapies I have mentioned under Eastern medicine.

I had a friend who was 90 years old and used a walker to move around. He had a session of chiropractic manipulation done and was able to walk without the walker immediately. This is a small example of the efficacy of this discipline.

Herbs

Herbs are prescribed by several alternative practitioners including Naturopathic physicians, traditional Chinese practitioners, Acupuncturists, and Ayurvedic practitioners. Herbs help strengthen various organ systems. It is beyond the scope of this book to detail all that herbs can do (or all the herbs themselves) to help the cardiovascular system. Herbs are taken orally and, therefore, one should be cautious in utilizing herbs on a daily basis. Unlike Homeopathy where only the energy of the remedy is transferred to you, you ingest the ingredients of the herbs and it's possible that you could experience side effects. Extra caution should be taken to understand interactions between not only various herbs, but also between herbs and Western medicines, as these interactions can result in serious consequences if you are not careful. You should consult with both your Western and Eastern medical practitioners when considering herbal therapy.

Yoga and meditation

This is another favorite of mine. Yoga enhances mind-body union. Yoga exercises benefit the entire person in several ways. And if there is one system of physical activity that combines the union of mind and body, it is Yoga. Especially, if one includes meditation in the practice of Yoga.

Tai Chi, an ancient Chinese tradition of exercise and breathing, is another discipline where intense focus and attention is required during the movement. Yoga and meditation have been shown to help stabilize a person's heart rate, regulate blood pressure, and help with overall well-being and the ability to face the stressors of day-to-day life. When you practice Yoga on a daily basis, you will begin to handle daily stressors as though you are taking care of another person's problem instead of your own. In other words, it helps you detach yourself to better handle an issue without getting emotionally involved and allowing emotion to direct your response by reflex. It gives you clarity in thinking. It allows you to be mindful. It gives you the ability to pause in the face of a stressful situation. It surely helped me on October 11, 2006.

Ayurveda

Ayurveda is a system of practices that originated in ancient India. I grew up in this tradition. The system involves not only natural remedies for the treatment of various ailments, but also includes a system of living that promotes health. Most of the modalities used are related to cleansing the body by various means to get rid of the accumulation of unwanted toxins. This allows your body to regain its full, functional potential. Additional modalities within Ayurveda tradition include adjustments to a person's diet to suit his or her temperament and the ingestion of various supportive remedies for the maintenance of wellness.

At this point, you should have a good idea of what Eastern and Western medical systems can offer you as tools to take care of your health. It is obvious, I believe, that in comparison to Western medicine, Eastern medicine offers a multitude of modalities that you can choose to enhance your health and well-being—and strengthen yourself.

I was using all of these modalities, with the exception of Chiropractic therapy, prior to suffering my heart attack. What astounded me was the fact that none of this prevented or protected me from heart attack.

I do believe, however, that these modalities aided in minimizing the intensity of the heart attack, my ability to recover from it—and could have even played a role in the fact that I lived to tell my story.

That is when I realized that, while these Eastern and Western treatments and therapies are very useful and beneficial, the full benefit of these efforts can only be realized when you combine these efforts with becoming a *proper being*. This is what I meant by my statement: **It is not what you do that impacts your health, it is who you must be.** When I changed my being and then combined the techniques and treatments of East and West, the benefits of these efforts multiplied significantly. In fact if you have the right *being*, you may not need a lot of doing.

The next section deals with your *being*... related to heart disease.

Handling your You Power

Your You Power is perhaps the most important aspect to develop and cultivate in your life related to health, wellness, and well-being. It can impact not only health, but every aspect of life. Your You Power underlies and influences the degree of benefit we can reap from using the Western and Eastern modalities that I have outlined in this chapter. Your You Power reflects the way you are wired. If you do not have the optimal being that is unique to you, then no matter how many of the above modalities you choose to use, there will be no optimal benefit. Certainly, you are likely to see some benefit, but it will not be optimal.

Our optimal being is affected by two things. First, by the constant internal dialogue that goes on in our head. And, secondly, by our personality that has to adapt and adjust based upon how we want to project ourselves to the world.

Internal dialogue or Primal being

The emotions that are associated with the heart are love, joy, anger, and fear. Of these emotions, love and joy are directly associated with heart. Anger and fear are indirectly associated, via the liver and kidney respectively. In my experience, as I have stated on the opening page of this chapter, most patients with heart disease tend to have an internal dialogue of "I am not loved enough" going on within themselves. On the other hand, they are also likely to have problems allowing other people to love them. This internal dialogue goes on within themselves on a daily basis, underneath their consciousness, without their being aware of it. Over time, this battle within themselves erodes the heart.

In order to correct this internal dialogue, and to prevent heart energy from draining or dissipating, one must change the dialogue. This involves what I call an *emotional cleanse*. This term is very new to a lot of people. It means you should seek help from a counselor who can help you eliminate or change this dialogue so that you can start believing that you are loved and so you can actually allow others to love you.

In difficult situations when changing this dialogue is challenging, one may have to resort to cognitive therapy or even hypnosis to get to the root of it. Changing these internal dialogues is what *changing your being* means.

This internal dialogue exists in your *primal being*. No one else knows about or experiences this being except you. *Primal being* refers to our raw and unfiltered thoughts, desires, wishes, wants, and emotions. This includes thought processes that we would not share with the outside world.

What you do choose to show the outside world is known as your *social being* or your personality. Your social being is the "politically correct" (or incorrect) behaviors, actions, and thoughts...or how others see you. People look at what you show them about yourself and determine what kind of personality you have.

Personality or Social being

Personality refers to an individual's characteristic pattern of behavior *driven* by their deeper thoughts and emotions, but modified by their rules of conduct to suit the outside world. In other words, it is the primal self, modified to be acceptable in the outside world and within society. The primal being in all of us is essentially the same, but what differs are the rules of engagement that we all have acquired through differences in upbringing, culture, education, religion, and the like. These factors and experiences determine our individuality with regard to our unique personality.

Do you know what type of personality you are? It's hard to correct your being if you do not even know what type of being the world perceives you as. There are personality tests that can be done to ascertain what type of personality you are. The first step in learning to change your being is to understand what type of being you currently are. Once you determine that, you can then perform an emotional cleanse and progress on the path to fully understanding yourself.

Many people have already taken a Personality Test or Index. And many people find them very enlightening—even validating. If you choose not to do a personality test, I suggest basic counseling to begin the process of looking within yourself to identify the constant triggers that steal your spirit and precious vital energy as a first step to a tremendous improvement in your current assessment of YOU.

Chapter Two

Liver

The Bleeding Killer

I don't want to face life.

The liver is a single organ that is located in the abdominal cavity. It is the largest internal organ in our body and is considered the largest gland as well. The function of the liver, as an important organ in the purification of our body, is complex. One of the functions of the liver is to receive all the digested and absorbed nutrients and other substances from the gastrointestinal tract, metabolize these materials, and then distribute them throughout the body.

The liver is also involved in the detoxification of the body. Most of the drugs we take for illnesses, either by mouth or intravenously, are degraded and metabolized in the liver. This means that, thanks to our liver, the drugs we ingest become active, functioning chemicals that address a specific abnormality in our body or are degraded so that they can be eliminated from the body via the gut (in the stools) or via the kidney (in urine). The entire description of the liver's functions is beyond the scope of this book, and for our purposes we can think of our liver as an organ that functions like a clearing house.

Eastern and Western medicines look at the functions of the liver very differently on the surface, but I think you'll see that there are similarities in both thought processes.

The American Liver Foundation reports that every year, approximately 1,500 people in the United States die waiting for a liver transplant[1]. And each year, about 17,000 adults and children are on a waiting list for liver transplants in the United States[1]. This waiting list continues to grow every year. Since 2004, an average of 6,000 liver transplants are performed each year[2]. There are always more transplant candidates than donors and oftentimes the waiting list for a viable liver is a long one.

An interesting fact about the liver is that it can actually regenerate itself by growing new cells. In comparison, organs like the heart and kidneys are not able to regenerate and replace lost cells. Once lost due to injury or illness, areas of heart and kidney are replaced only by scar tissue, not new cells. This is why a person who donates a part of his or her liver to someone in need of a transplant can not only survive but continue to lead a normal life. The donor's liver regenerates and can support the donor sufficiently.

One of my patients, a man in his thirties, was in the prime of his life. He was well-educated, had a great job, and an outgoing personality However, whenever he was out with his friends having fun, he would get so intoxicated that he was not aware of his surroundings most of the time. For him, "fun" was deadening himself to his surroundings through alcohol. As a result, he had trouble keeping up with the responsibilities of his job and tended to change jobs quite frequently. He had trouble maintaining meaningful relationships with his partners. He had what most people would call an *anti-social personality*.

Over the years, as I got to know him better, I learned that he felt as if he was punished excessively as a child. This feeling was born out of real experience; he *was,* in fact, excessively punished as a child. But the important observation I made was that he continued to feel that way even as an adult—even in the absence of ongoing punishment in his adult life. He had trouble trusting people and facing the real world, even though it was not readily apparent to those who interacted with him. He had trouble separating what was true and what was not true related to what he thought about himself.

As time went on, and as his drinking continued, he was unable to keep a job. He became unemployed and developed liver disease from alcohol abuse. His skin color changed, he was jaundiced (yellowed skin), and his energy level plummeted. He kept telling me "Don't worry, I am a happy guy." And he was very happy—as long as he escaped from the world. And his escape was alcohol.

Several attempts to address the addiction failed and he died, in his forties, from end-stage liver disease. At the time of his death, he had uncontrollable bleeding from all the orifices in his body. As will be discussed later in this book, one of the major issues with end-stage liver disease is uncontrollable bleeding that can lead to death despite the best medical efforts.

This story may seem like an extreme example, but I think we all know someone who reminds us of this wonderful man. We all know someone who is headed toward this path, or already on it.

Once the disease developed, his Western medical practitioner took his personality for granted. His alcoholism was taken for granted. He was advised to stop drinking—without anyone looking into why he was resorting to alcohol. The person, the man he was, was not treated. Because he did not have anyone to tell him what was wrong with him as a person, he handled the situation, his internal dialogue, the best way he knew how. My advice: Don't take anything for granted and do not rely on one point of view, one source of advice. Strongly consider the importance of the Eastern medicine philosophy of "treat the patient—not the disease" and the importance of You Power in your health and fight against disease.

The Western side of the liver coin

With regard to the patient example we just reviewed, in Western medicine we look at the causes of liver disease, its symptoms, and how to diagnose it. Then we decide the treatment for the disease. There are several factors that can affect the liver and cause disease. The common causes of liver disease include the following:

- Alcohol abuse – the most common cause in North America
- Excessive doses of medications that are toxic to the liver – such as Acetaminophen, an ingredient in Tylenol
- Viral infections of the liver such as hepatitis (*hepa* means liver and *itis* means inflammation due to any insult). These are hepatitis A, B or C, D, or E.
- Cancers of the liver

Each of these causes has its own risk factors and behaviors that predispose people to get ill. For example, alcohol abuse is related to an abnormal behavior of a person. Likewise, acquiring the hepatitis B or C virus requires the virus to be introduced into your body via body fluids from infected people. This happens when people share needles related to recreational drug use, engage in unprotected sexual activities, or receive a contaminated blood transfusion. Today, many safeguards are in place for transfusions and the use of infection-free blood in those transfusions. That said, I have treated patients who have contracted liver disease from infected blood they received before protocols and new standards related to blood donors were in place.

Symptoms of liver disease include:

- Fatigue and weakness
- Nausea and or vomiting
- Weight loss
- Yellow coloration of the skin called *jaundice*

- Tendency toward bleeding
- Pain in the upper abdomen

Simple blood tests can identify abnormal liver function and recognize the problem.

At the beginning of this chapter, I described the main function of the liver and I will expand on those functions here so that a comparison between Western and Eastern understanding of the functions of the liver can be made. These functions are:

- Production of a substance called *bile* which is necessary for the digestion of fat
- Storage of extra glucose and supply of more glucose when needed
- Production of blood clotting factors – If these factors are not produced by the liver, due to liver failure, a patient can bleed uncontrollably.
- Processing of iron to help make red blood cells
- Manufacturing of cholesterol
- Metabolitization of medications and other toxins for elimination

Once liver disease is diagnosed, Western medicine recommends that the underlying cause of the liver disease be treated. People are advised to stop alcohol consumption or stop taking excess doses of the medications. Hepatitis is treated with powerful anti-viral medications. When the disease progresses to an end stage, the only form of advanced therapy is liver transplantation. The concern in Western medicine is related to biochemical changes, structure, and function. As a result, the recommendations for the restoration of health are limited.

Eastern side of the liver coin

In Western medicine, liver refers to an organ and its functions. Although Eastern Acupuncture medicine has a concept that is addressed in modern times as *liver*, it encompasses more of the energy and functional aspects and, therefore, it is defined by several functions rather than as an anatomical organ.

In Eastern medicine, the liver is defined by several functions. The main function is to ensure the smooth flow of energy in our entire body. In Acupuncture, the blood is said to carry one form of our energy throughout the body and, therefore, the liver is concerned with the smooth flow of blood via the storage and release of blood and body fluids in the circulatory system.

Using the example of my patient's story, as he became severely ill, his lack of energy became apparent. The change in the color of his skin was noticeable and his eyes had lost their luster as a result of his lower energy level. His energy was so low that he contracted infections easily and had no resistance to fight them off.

The story is similar when it comes to another major Eastern discipline called Ayurveda. Ayurveda confers similar principles to the functions of the liver. The liver organ falls into the characterization of *Pitta* in Ayurveda. Pitta is concerned with all transformations in the body. For example, the transformation of digested food and fluids, the transformation of light in the retina into sensations, the transformation of triggers into thoughts at the level of the brain, and so on. It is concerned with the aspect of transformation wherever it exists in our body. As you may recall, this is similar to what is proposed in Acupuncture. The liver falls under Pitta in this regard and imbalances in Pitta can initially lead to energetic imbalances followed by abnormal function and then destruction of the organ, the liver, if left unchecked.

This is a good point at which to emphasize that in the descriptions regarding individual disease examples and throughout this book,

I have alluded to an energy imbalance preceding the development of the organ disease that is later diagnosed by Western medicine. You will also notice a connection between these energy imbalances and emotional changes and subsequent behavior changes. The concern here is how an energy imbalance leads to abnormal function and then leads to structural abnormality. As we compare and contrast the differences between Eastern and Western thinking, this connection becomes very clear. In Western thinking, a functional abnormality develops first and then leads to a structural abnormality whereas in Eastern thinking, an energy imbalance develops first followed by functional abnormality and then progresses to structural abnormality.

The *liver* in Acupuncture has deeper and more complex explanations and descriptions that are beyond the scope of this book. For our purposes here, the liver-type patients in Acupuncture tend to prefer the climate of the Spring, the color blue-green, and the taste sour. The emotion associated with the liver is anger. Healthy nails indicate the energetic level of the liver and the liver is said to control our tears. For example, if you have problems with tears, such as excessive tears or lack of tears, in Acupuncture this indicates an imbalance of the *liver* organ.

Interestingly, Acupuncture does not describe causative factors for liver abnormality, with the exception of emotions such as anger, frustration, and resentment. Ayurveda, on the other hand, describes some causative factors with regard to liver disease patterns. These Ayurvedic factors include competitiveness and drinking too much alcohol, which can lead to too much Pitta in the body. It also identifies eating too many tomatoes, chilies, eggplant, spinach, and onions—as well as, too much exposure to sun—as giving rise to Pitta abnormalities.

You Power • The third side of the liver coin

As a heart transplant cardiologist and pulmonary hypertension specialist, I have the opportunity to see liver transplant patients in consultation when they need cardiac clearance to undergo a liver transplant. There is a recognizable pattern in these patients. The liver failure patients I have seen exhibited a consistent and common emotional or personality undertone. It is important to note that the majority of patients I have observed had liver failure as a result of alcoholism or hepatitis acquired from poly-substance abuse. The following are those tendencies:

- A tendency to avoid the rest of the world and shy away from it is often the most predominant. These people would be happy to lock themselves in a room or crawl under the bed and not face the world. But they don't do that. They may appear to be very outgoing people, but they block out the world by deadening their awareness with addictions to substances such as alcohol.

- A tendency toward poly-substance abuse, predominantly alcohol. Also a tendency to abuse other substances such as recreational drugs in an effort to avoid the world or distance themselves from the surroundings.

- A tendency not to follow through with actions recommended by doctors or care providers—what we call *non-compliance* in medicine. This characteristic not only relates to medicine and medical opinions, but also to other aspects of their lives.

This is just a snapshot of patients who have liver failure due to alcohol abuse and hepatitis. There are other causes of liver disease, including inherited disorders of the liver itself. The considerations that lead to the development of liver impairment in those patients are too numerous to list. However, a general tendency and personality pattern can be drawn from these examples while keeping in mind that the tendencies can have several shades, ranging from those that are readily obvious to those that are very subtle and difficult to detect.

This was the case with the patient in the example I shared earlier. It was hard to conceive what he was going through internally during his childhood and how he carried those experiences and memories into his adult life. He was well dressed and had a great demeanor and a well-paying job. To a casual observer, he appeared to be just like you and me. His internal dialogue—his desire not to face the world or life—was not communicated to the external world except when he distanced and deadened himself by getting drunk.

When this behavior happens, in Western medicine we advise the patient to stop drinking. That's all. We do not address why this person is drinking or what is at the root of this behavior. We blame the addiction without looking at the root cause. The trigger is the internal dialogue that results in a social behavior, or what we call *personality*. In the case of patients with liver disease, they tend to have what we call *anti-social personality*.

The question of whether these tendencies give rise to liver abnormalities—or whether the liver abnormalities give rise to these tendencies—is an ongoing debate as the Western world has not collected enough data to support either position. The accumulating data, however, tends to point toward the personality being at the core of the development of disease states.

In Eastern medicine, the emotional tendencies not only play a role in the initiation of imbalances, but also in how the disease manifests. In other words, continued extreme emotional imbalances indicate an imbalance of the associated organ. Therefore, if we are able to identify the predominant emotions that we feel the majority of the time, we may be able to recognize that our liver function at a subtle level, at an energetic level, may be altered. For example, from an Eastern perspective, if you feel frustrated and angry most of the time, it is time to take action to balance the energy of your liver before it progresses to a structural abnormality of the organ itself. The way to deal with it is to handle the cause of your anger right away, rather than ignoring it or just putting up with it.

I want to emphasize the principle taught by Eastern medicine that the relationship between emotions and the function of an organ is mutual. In other words, extreme emotions that continue over a long period (called *mood*) can unbalance the organ to cause dysfunction and, conversely, an imbalance of an organ can result in the excessive expression of a particular emotion associated with that organ.

What can you do?

The first step is easy: Understand that there are three sides that need to be considered. These are: Western medicine (a teammate), Eastern medicine (a teammate), and The You Power (the team captain). Western medicine is only 30 percent helpful when it comes to your healthy future. When you receive recommendations from a Western medical practitioner, only one-third of your problem is taken care of. If you want to help another 30 percent of your being, then you need to seek out help from your the Eastern medical teammate. However, if you want to be successful in accomplishing your goal of optimum health and reaping the benefits of both Western and Eastern medicines, you need to pay attention to You Power. Your ultimate success or failure in either overcoming a disease or maintaining health depends on how well you can influence your You Power—and the critical role each of us plays in maintaining or restoring our health. This was the problem with my patient who faced liver disease. Several attempts to get rid of the addiction were not successful because his internal dialogue (part of his You Power) was never fully and successfully addressed.

What can Western medicine offer you?

How would a Western medical practitioner address my patient? First of all—and this point underscores a key difference between a Western medical perspective and an Eastern medical one—a Western medical practitioner won't even consider addressing any issue unless there is a symptom that can be a starting point for a diagnosis. Once symptoms develop, you and I know that functional and structural changes have already occurred in the at-risk organ. We have already missed a golden opportunity to address and reverse the problem—had we only identified it earlier through other subtle abnormalities such as emotional changes, mood level, or energy level. Nevertheless, once the problem is identified, the Western medical practitioner will use the following treatments.

Medications

A Western medical practitioner will prescribe medications based on your blood test results and other investigative findings. For example, if you have hepatitis, medications to treat hepatitis will be prescribed. Medications to prevent and control bleeding or medications to reduce swelling can be prescribed. Additionally, medications to eliminate some toxins that are not readily eliminated due to liver dysfunction can be prescribed. Interestingly, Western medicine recognizes end-stage liver disease to be associated with the development of abnormal function of the lungs due to increased pressure in the lungs, and dysfunction of the right side of the heart that causes heart failure and leads to kidney failure. These associations have already been described by ancient Eastern medical disciplines such as Acupuncture many years ago. Most of what is prescribed by Western medicine is done to control the consequences of liver disease—not to correct it. Only recently do we have medications that seem to eliminate diseases such as Hepatitis C. Even then, the damage to the liver organ by this disease may have already been completed.

Diet

Diet is a major contributor to abnormal liver health. Diet helps in several ways. Up to this point, we have concentrated on liver damage caused by alcohol. Dietary habits can also cause liver damage and lead to what is called *non-alcoholic fatty liver disease* (NAFLD) in the Western medical world. Simply put, NAFLD is the excessive consumption of certain types of food that can cause the liver to turn into fat. You may be familiar with the 2004 documentary titled *Supersize Me* in which the director ate all his meals at McDonalds and did not exercise for a month. He gained weight and developed high cholesterol and fatty liver (NAFLD). These findings have been subsequently corroborated by other studies by Western medical researchers[3]. It appears that a steady consumption of fast food, artery-clogging fat, and sugary drinks can lead to liver function abnormalities. Even worse, the risk from these types of diets increases for those older than 40.

If what you've just learned about diet concerns you, try eating fewer foods containing saturated fats and transfats, and minimizing fast food consumption, and sugary drinks such as soda and fruit juices. You can also increase the intake of omega 3 fatty acids and fiber in your diet.

A word of caution on supplements—especially dietary supplements taken for weight loss: These supplements can cause damage to the liver.

We all know that there are several natural ways to lose weight. In my opinion, if a person needs to resort to dietary supplements to lose weight, there is something seriously wrong with that person's being. The best way to address this issue is to address the underlying You Power, rather than ingesting harmful supplements to correct the problem of excess weight. If you choose to use supplements and not address the underlying cause, the fight against weight is going to be a lifelong battle.

Several medications prescribed by Western medical practitioners for different disease conditions can affect the function of the liver and can lead to damage if liver function is not checked on a regular basis. I encourage you to be aware of medications that can cause liver damage. Remember that, because the liver functions as a clearing house or factory clearing these medications from the body, it can be overwhelmed by medications that affect the organ liver. Ask your health care provider about the side effects of any medications you may be taking, related to the liver.

Exercise

Regular, moderate exercise is one of the best ways to improve your overall health. Interestingly, the studies mentioned above related to diet combined both the consumption of fast food with restrictions on regular exercise. A combination of fast food and lack of exercise resulted in abnormal liver function. This underscores the importance of exercise for liver health.

In the case of my patient, he did exercise but did not do so regularly. In his case, as I have alluded to repeatedly, what he did—or did not do—was only part of the problem. His primal self and his being were the main problems that led to his demise.

Alcohol and Drug Consumption

Where the liver is concerned, the prescription for alcohol and drugs is pretty straightforward: Stop drinking alcohol and using recreational drugs, if you are using them. Instead, ask yourself what internal dialogue or conflict is being numbed by the effect of the drugs or alcohol.

There is clear evidence that alcohol damages the liver and can lead to the development of liver cirrhosis and end-stage liver disease requiring a liver transplant. Even if you do not have liver disease, but take medications for other diseases, alcohol interferes with the breakdown and elimination of these medications by the liver and can result in the abnormal handling of these medications. This can lead to reduced efficacy or toxicity of those medicines. Recreational drug use can affect the function of the liver in similar ways. Another problem with recreational drug use is that it increases your risk of contracting hepatitis through needle sharing. Overall, addiction to any substance—food, excessive supplements, alcohol, or recreational drugs—is not good for you or your liver.

What can Eastern medicine offer you?

There are a myriad of Eastern medical disciplines that one can choose to use, either alone or in combination, to help you continue to address your liver disease or simply to maintain a healthy state.

Acupuncture

An Acupuncturist understands the liver from its function. The liver is responsible for the smooth flow of blood and energy (*Qi*—pronounced *Chi*). It is interesting to note that even in Western medicine, it is a well-known fact that bleeding complications are very frequent when a person has end stage liver disease. An ancient observation is not far from what we practice in Western medicine today. An Acupuncturist will examine your eyes, nails, as well as the color of the skin and other physical aspects before moving on to questioning you about your favorite color, taste, season, and so on. If these indicators point to an abnormality of the organ liver, then treatment will involve inserting needles along the channel that pertains to the organ liver on your body. The Acupuncturist may use an associated organ channel to treat you as well. In the case of the liver, the paired or associated organ is the gall bladder. The channels pertaining to both of these organs are situated on your lower extremity and the trunk. In the case of the gall bladder, the channel starts on your foot and runs all the way up to your head.

If you have liver disease, let the Acupuncturist know about your condition. It is also important to let the Acupuncturist know that you may bruise easily and have bleeding tendencies. This knowledge will allow the Acupuncturist to adjust the treatment program accordingly or use other methods such as acupressure or laser stimulation of the pressure points instead of needles.

Some Acupuncturists may use reflexology to help in cases where needling is not possible.

Massage

Massage on a regular basis can influence your stress and aid in better handling of the emotions associated with the liver such as anger, frustration, and resentment. As I have already stated, this can help to address your You Power more effectively, especially when a fluctuation in your emotional state arises. Additionally, a massage therapist can stimulate channels that pertain to the liver and gall bladder channels to invigorate the flow of energy along those channels. I would submit that an addiction to massage—rather than food, alcohol, or recreational drugs—may positively influence your health and your You Power to benefit a healthy life.

The idea of employing Eastern medical disciplines in your life is to *prevent* developing liver abnormalities. However, if you do have liver disease and want to use massage, Eastern modalities can still help to support healing and well-being. When having a massage, it's important to tell the massage therapist that you have liver disease. Make sure that the therapist adjusts the pressure of the massage to reduce the chance of bruising, as you may bruise easily and have bleeding tendencies. Another issue with liver disease is that you may have a swollen abdomen and, in this case, positioning yourself for massage becomes a very important consideration. Find a comfortable position that can be tolerated for the duration of the therapy.

Homeopathy

Homeopathy can be used at early stages of liver abnormality detected by Eastern medical practitioners. However, if you have developed structural liver disease and have a Western medical diagnosis of liver disease, Homeopathy can still be a great adjunct.

Most patients with liver disease have abdominal complaints such as appetite changes, problems with bowel movements such as diarrhea or constipation, and nausea. In these cases, Homeopathy can be used only as an adjunct to Western medical therapy in discussion with your doctor.

One of the advantages of Homeopathy in patients with liver disease compared to herbal therapy is that Homeopathy is an energy medicine. As such, no significant amounts of the remedy are administered to you and it's likely that there will be few side effects or interactions with medications prescribed by Western medical practitioners that you may already be taking. Be sure to let the Homeopath know about your Western medical diagnosis if you have one, and let your Western medical doctor know about the use of Homeopathy. The important point here is to let your teammates know about the rules under which the game is played. If you don't, the only person who will lose is you.

I have used Homeopathic remedies for liver abnormality diagnosed via energy imbalance (when liver function blood tests were normal) and have seen significant changes in the way I experienced and handled emotions, diet, and my energy level after the conclusion of the treatment.

Chiropractic Care

Liver dysfunction and its progress, which can lead to death or require a liver transplant at its end stages, can be significantly influenced by a chiropractor. First of all, in early stages of liver imbalance, which have not yet resulted in any structural changes in your liver, optimizing the nerve supply to the liver can result in a reversal of the imbalance and set you on the path to liver health.

For example, let's say you have minor symptoms and went to an Eastern medical practitioner who told you that you have liver imbalance. In this situation, the first thing to do is to seek out your Western medical practitioner and obtain necessary investigations to ascertain that the energy imbalance diagnosed by the Eastern medical practitioner has not resulted in structural and biochemical changes in your liver. Once you confirm the absence of structural and biochemical abnormalities, the use of chiropractic therapy can put you on a path to health and make your symptoms better. Remember, in this situation a Western medical practitioner won't be able to help you a lot because the symptoms are very non-specific and no identifiable liver abnormalities can be confirmed by testing.

On the other hand, if your Western medical practitioner confirms structural and biochemical changes in your body related to your liver, then you will use recommendations from both disciplines. In this situation, the function of other organs may begin to be affected as well, due to the liver dysfunction. A chiropractor can optimize the nervous input to all of your abdominal organs—heart, lungs, and kidney—through manipulation. It is important to optimize all organs that are affected in order to have a combined optimization, which has a better chance of improving your condition. Keep in mind this important fact: Your body functions as a unit with multiple organs that are meant to perform their action in synchrony and unity.

I see this situation all the time in my heart patients. Severe heart failure affects other organs such as kidney, liver, and lungs. Most commonly, the treatment (even in Western medicine) is to treat all affected organs in a combined fashion. The thought behind this strategy is that if you treat only one affected organ and leave the others unattended, the patient's health is not optimized and he or she stands to lose. Even in the transplant world, it is not unusual to perform a combined heart and kidney transplant. And combined heart, kidney, and liver transplants have been performed in this country.

Herbs

Herbs are prescribed by several alternative practitioners including Naturopathic physicians, traditional Chinese practitioners, Acupuncturists, Chiropractors, and Ayurvedic practitioners. Herbs have a role in liver imbalance when there is no structural and biochemical change in the liver function. This is an area where you should use utmost vigilance if you have a liver abnormality. Herbs—wrongly prescribed or in excessive amounts—can not only affect your liver and cause liver abnormality but can also interact with other medications that you may currently be taking, even if those medications are not related to your liver.

This is because the liver functions as a clearing house and works overtime to handle all the substances we put into our body. It is therefore important to discuss the use of herbs carefully, not only with your Eastern teammate but also with your Western medical practitioner as well. Having said that, in the absence of structural and biochemical changes with regard to liver (at an energy imbalance level), herbs can help cleanse the functions of the liver just like Homeopathy and a Chiropractic therapy can help strengthen the organ and its associated functions.

Remember, you want to maximize your benefits from having two teammates. Do let each of them know that you are playing with both teammates and they will advise you how to incorporate their contributions. If they cannot, it is time to look for a new teammate. What is most important is to have a practitioner who is unbiased, balanced in his or her approach, and has your best interest in mind.

Yoga and Meditation

Yoga is very gentle and can be adjusted to focus on your particular liver disease. There are several Yoga exercises that benefit the organ liver. As an organ in the abdominal cavity, the liver can be exercised by various Yoga postures. The most important exercises are forward-bending and backward-bending postures. When you bend forward and suck your belly in, it squeezes the liver and expels blood out of it. When you come out of this position and bend backwards, it allows a rush of blood into liver (a process called *hyperemia* in Western medicine). This helps flush out the liver and invigorate it for a healthier function. Additionally, forward bending and backward bending help invigorate the nerves coming out of your spine and help invigorate all organs in the abdomen. This is similar to having a Chiropractic manipulation. The good news is you don't need a Chiropractor and can learn to do Yoga yourself every day, versus Chiropractic manipulation which is done every few months or so.

Ayurveda

Ayurveda uses a system of healthy living to promote the health and well-being of a person. This system utilizes various cleansing methods to purify the body of its toxins and unwanted substances on a regular basis. As such, it is a very helpful adjunct to maintaining a body free of impurities that, in turn, allows optimal function of the organs.

For example, an Ayurvedic physician will consider a liver cleanse in a person with liver disease. Once the liver cleanse is completed, it is expected that the combined function of all of liver's activities are enhanced. This may result in better digestion and assimilation of food as well as better mental acuity and focus by cleansing the blood of impurities. It can also aid in the better handling of medications. Once the cleanse is done, Ayurvedic herbal remedies can be used to treat the underlying liver disease. However, as I've stressed, I would use caution in this situation in order to avoid interactions. Ayurvedic treatments can be used as an adjunct or alone, depending upon the person's degree of liver dysfunction. Again it is important to inform both your teammates about the interventions you are using from Western and Eastern sides.

In the modern world, we are surrounded by chemical toxins from prepared and packaged food, alcohol, bottled and packaged juices and drinks, unregulated supplements as well as toxins absorbed through our skin from the our soaps, deodorants, and lotions. Additionally, we live in a frustrating world where anger, resentment, and similar emotions are induced on a daily basis. Can you recall a single day when you did not feel angry or frustrated at something or someone? For most of us, the answer is no.

As a result, most of us are walking around with some degree of liver imbalance. This imbalance, in turn, can cause us to react with more anger and frustration than we typically might to the same degree of stimulation. It is for this reason that I recommend a periodic liver cleanse throughout the year to optimize and take care of your liver. Intervention of this kind exists only in the realm of Eastern medical practice. For Western medicine to kick in, you must first have a symptom.

Handling your You Power

The You Power is perhaps the most important aspect to develop and cultivate, not only when it comes to health but in every aspect of life. I have known people who drank alcohol like a fish and never developed liver disease, as well as those who drank moderately (or for only a short time) and developed liver abnormality. The difference between these two types of people was their You Power.

Keep in mind those people who never drank alcohol but who developed liver disease, and those whose diet or use of supplements has negatively impacted their liver function. The pivotal question is: What is it—within you—that drives you to drink or to engage in addictive behavior? It doesn't matter whether it's alcohol, recreational drugs, fast food, sweet drinks, or diet supplements.

The answer to this question may seem easy or obvious, but getting to the true cause may not be as easy as it seems. I believe it is the internal dialogue (from our primal being) that leads to a specific type of behavior (as a social being) which, when perpetuated, leads to the depletion of the vitality of any organ in which we have a predisposed weakness.

As a result, it is not the alcohol, but the *reason* we get addicted to it that becomes the important question. Remember, Western medicine actually recommends that moderate consumption of alcohol is beneficial for health. While that may be supported by current research, my recommendation is to consume alcohol only if you fully understand why you are doing it. If you do not understand your motivation or if you feel addicted to it, then question yourself before continuing to consume alcohol.

If you feel you have a tendency toward addiction to the substances we've discussed, take a look at the internal dialogue that is triggering you to act in a certain way. You are either trying to avoid an internal conflict or continuously battling a conflict.

Internal dialogue or Primal being

In the case of my patient, he felt ashamed because of punishment he received as a child. He was afraid of being judged and punished as an adult. As a result, he did not want to face that experience again. The scar that was formed in his mind in his childhood affected him into his adult life. It always does, in all of us.

There is a concept in the world of psychology that refers to adults who behave like children as *adult children*. This assessment is determined by a person's observable behavior, or their *social being*. But what about my patient? He did not behave like a child, yet he had an addictive tendency. In fact, he was a perfect gentleman.

I would therefore submit that *all* adults are adult children carrying scars, memories, bags and baggage from our childhood. Some of us carry it as an internal dialogue and others exhibit it to the outer world by their behavior. Those who exhibit to the outside world are described as *adult children* because all the world perceives their behavior.

The internal dialogue in people with liver disease tends to be associated with facing the world or others. Internally, they are telling themselves "I don't want to face the world or life. I am ashamed, and I do not want to be judged." They are happy to distance themselves from the outer world as permitted by society, and then progress to be numbed as much as possible as the addiction tightens its grip on them. At this point, they are even immune and deadened to their own behavior, or whether their actions are socially acceptable or not.

The key is to learn to identify this internal dialogue. It takes effort. Emotional levels, moods, and tendencies toward addiction can give you a clue to the fact that you are battling an internal dialogue. If you recognize this, do not just ignore it and go on with your life. It may be time to do an emotional cleanse. This is done by seeking help from a counselor or psychologist to work through the emotional conflict that you are carrying.

One of the reasons that Alcoholics Anonymous (AA) is successful in helping people obtain long-lasting results in abstaining from their addiction is because AA's fundamental principle aims to remedy and reinforce your You Power.

Personality or Social being
Personality refers to an individual's characteristic pattern of behavior *driven* by their deeper thought and emotions, but modified by their rules of conduct to suit the outside world. In other words, it is the primal self, modified to suit the outside world and be acceptable within society.

Try your best to understand what type of person you are. Learn how you handle external stress and internal conflicts. Personality will tell you about your prototype for handling life stressors and conflicts. You can obtain this knowledge by being mindful of your feelings and actions, by taking a personality test and studying the results, or by seeking help from a counselor or psychologist. From there you can work your way toward a state of better health.

What is most important is that your You Power determines how much benefit you will reap from the tools that both Western and Eastern medicine can offer you.

Chapter Three

High Blood Pressure

The Silent Killer

I cannot deal with my emotions today.

One in five Americans does not know that they have high blood pressure[1]. Most of my patients admitted that they found out that they had high blood pressure at the time they were being treated for some other problem. These "other problems" were often a heart attack, abnormal rhythm of the heart, kidney problems, diabetes, or a stroke. The problem with high blood pressure is that it does not provide any symptoms, and then progresses—undiagnosed—to a point where complications develop like a heart attack, stroke, or kidney failure...which can lead to death. That's why it is often called *the silent killer*.

High blood pressure is called *hypertension* in the medical world. In 2013, there were about 1,000 deaths per day in the United States that included a diagnosis of hypertension[1]. One in every three adults in the United States has high blood pressure[2]. This amounts to about 29 percent of adult Americans, or 70 million people. African-American and Mexican-American communities especially are at high risk of developing hypertension[1].

High blood pressure puts you at risk of developing a heart attack, stroke, heart failure, and kidney disease. In fact, in a majority of diagnoses—7 out of 10—high blood pressure is often first discovered only when a person has their first heart attack[1]. Keep in mind that this is only in the 50% of the heart attack patients who survive long enough to get to the hospital. This number rises to 8 out of 10 for those who have their first stroke. As you can see, high blood pressure is a condition that creeps up on us—without producing any symptoms. If you are someone who does not regularly see your doctor for a physical exam, you may be at risk of this silent killer.

Several years ago, I was consulted and asked to see a 36-year-old man in the ER. He had no history of medical problems until that day when he came to the Emergency Room at the hospital. Apparently, he was at home one evening when he noticed bleeding from his nose. He went to the ER for further care. The ER staff promptly took care of his nosebleed, but during the process of evaluating him, they learned that he had very high blood pressure. His blood pressure was 240/135 mm Hg.

This is well above what is considered normal or optimal. If he had bled in the brain instead of the nosebleed, he would have suffered a stroke. However, at the time of this diagnosis he did not have any heart, kidney, or brain problems and was otherwise healthy. He was admitted to the Intensive Care Unit for careful administration of medications, via IV, to control his blood pressure. A couple of days later, he was transitioned to oral medications and was discharged, with a follow-up visit as an outpatient.

He did not show up for his first follow-up appointment. We called him and made another appointment for follow up. When he came in for that appointment, he was asked about the medications he was taking. He stated, very matter-of-factly, that he did not bring them with him and could not remember which medications he was taking.

As I followed his progress and care for several years, I found him to be a very nice and polite young man, but he was disorganized. He did not pay attention to our recommendations and always had an excuse for not complying with them. He did not come in for his follow-up appointments regularly, but when he did, he was very respectful, pleasant, and accommodating.

His blood pressure was always uncontrolled during the office visits, meaning it was consistently in the high and abnormal range. I had a hard time managing his medications because he was unaware of the medicines he was taking at the time of the visit. We had discussed extensively the consequences of uncontrolled hypertension. On most occasions, he verbalized his understanding of the information he was given. Yet again and again he would fail to follow through.

We discussed a regular exercise program, a low-salt diet, and relaxation techniques. He showed a lot of interest in learning those techniques, but never did them. Over the years, I learned that as a child he was considered a failure by his parents and siblings. He grew up with a family who made him believe that he could do nothing right—and was bullied about it. His internal dialogue was "I am not good at this. I will do it later, when I can do it better." Hence, he grew up to personify passive-aggressive behavior and procrastination. His first reaction to any task was to postpone doing it.

Throughout the years, we continued to have difficulties controlling his blood pressure. There were times when it was controlled, within normal ranges, but many times it was not. Years later, he developed heart failure and subsequent kidney failure as a result of his high blood pressure. A few years after developing organ failure, he underwent a heart-kidney transplant. Three years after the transplant, his transplanted kidney failed, and he now lives on dialysis three times a week. He has been denied consideration for a kidney re-transplantation because of his past non-compliant behavior.

The Western side of the high blood pressure coin

In Western medicine, high blood pressure is a growing problem. It is considered to be, primarily, a problem related to aging. When high blood pressure is diagnosed in older patients and when no cause is identified, it is called *essential hypertension*. As we age, we tend to develop high blood pressure due to the hardening of our blood vessels. One of the reasons blood vessels harden with age is because cholesterol deposits build up in the lining of the wall of the blood vessels. Therefore, high cholesterol puts us at risk of high blood pressure later in life. Other risk factors that put us at risk of developing high blood pressure include diseases like:

- Diabetes mellitus
- Prehypertension – A condition where your blood pressure is higher than normal, but not high enough for a diagnosis of hypertension by current standards.
- Obesity

Other risk factors include behavior patterns like:

- Sedentary lifestyle or physical inactivity
- Smoking
- Consumption of high-sodium or low-potassium food
- Excessive alcohol consumption

Because high blood pressure does not produce any symptoms it can be a silent killer, and the only way to identify it is to measure blood pressure. Measuring your pressure is a painless procedure and easy to accomplish. You can even measure it yourself with automated home kits or using Blood Pressure kiosks at some pharmacies or grocery stores. A blood pressure reading gives you three numbers: Two numbers for your blood pressure and the other for heart rate. The two blood pressure numbers consists of an upper value and a lower value. The upper value is called the *systolic blood pressure*, which indicates the pressure in your blood vessels when the heart contracts and pumps the blood into the major arteries. The lower value is called the *diastolic blood pressure* and indicates the pressure in your major arteries when the heart relaxes. The *heart rate* is how many times your heart beats in one minute. Therefore, a reading on the screen of a machine may look like this:

S 120

D 80

HR 70

The S indicates systolic pressure and the D indicates diastolic pressure. The HR reflects your heart rate. The blood pressure is measured in units of millimeters of mercury (mm Hg) and the heart rate is estimated at heartbeats per minute. Once you have these values, you can determine whether your blood pressure is low, normal, or high based on current guidelines as detailed in Figure 1 below.

Normal	Systolic: less than 120 mm Hg Diastolic: less than 80 mm Hg
Prehypertension or At Risk	Systolic: 120 – 139 mm Hg Diastolic: 80 – 89 mm Hg
High	Systolic: 140 mm Hg or higher Diastolic: 90 mm Hg or higher

Figure 1: Basic parameters for the diagnosis of high blood pressure.

Blood pressure measurement is part of an annual physical exam; for many people, it is part of a normal wellness program with their family physician. Not surprisingly, some patients have high blood pressure in the physician offices but have normal pressure at home. This is called *white coat syndrome*. Due to the anxiety and stress of being at a doctor's office, patients tend to exhibit higher blood pressure levels than normal, which can be erroneously diagnosed as high blood pressure. Likewise, there is an opposite circumstance in which a patient may have normal pressure at the physician's office but have high pressure in his or her home. This is called *masked hypertension.* In these types of cases, a diagnosis of true hypertension may be missed. Neither *white coat syndrome* nor *masked hypertension* are optimal and can be easily addressed by doing what we call an *ambulatory blood pressure monitoring.* This process involves wearing a blood pressure monitor for 24 hours at home. The blood pressure readings that are recorded during that period are then evaluated by a physician to determine if it is a case of true hypertension.

After a diagnosis of high blood pressure is made, the patient is given either lifestyle behavior recommendations (if the pressure is not very high), or medications (if the pressure is high), or a combination of both, based on the physician's evaluation. Recent studies indicate that a blood pressure close to 120/80 mm Hg results in longer life, compared to aiming for a blood pressure close to 140/90 mm Hg, as it is currently recommended. These latest recommendations have not been included into the current guidelines for physicians.

The Eastern side of the high blood pressure coin

Just as with strokes (which we will cover in the next chapter), Acupuncture evaluates hypertension based upon the underlying pattern of the interactions among different organs. It is not considered to be a pattern of a single organ, but rather can be a pattern that results from collective Yin and Yang imbalances of different organs. As such, the patient is evaluated according to the Five Element principles of the Acupuncture philosophy to make a diagnosis pertaining to the underlying patterns that may give rise to high blood pressure.

Five Element theory is used to explain any phenomena in the Chinese tradition. In the case of traditional Chinese medicine, the Five Element theory is used to describe the relationship between the organ system and the development of imbalances. The five elements are wood, fire, metal, earth, and water. Each element is assigned an organ along with an emotion, color, taste, a sensory organ (eyes, tongue, skin, ears, etc.), climate, and sound. Analyzing the human body using this theory helps determine internal disharmony in the body and thus an energetic diagnosis.

Specifically, the liver and kidneys are the main organs that are associated with the development of high blood pressure. Interestingly, the liver in Acupuncture is associated with the emotion anger and the kidneys are associated with fear. Both these emotions are known to elevate our blood pressure. Fear, as we know, is the underlying emotion that triggers a fight or flight reaction within us. This reaction involves physiological changes such as increased heart rate, increased blood pressure, and increased blood supply to the skeletal muscles. This reaction is an outcome of the activation of our sympathetic nervous system. Increased sympathetic activity results in elevated blood pressure. It can therefore be extrapolated that the chronic presence of these emotions (fear and anger) can result in a chronically-activated sympathetic response, which will tend to elevate the blood pressure and cause hypertension.

Ayurveda, on the other hand, attributes the development of hypertension to potential imbalances of all three energy regulatory systems—Vata, Pitta, and Kapha. This is very similar to Acupuncture's assessment of hypertension as a result of imbalances of multiple organs. However, Ayurveda tradition notes that the condition of high blood pressure has a close relationship to Vata, as Vata is related to the nervous system—and the nervous system has a great influence on blood pressure. As with Acupuncture, a practitioner of Ayurveda will tend to evaluate the person as a whole prior to making a diagnosis and prescribing appropriate therapy. Once the underlying energetic diagnosis is made, both disciplines use the principle of strengthening the underlying *person,* rather than treating a disease. While Acupuncture uses herbs and needles, Ayurveda uses herbs and various cleansing practices.

As we can see, specific descriptions explaining the development of hypertension are missing in both of these Eastern traditions. This is because the energy imbalance that underlies this condition is general in nature, involving the entire organism (the entire body) rather than a particular organ or organ system. And while we can see the similarities between the Eastern and Western thought processes, keep in mind that the former is based on energy balance and the latter is based on biochemical changes.

You Power • The third side of the high blood pressure coin

As a cardiologist, 9 out of every 10 patients I see on a daily basis have high blood pressure. According to national data, 7 out of 10 people with heart failure have high blood pressure[1]. As a result, my exposure to high blood pressure, while extensive, has been masked by the presence of other more serious diseases such as heart failure, heart attack, kidney disease, and stroke. During my practice, there have been prominent characteristics that are prevalent in this population. I have made the following observations:

- They were well-behaved but disorganized.
- They had a negative outlook on life and were distrustful of others.
- They had an internal sense of self-doubt, even though they had experienced successes in life.
- When it came to expressing their feelings and emotions, they tended to suppress their feelings and not express themselves openly, or they over-expressed their feelings.

The patient I described earlier in this chapter shared some of these observations. Obviously, the patient example I've used is very extreme and used to make an important point about hypertension. This does not mean that every patient with hypertension must have these characteristics or to the exact same degree. It should be noted that these characteristics exist at different levels in different people and may not always be obvious in people with hypertension.

In studies that looked at behavior patterns in patients with high blood pressure, two personality patterns emerged as being predominant.

These are the same characteristics that were also present for heart disease, kidney disease, obesity, and stroke. There were only minor differences between the two personality characteristics of these patients. Those characteristics are:

1. **Prone to stress and worry:** These individuals tend to be anxious people who are apprehensive and worry a lot. They can get frustrated easily, feel irritable, and are quick to get angry with others. They are also prone to feel lonely, sad, and rejected. They tend to have difficulty controlling their impulses, wants, and wishes but have no problem handling normal, day-to-day stress.

2. **Spontaneous and careless:** These people tend to lack organizational capacity, are not efficient in making rational decisions, tend to not meet their obligations, and lack self-discipline and motivation.

It should not be surprising that these characteristics are shared by patients who had heart disease, kidney disease, and strokes. As we already know, high blood pressure often leads to these diseases. In my opinion, high blood pressure is like a warning sign before the other catastrophic diseases happen. Therefore, it is imperative to be aware of your internal dialogue and behavior if you have high blood pressure.

Research indicates that a person's personality often changes after intense personal disasters, natural disasters, or structured behavioral education and training. The good news is that even if you remain a person who is prone to stress and worry, by changing the other characteristic (ie: #2 above... the tendency to be spontaneous and careless) in the opposite direction, you can reduce the risk of a catastrophic outcome[3]. In other words, if you learn to be organized, motivated, and prompt in doing tasks without procrastination, you can minimize the consequences of high blood pressure and be able to achieve better blood pressure control[3].

From a psychological perspective, high blood pressure means an unaddressed emotion that is deep-seated within our internal being. These emotions, either fear, anger, or a variation of the two—such as irritability, frustration, and anxiety—result in continued hyperactivity of your autonomic nervous system. Heightened sympathetic activity has been shown to be associated with high blood pressure in Western medical research.

The patient I treated exhibited both the characteristics I've described. He had a tendency to procrastinate. He carried intense negative emotion with regard to his childhood experiences. He expressed anger in a passive-aggressive manner. This prevented him from being able to successfully control his blood pressure, even with the help of medical therapy. This illustrates the fact that—even with the assistance of Western medical therapies—if you don't optimize your You Power, you may not achieve maximum benefits and results for your efforts.

What can you do?

Let us take another look at the patient I described at the beginning of this chapter. He was young and had access to the best that Western medical therapy had to offer for treating his high blood pressure. However, his You Power was not optimized to reap the benefits of the resources that were available to him. If he had learned to be organized, motivated, and compliant he may have had a better chance to avoid or delay the progression of the high blood pressure that led to the need for a heart and kidney transplant. In fact, if he had been complaint, he would not have been turned down for second kidney transplant. As I have referenced previously, personality does play a role in how successfully high blood pressure can be controlled with medical therapy[3].

In the case of my patient, he used only the Western medicines. He played with only one team member. Let us now contrast the first patient with another patient of mine.

This second patient was a very busy professional in his late forties. He came to see me for his high blood pressure because he did not want to take Western medicines. He wanted to explore alternative methods of treating his high blood pressure. His blood pressure was not as high as my other patient example and he did not present with a nosebleed (evidencing the severity of uncontrolled blood pressure). His high pressure was diagnosed—incidentally—during a physical exam for life insurance coverage.

We discussed the various methods that he could try as alternative interventions to treat high blood pressure. My initial recommendations to him included the following:

- A no-salt diet and a dietary cleanse
- Regular aerobic exercise of moderate intensity for at least 30 minutes each day.
- Use of a device called RESPeRATE® at least once a day. This is a device that is used to guide you to breathe according to pre-recorded music. This device is approved by the FDA (Food and Drug Administration) for use as an adjunct therapy for high blood pressure.
- The regular practice of Yoga and meditation—or Tai Chi.

I suggested that he should try these recommendations for three months and then follow-up with me to further explore other natural ways, if needed, to control his blood pressure. The other disciplines we planned to consider were Acupuncture, herbal therapy, Ayurveda, relaxation techniques, biofeedback, and homeopathy.

He was thrilled with the possibility of treating his blood pressure with natural efforts and was eager to start the strategy I prescribed.

I did not see him three months later, as planned. In fact, I didn't see him again for nearly a year. One day he turned up at my office for a follow-up visit. His blood pressure was 155/95 mm Hg.

Naturally, I asked him if he was doing the interventions I had suggested nearly a year ago. He said, "I used the RESPeRATE for a few months, but not consistently, and have been meditating but cannot keep up with it on a regular basis because of my hectic schedule." I asked him about his diet and he said, "It's hard to adhere to a no-salt diet when I travel...and I travel a lot."

Do you see a pattern here? What, specifically, do you see?

This is an example of a patient who was trying to win the game—the battle against high blood pressure—while playing with only one team member. In his case, Eastern modalities could not deliver their maximum benefits because of *who he was*. His You Power was not at optimum level to gain the best result from the available resources. He was not committed and his motivation was not sufficient enough to achieve optimal results.

This is a very important point: It is not the resources you have, but how well *you* are using them. This second patient also kept making excuses and did not show up for his regular follow-up appointments as recommended. These were patients who could, quite likely, see positive results from the recommendations for control of their high blood pressure. Yet they did not. Who do you think is at fault? Western medicine, Eastern medicine... or their You Power? The key is not to try to determine who is at fault, since we all make mistakes. The critical factor here is to investigate and understand the reason for the failure of the You Power in both these patients—what internal dialogue was keeping them from realizing their full potential?

What can Western medicine offer you?

How would a Western medical practitioner address the health challenge faced by my first patient? Just as I addressed it, I would expect. Prescribe medications, schedule follow-up visits to make sure the drugs are working, educate him on the importance of a low-salt diet, regular exercise, and screening tests to make sure that other organs such as heart, kidney and blood vessels are not being affected.

Medications

There are many medications available on the Western-medical market for the treatment of high blood pressure but they are too numerous to describe in this book. In most cases, it takes at least two different types of medications to get full control if your blood pressure is at a level where drug therapy is needed. One type of medicine called a *diuretic* is sometimes used as a first line of therapy. A diuretic is a drug that makes you urinate a lot and therefore gets rid of excess salt and water from your body. Your practitioner may prescribe additional medications as needed.

Sometimes up to four medications are needed to control blood pressure. If you need more than three medications for blood pressure control, I'd suggest that it's time to investigate what we call *secondary hypertension*. This means that your elevated blood pressure could have another cause that may be correctable or treatable. If you think this could be the case, I recommend that you discuss this with your physician and he or she will then recommend what needs to be done.

Diet

Most patients with high blood pressure are advised to eat a low-salt or no-salt diet. Salt is strongly associated with high blood pressure. However, there is emerging evidence that brings into doubt the degree to which salt intake affects blood pressure.

Additionally, different races respond differently to the effects of salt in the diet. That said, the impact of salt is so important that New York City Health Council decided to request that chain-restaurant owners disclose the amount of salt in each menu item that contains more than 2300 mg of sodium. Most nutritionists agree that 2300 mg per day of salt is the healthy limit. But for an entire day's intake—not just for one item or meal!

I am not sure if all the patrons will pay attention to the salt listings on the menus of the New York City restaurants, but at least it will help people like my second patient, who travels a lot, and who are at least attempting to initiate changes in their diets.

I would also recommend that those faced with high blood pressure should consider a low-fat, low-cholesterol diet. Another recommendation related to diet includes losing weight by calorie reduction. I have known several patients who moved from high blood pressure levels to normal levels by simply losing weight and exercising regularly.

Coffee, especially drinking more than four cups a day, has been associated with the development of high blood pressure, according to the National Health Services of England. Excessive alcohol also is associated with the development of high blood pressure.

Exercise
Regular moderate exercise is one of the best ways to improve your overall health. I cannot emphasize the importance of regular aerobic exercise. As I have mentioned, I have known patients who were successful in controlling their blood pressure simply by exercise and weight loss. Exercise has benefits in helping you to deal with stress better, helping to cultivate emotional stability, releasing anger, and losing weight. Above all, the arteries in your body dilate (or expand) when you exercise regularly and thus help

control blood pressure.

Another cause of hypertension and cardiovascular disease is heavy-metal poisoning. We are all exposed to environments and foods that contain heavy metals. Most often, the question is not whether you have heavy metals in your body, it is how much heavy metal is in you. Arsenic, lead, and cadmium are some of the heavy metals that are associated with high blood pressure[4].

Aerobic exercise can also help excrete some of the heavy metals, since small amounts of these heavy metals are eliminated in our sweat. There are other ways to eliminate heavy metals and these include salt baths and chelation therapy.

Stop smoking

Smoking is strongly associated with high blood pressure. Your blood pressure increases with each cigarette you smoke, then decreases after a few minutes. The rise in blood pressure is higher if smoking is combined with drinking coffee[5]. If you smoke more than 15 cigarettes a day, your chances of getting high blood pressure are high[6]. Smoking actually makes your arteries stiff and this stiffness can last for decades, even after you stop smoking[7]. I consider smoking to be a habit arising out of nervousness. The question to ask yourself is, *What is in your mind that is making you so nervous that you resort to smoking as a means of dealing with it?*

Smoking is not only associated with high blood pressure. It is also associated with stroke, heart attack, kidney failure, lung cancer, peripheral arterial disease (narrowing of the blood vessels in the legs and arms), and possibly other cancers as well. Therefore, it is wise to stop smoking if you have high blood pressure or any of the conditions mentioned above.

I would submit to you that you should quit smoking by dealing with your internal dialogue through emotional cleansing rather than continuing to smoke in order to deal with the internal dialogue.

What can Eastern medicine offer you?

The second patient I described earlier in this chapter was seeking alternative therapy to Western medications for the treatment of his high blood pressure. As you may have realized in reading about the Eastern medicine philosophies related to high blood pressure, my patient had several treatment options available to him because his blood pressure was not very high at the time of diagnosis. If you have very high pressures at the time of diagnosis, you should begin with Western medical therapy. If, on the other hand, your pressure is not very high, then alternative methods can be entertained. Your practitioner will recommend the appropriate path to take. It is wise to consult a practitioner who understands both sides of the medical coin if you are considering alternative treatment methods.

Acupuncture

Acupuncture is very useful when it comes to the treatment of high blood pressure. That said, the correct energetic diagnosis needs to be made for this treatment to be successful. The evidence for the efficacy of Acupuncture in high blood pressure has shown mixed results because of several inconsistencies in the way the studies were conducted. As a result, even though the American Heart Association does not actively recommend this method for the treatment of high blood pressure, no major harm has been documented[8]. I have seen success with Acupuncture therapy. Therefore, in my opinion, individualized Acupuncture therapy may be considered either as an adjunct or as a lifestyle-modifying strategy. Acupuncture, at a subtle level, improves your emotional well-being thus helping control elevations in blood pressure.

Your practitioner may evaluate you with regard to energetic influences using Yin Yang imbalances, as well as the Five Element Theory of Acupuncture, to arrive at a conclusion. Remember, hypertension is considered to result from various energetic imbalances based on the individual influences. Therefore, the number of needles and Acupuncture points used in one patient may be totally different for another patient, even though both may have high blood pressure.

Massage

Massage on a regular basis can influence your stress and aid in better handling emotions associated with high blood pressure such as fear, anxiety, and anger. This technique falls under what the medical world collectively calls *relaxation techniques.* As mentioned with Acupuncture, an associated channel with the kidneys, the bladder channel, runs on the back of our body along either side of the vertebral column to reach the neck and head. A massage therapist can use these channels and the points along these channels to help relieve blockages and stimulate the energy flow along the channel to harmonize the entire body. In addition, the general effects of massage —such as reducing stress and stress-related tension—will help reduce surges in a hormone called *cortisol,* a stress-related hormone in our body that has been linked to the development of high blood pressure.

Homeopathy

In my opinion, Homeopathy is very useful in treating blood pressure. During the two years I worked with my friend Ravi at his clinic in London, I saw some impressive results with Homeopathic remedies when used properly. The British Homeopathic Association recommends several medications for the treatment of high blood pressure.

As is customary in Homeopathy, you will be treated with a remedy for the constitution first, and then additional remedies may be prescribed to unlock and release several emotions that are associated with the development of high blood pressure. These emotions all have their own remedies. For example, anger can be treated with *Nux Vomica*, grief with *Ignatia*, and anxiety with *Arg nit*. Consult with a qualified Homeopathic practitioner to obtain proper assessment and treatment. As always, it is important to inform your Western practitioner about the incorporation of Eastern modalities for the control of blood pressure. There are several Western-trained physicians in this country who also incorporate Homeopathy in their practice.

Chiropractic Care

The principles of treatment with Chiropractic therapy are much the same for high blood pressure as with other diseases. Chiropractic therapy is used to invigorate the nerve supply to the organs. In the case of high blood pressure, the organs involved (from an Acupuncture perspective) are the liver and kidneys. Experienced chiropractors can perform necessary manipulation without much discomfort and will exercise caution related to the severity of your illness. The manipulation of the entire vertebral column helps relieve tension on the nerves that supply the kidneys, as well as the bladder channels. Many Chiropractic physicians are also trained in Acupuncture and may be able to offer both therapies. They may have additional training in herbs and Homeopathy as well.

Herbs

Believe it or not, about 75 to 80 percent of the world's population uses herbs for the treatment of high blood pressure. This data is derived mostly from the developing countries[9]. Several Eastern medicine practitioners such as traditional Chinese practitioners, naturopaths, chiropractors, and even some Western medical practitioners use herbs either as primary treatment or as adjunct for various illnesses.

Caution should be used when combining Western pharmacological medications and herbs in an effort to control blood pressure. The drug interaction between Western medications and herbs should be carefully assessed. It is imperative that you communicate with your Western practitioner about the Eastern medications that you are taking and talk to your Eastern practitioner about the possible interactions with the Western medicines you are taking. A well-qualified naturopathic practitioner will be able to understand and give you directions on both medications.

Yoga and meditation

Yoga exercises are excellent for maintaining overall health and wellness. When it comes to the treatment of high blood pressure, Yoga and meditation are great assets. These practices affect the blood pressure by reducing stress response and thereby reducing sympathetic activation (via other biological pathways) to help reduce blood pressure. Several poses (*asana,* for example) have been documented to result in a relaxed state that, in turn, can affect your blood pressure.

One of the problems with the studies that have evaluated the practice of Yoga and meditation is that the training and frequency of practice among the sample patients in these techniques was not robust. Most studies had mixed results because of this variability and inconsistency. These Yoga techniques are not as easy as swallowing a pill. When it comes to Yoga and meditation, patients need to be organized and motivated toward daily practice. Imagine trying to ensure that your patient practices daily Yoga, when they do not have the organizational capacity or motivation to perform a task as simple as swallowing a pill at the same time every day! This is the same problem that has come to light related to research in this area. As we have seen before, most patients with high blood pressure have what can be described as a spontaneous and careless attitude, characterized by poor organizational capacity, motivation, and personal discipline—the very attributes that are needed for someone to practice daily Yoga.

After doing Yoga and meditation for over 30 years, I still sometimes have problems maintaining practice on a daily basis. And I *know* that the most benefits are seen only when these practices are done on a daily basis. Not twice a week or three times a week—daily!

Another modality that may have similar benefits is Tai Chi. This discipline involves slow movements coordinated with breathing and mindfulness. There are some studies that indicate that the practice of Tai Chi benefits patients with high blood pressure to help reduce their pressure.

Other practices that come under this section, but may also fall under relaxation techniques, are aromatherapy, music therapy, spiritual therapy, and biofeedback.

In fact, biofeedback is recommended as adjunct therapy for high blood pressure[8].

Ayurveda

Ayurvedic recommendations for high blood pressure tend to include diet, Yoga, and meditation as mentioned previously, as well as natural Ayurvedic remedies. Part of the Ayurvedic lifestyle includes what has been taught in Yoga, such as mindfulness and truthfulness. Additional techniques include various cleansing practices that are used to elevate a person's mood and well-being, thereby reducing blood pressure. I have known patients who went through a complete Ayurvedic regimen and came back from India with normal blood pressure.

I believe that the main effect of Ayurveda appears through behavior changes in the person. In other words, at some point through these strict practices, the individual develops better coping mechanisms, organizational capabilities, motivation, and discipline. These changes help the individual to optimize his or her You Power, which leads to the desired results.

Handling your You Power

As we will continue to discuss in great length, the importance of You Power in the management of health and disease cannot be understated. You Power is perhaps the most important player in the outcome of dealing with disease. In fact, it is probably *the* most important factor in not developing disease. Therefore, it is important to address The You Power— your internal dialogue (part of your primal being) and your personality (your social being).

Internal dialogue or Primal being

In my first patient, you may recall that he had internal conversation from his childhood experiences telling him that he was not good at accomplishing anything. His internal dialogue appeared to be "I cannot deal with this today." This conversation resulted in procrastination and non-compliance. These characteristics, coupled with a negative tendency towards life, led to the development and perpetuation of disease. Most patients with high blood pressure appear to share similar characteristics at varying degrees. The degree to which one exhibits these characteristics seems to have an influence on the degree of complications they may develop later in their life. During this process, if they get a chance to change the way they think and behave, then there is a chance to make improvements in their condition.

In looking at both patients described in this chapter, I think we can see that their problems were not related to whether they had access to Western medicine or Eastern medicine. It was whether they could use those disciplines to their benefit. What prevented them from reaping these benefits was their You Power.

Personality or Social being

You will recall that personality refers to an individual's characteristic pattern of behavior *driven* by their deeper thoughts and emotions. This is modified by their rules of conduct to suit the outside world. In other words, it is the primal self modified to suit the outside world and society in order to be accepted.

If you think that descriptions relating to You Power have a way of repeating themselves, you are right. This is because it is related to you—and since there is only one version of you, there cannot be multiple descriptions of your You Power. The overall suggestion may be the same, but the techniques used by counselors, psychotherapists, cognitive therapists, and hypnotists may be different to achieve the desired end result. The descriptions of these different techniques within the realm of psychological counseling is beyond the scope of this book.

By understanding your personality and recognizing certain tendencies, you may be able to recognize abnormal coping mechanisms. This understanding may help you to deal with your negative internal dialogue better and may even help you get rid of it.

Learning about your personality, followed by a good emotional cleanse, and learning coping mechanisms to deal with external or internal stressors, will help you avoid conflicts. Avoiding conflicts is the first step in reducing the emotional baggage that we carry with us in our lives. Your partner in identifying conflicts and changing your coping mechanisms to such conflicts is a counselor or a psychologist. Mindfulness, meditation, and Yoga exercises can also aid in creating clarity of thinking, which makes it easier to identify your internal conflicts and emotional imbalances.

Remember, the real value of these practices comes when they are done daily, not periodically. Periodic practice is acceptable, but do not expect benefits to occur in leaps and bounds. These techniques provide benefits slowly over a long period of time. Conflicts and emotional imbalances that remain unaddressed often lead to illness down the road. Abnormal behaviors are known to predispose people to different diseases. Addressing them is the first step toward optimal health and wellness.

Chapter Four

Stroke

The Paralyzing Killer

I've lost my purpose in life and feel trapped.

S troke, also known as a *brain attack,* is the second leading cause of death in the world[1]. When the blood supply to any part of the brain is suddenly cut off, a brain attack happens. If this happens to you, you've had a stroke and must seek emergency care immediately.

The blood supply to the brain can get cut off in two ways. One is when an artery that supplies the brain with blood becomes blocked, and the other is when one of the tiny blood vessels in any part of the brain ruptures or bursts, causing bleeding in the brain. The most common cause of strokes is blood vessels becoming blocked by cholesterol plaque or a blood clot, which is called an *ischemic stroke.* This type of stroke accounts for 87 percent of all strokes[2].

One out of every 20 deaths in the United States is due to stroke[2]. Every 40 seconds an American experiences a stroke, and one American dies from a stroke every four minutes[3]. The American Stroke Association reports that it is the fifth leading cause of death in the United States[3]. In the United Kingdom, it is fourth leading cause of death[4]. Strokes kill twice as many women as breast cancer and more men than prostate cancer and testicular cancer combined. In Canada, stroke is the third leading cause of death[5].

When you have a stroke, it manifests in several ways. A person can experience impaired or slurred speech, weakness or paralysis of the body, impaired vision, sudden severe headaches, difficulty swallowing, loss of sensations, or dizziness and unexplained falls. Because of the loss of brain tissue that controls many of the functions of our body, we can become paralyzed and disabled from a stroke. One in three stroke survivors suffer paralysis and two out of three require assistance with mobility.

Once a person becomes paralyzed, they become dependent on others and arrangements need to be made for their care. Many stroke victims become wheelchair-bound and performing the daily tasks that we take for granted becomes a major production.

I have been monitoring a 62-year-old man for his high blood pressure and high cholesterol issues for many years. He is a "go-getter" type of person—a successful businessman who had been on the go for many years. In fact, his high blood pressure was associated with the stress he experienced related to his work. Every time he visited the clinic he would share his business accomplishments. He was an aggressive person who was motivated and organized. As such, he was conscientious related to all of his medications and turned up for all his follow-up visits.

He retired at age 65. Subsequent to his retirement, he became quite distressed with the feeling that his life was on hold. He was a man accustomed to action and activity. Although he was constantly talking about having more time to spend vacationing, with grandchildren, and enjoying life, he would often comment on how much he missed his work. He confided to me that he felt he had lost his main purpose in life and was looking for something to do with the rest of his life. Even though his business was doing well, he missed being at the helm of that ship. I asked him why he decided to retire from running his successful business. He said that he had been away from his family so much during the years he was building the business that his family had insisted it was time to devote some time to them.

A few years after his retirement, he suffered his first stroke. As a result, he had right-sided weakness that eventually improved with physical therapy. He returned to his life as a retiree.

We met a few times after his stroke. I saw a man who had lost his vitality and energy —and who looked as if he was trapped in a "no-man's land." We talked about many things, including the option of going back to work, taking long vacations, relocating to another country, and spending time with the grandchildren. A few months after our last visit, he suffered his second stroke, which resulted in him becoming wheelchair bound. He became totally dependent on others for his care. This was a man who cared for and commanded other people in his business and was now dependent on others for his care.

I was devastated with this news. It was incomprehensible. I could not understand how this could happen to such a strong and vibrant man who did everything he was supposed to do and was very compliant with all the recommendations I made related to his health. He passed away in his early seventies.

Could I have predicted this event? No. Not with the tools available to me in Western medicine. We knew that he was at risk for a stroke because of his high blood pressure and high cholesterol. But both of these conditions were adequately treated and maintained. On the other hand I have known patients who have not suffered a stroke, even though their blood pressure was totally out of control for several years.

During our conversations, I had recognized his internal sense of distress and realized that it was consuming him. During those days, I recommended that he take up Yoga and meditation to reduce his internal distress and start enjoying his free time, spending it getting in touch with his inner self. He was not inclined to do that, saying that he could not sit still without doing something. I recommended taking up Tai Chi, but he said it was too slow for him. We discussed plans to get together with his friends to play tennis or racquetball. He said he had no time for those activities.

I remember thinking, *Here is a man who misses his work and feels as if he has lost his purpose in life...but does not have time to engage in activities that will improve the health of his body and mind.* At some point I even thought that he just didn't like spending a lot time with his family. He was a man who just didn't know what to do with himself after retiring and was distressed about it. To me, it appeared as if he lost his purpose in life after retirement and felt trapped in his new environment and family duties.

Western side of the stroke coin

How does Western medicine look at stroke? It looks for predisposing factors and considers people with those predispositions at high risk of stroke in their lifetime. Predisposing factors do not confer disease development but they confer a high risk of developing it. As with any disease, the established predisposing factors for stroke can also be divided into modifiable and non-modifiable groups[3].

The modifiable risk factors for stroke include:

- High blood pressure – the leading cause of stroke.
- High cholesterol level – which leads to cholesterol plaque formation in the blood vessels. These plaques can break and block the vessels that supply the brain, causing a stroke.
- Smoking – the chemicals in smoke (nicotine and carbon monoxide) damage the lining of the blood vessels and make them susceptible to the formation of clots.
- Diabetes mellitus – this disease is commonly associated with high blood pressure, high cholesterol, and obesity.

- An abnormal rhythm of the heart called *atrial fibrillation*. This abnormal rhythm puts you at high risk of forming clots in your heart that can break off and cause you to have a stroke.

- Poor diet – high fat and high cholesterol intake can increase cholesterol levels in your blood and lead to plaque formation.

- Physical inactivity – this factor puts you at risk by leading to high blood pressure, high cholesterol, and obesity.

- Abnormal heart function – heart failure can put you at high risk.

The non-modifiable factors include:

- Age – The chance of suffering a stroke doubles every 10 years of your life after the age of 55.

- Family history – If you have a family member who suffered a stroke, then your chances of suffering a stroke are also high.

- Race – African-Americans are at higher risk of dying from stroke compared to Caucasians.

- Sex – Women tend to have more strokes than men.

- Prior stroke or mini-stroke – Having a prior stroke or a mini-stroke increases your chance of having another stroke.

The clinical presentation of a stroke can be as subtle as experiencing numbness of your arms, legs, or face, slurring of speech, or drooping of the face (where your face looks asymmetrical). If you experience these symptoms, you should call 9-1-1 immediately. The other presentations have been described at the beginning of this chapter.

The patient I've described had high blood pressure and high cholesterol prior to his stroke. He was of African-American descent and someone you would want on your team if you were in the world of business and finance.

In Western medicine, the prompt diagnosis of a stroke is imperative. This diagnosis is confirmed by doing a CAT (computed automated tomography) scan of your head. Once you have a stroke, your survival and the degree of disability you will experience depends on how fast you get treatment. There is a saying in the medical world, "time is brain!"— which means we must act fast! As soon as a diagnosis of stroke is made, there are several ways treatment is administered.

If you are in a window of time where the blood clot can be removed or dissolved, actions will be taken to achieve that. In the case of removing the clot, you will be taken to the operating room for a procedure called a *thrombectomy* where doctors will remove the clot from the blood vessels in your brain. Full recovery has been reported with this method. This procedure is similar to how we treat heart attacks. If no procedure is planned, then "clot-busting" medications can be administered through the veins to try to dissolve the clot.

Finally, you will be admitted to the hospital and monitored for complications and evolution of the stroke. Patients who have a stroke can develop complications such as a respiratory infection called *pneumonia,* especially if they are in the hospital and somewhat immobile for any length of time. These complications can be life threatening. As part of your treatment regimen, you will be given medications for high blood pressure, high cholesterol, as well as medicines to help keep your blood thin so that it does not clot easily. After a few days of observation, you may be discharged with a recommendation for occupational and physical therapy.

Western medicine excels in treating this disease and has made many advances in this respect. When I was a medical student—30 years ago— we did not have the ability, the tools, or technology to go into the blood vessels to remove the clot with a catheter. Today, this procedure not only saves lives but also decreases the residual effects of a stroke and gives patients a chance at full recovery.

Typical post-stroke care in the United States involves about seven days in a hospital followed by about two weeks of rehabilitation in a facility that offers physical therapy, occupational therapy, and speech therapy. In some cases, patients are offered a few more weeks of home rehabilitation. Once completed, you are on your own and will be managed by a Western medical practitioner with medications and basic education for ways to prevent a second stroke.

Eastern medical side of the stroke coin

Just as it is customary with Eastern medicine related to other diseases, stroke is considered to reflect an underlying imbalance within the person. In Acupuncture, stroke is not assigned to an organ because it is a disease and there is no specific organ that is affected. The brain is described as *marrow,* and kidneys control the marrow. Therefore, an associated organ system for abnormalities of brain would be the paired organs of kidney and urinary bladder.

Acupuncture views stroke as a deficiency of energy (Qi) with the accumulation of internal heat and wind. The concept of stroke in Acupuncture is quite complex. For our purposes, it is sufficient to say that it is a manifestation of Yin Qi deficiency and Yang excess activity in the brain area. As a result, there is retention of wind and phlegm in the internal channels of the affected and paralyzed limbs.

Western medical blood tests indicated that my patient did have mild kidney insufficiency, but he did not have kidney failure. His kidney insufficiency was attributed to his high blood pressure that was uncontrolled at times, despite medical therapy.

The Ayurveda concept is similar. It describes stroke as a manifestation of abnormality of the VATA energy axis, which regulates the functions of the brain and is related to the nervous system. Most of Ayurveda's treatment modalities are related to treating this aspect of VATA.

You Power • third side of the stroke coin

Stroke is one of the diseases that I have been very interested in because of my exposure to my father, who had a stroke, and several other stroke patients at the Acupuncture clinic in Sri Lanka. At that time (in the 1980s), stroke care by Western medicine was not as robust as it is today. Most patients who suffered a stroke were paralyzed and disabled. As such, I had several patients who came for Acupuncture therapy at the clinic hoping to improve their weaknesses in the arms, legs, or both. The types of people who have strokes has been very puzzling to me.

I treated a young man in his fifties whom I met after he was admitted to the Emergency Room. He came to the ER with chest discomfort. When I met him, he was seated in a chair in a suit and tie with his computer and phone beside him. The computer was open and it appeared as though he was working when I arrived. He was well spoken, well mannered, and polite. After initial introductions, I took his history, did a physical exam, and I told him that he was going to be admitted to the hospital for two to three days for further testing and work up. He was not happy about this, but agreed to the recommendation and made me reassure him that we would discharge him in two to three days. In taking his history, we learned that he used cocaine for recreation.

Two days after his admission, when I visited him in his room, he seemed happy and wanted me to discharge him that day. I could not do so because of pending tests. Early that afternoon, he discharged himself from the hospital against medical advice.

Later that same day, in the early evening, I received an urgent page to the ER. When I arrived in the ER, I saw my patient unconscious on a stretcher undergoing emergency resuscitation. He could not be resuscitated and subsequently passed away.

Later, I learned (from a CAT scan of the head done earlier that evening in the ER) that he had had a massive stroke due to bleeding inside his head. I was also told by his friends who were in the ER with him that he had gone directly from the hospital to a friend's house and was using cocaine when he collapsed. They also told me that he was to get married the following week.

When events like this happen, you question life and the decisions people make. What prompted him to leave the hospital that day, against medical advice? What prompted the stroke at this time in his life? This man, like my other patient, seemed to have everything going for him. They were both accomplished go-getters.

Researchers have questioned whether or not personality traits can predict the chances of people suffering from stroke. While there are not a lot of studies in this regard, there are some indications of personality preponderance or pre-disposition towards stroke. One of the published studies is from a pooled analysis of three studies comprising about 25,000 patients[6].

The researchers compared the personality characteristics of patients who die from heart disease and stroke and came up with some very interesting findings. Here are the characteristics that were found to be important.

1. **Prone to stress and worry:** These individuals tend to be anxious people who are apprehensive and worry a lot. They can get easily frustrated, feel irritable, get angry with others, and are prone to feel lonely, sad, and rejected. They tend to have difficulty controlling their impulses, wants, and wishes, but have no problem handling stress just like other people.

2. **Outgoing interpersonal attitude:** These types of people are affectionate, with warmth towards others, and enjoy being the center of attention. In fact, they may dislike a situation if they are not the center of attention. They have a tendency to please and seek approval from others. The stimulation of thrills and excitement has little appeal to these people and as a result they tend not to experience feelings such as joy and happiness.

3. **Spontaneous and careless:** These people tend to lack organizational capacity, are not efficient in making rational decisions, tend not to meet their obligations, and lack self-discipline and motivation.

What was astonishing was that people who had the combined characteristics of #1 and #3 had a high chance of dying from heart disease. To the contrary, people who *died* from stroke had combined characteristics of #2 and #3. Because heart disease is the #1 killer in the world—and stroke (brain attack) the #2 killer —it is not surprising to note that they share similar characteristics. That said, there are still key differences that may make them distinguishable. What is interesting about these findings is that all three of these characteristics are the same traits that are found in patients who are diagnosed with obesity and diabetes. In Western medicine, we know that diabetes and obesity significantly contribute to both heart disease and stroke.

Having said all of this, we also know that not everyone who has diabetes and obesity gets heart disease or stroke. Therefore, it is important to note that personality may not be the only factor, and that a *combination* of personality and the internal dialogue of a person makes a big difference in disease development and progression. In other words, just because you have the personality type that's prone to a specific disease does not mean you will develop a disease—unless it is combined with the right internal dialogue.

I believe that this is why some people get a disease while others don't, despite the risk factors. Personalities are derived from several factors based on rules of conduct we have acquired while growing up and from genetics. Therefore, personality may reflect different coping styles. However, I believe that it is the internal dialogue that acts as the catalyst for the occurrence of an event.

In the case of the first patient I described in this chapter, he found a loss of purpose in life after he retired. He was having trouble coping with that conflict in his mind. It was constantly worrying him. I did not get to know the second patient well, but his impatience and behavior related to insisting on being discharged within a few days led me to believe that his internal dialogue reflected a feeling of being trapped. Additionally, the second patient was about to get married. That begs the question, at least for me, of whether or not deep down, in his mind, he really wanted to make that commitment.

What can you do?

As with all the diseases covered in this book, the first thing we can do is understand that there are always three sides that need to be considered. These are Western medicine (a teammate), Eastern medicine (a teammate), and You Power (you... as the captain of your health team).

In the case of the first patient, Western medicine provided treatment to the fullest extent of its capabilities. And yet the man suffered a stroke. Could this have been due to chance? That's what we unofficially conclude in Western medicine, although I was not taught about *chance* in medical school. In other words, when events like this happen to our patients, we feel as if we did the best we could, from a Western medicine perspective, and it's just too bad that such an unfortunate event happened.

Health care providers do get devastated and feel terrible when tragic and life-ending events happen to our patients. Nevertheless, we just do not know where to attribute the reason for the event. We do know that people with high blood pressure and high cholesterol are at high risk of having a stroke, but the question is why this particular patient...and not another? Another question is, why at that particular time? The answer to these questions is chance or randomness, conditions that belong in our UNKNOWN level of existence.

It is the same with the second patient that I have described. Again, a well-educated, well-mannered, successful executive who decided to leave the hospital against medical advice. He went directly to substance abuse, and then died the same day. Go figure! The easy thing to do here is blame the patient and say that he brought about his own demise. That may be true, but why? I am sure that this is a question that his family is left to struggle with for the rest of their lives.

The answer to these questions lies within the internal workings of these two human beings. While it may be true that it's hard to figure out all the details that lead to life-changing or fatal events, why not take efforts to minimize the effects or even prevent such an event? We build levees and flood preventive mechanisms around rivers and dams, not because we know there will be a disaster or flood, but because nature is unpredictable. In other words, we do the best we can to prepare for and prevent a catastrophic event.

It is no different when it comes to the inner world of humans. Our inner world is as important as the world outside. It can have disastrous and turbulent conflicts that we may not be able to predict. The best we can do is to adopt mechanisms to minimize the consequences. If you look at the two examples of the patients I have described, one died immediately from stroke and the other lived for a few years after his stroke.

These two patients used only Western medicine. The one who survived used Western medicine to its fullest capabilities—and perhaps that helped him survive. The second man was not interested in using even *one* player on his team. In his case, the optimal strategy would have been to use not only Western medicine but also Eastern medicine—and You Power. Eastern medicines would have offered a chance to treat him as a person. In other words, most Eastern medical modalities strengthen and facilitate our You Power. They provide a levee system around our unpredictable internal dialogue.

What can Western medicine offer you?

We have explored what Western medicine can offer people with stroke. The most important question to ask is: What does Western medicine offer *before* a stroke?

Medications

Medications are usually directed at treating the underlying causes of stroke that have been addressed earlier in this chapter. You may be given medications for high blood pressure, high cholesterol, and diabetes depending upon whether or not you have one, or a combination, of these diseases. Subsequently, periodic follow-up at the doctor's office can make sure that these diseases are adequately controlled. Western medicine does not think that these diseases are curable but that they can be suppressed to a point where they pose minimal risk with regard to complications such as stroke.

If you suffer a stroke, Western medicine has excellent tools to minimize the catastrophic consequences you may be left with. It can use clot-busters, remove the clot, or manage you very closely in the hospital to make sure that you recover without further complications.

Diet

There are no specific dietary recommendations for stroke, per se. However, most recommendations for these patients are directed at the underlying causes of the stroke. Diet guidelines will be recommended to best treat a patient's high blood pressure, high cholesterol, diabetes, or obesity.

If you have developed chewing or swallowing problems after your stroke, a soft diet, like baby food, may be recommended to prevent aspiration and its complications, like pneumonia. In the event that you cannot swallow at all, a feeding tube may be recommended through which liquid food is administered via a tube (called *gastric* or *G tube*) that is inserted directly into your stomach through the front of your abdomen.

Exercise

Regular moderate exercise is one of the best ways to improve your overall health. Exercise plays a major role in the prevention of stroke and in the treatment of the underlying causes I have listed. It also helps us to better handle internal stress. Incorporating regular exercise into your life is a wise strategy.

Exercise plays a major role even after a stroke. In this case, *exercise* is delivered as physical therapy, occupational therapy, and speech therapy. These are provided by Western medicine in dedicated facilities (or in your own home) by a trained therapist. The frequency of this "exercise"—these therapies—is dependent upon several factors—one being your insurance coverage, of course!

Behavior and lifestyle modifications

If it seems that I am repeating myself here, you are right. I am. Because Western medicine focuses on disease, you will find that all the tools it offers are geared towards a particular disease. In the case of behavior modifications, you will be advised the following:

- Stop smoking, if you are smoker
- Lose weight, if you are obese
- Eat low-fat, low-cholesterol food
- Minimize sugar and carbohydrate intake, if you have diabetes
- Exercise regularly
- Eliminate the use of recreational drugs
- Take your medications regularly

With these recommendations, you are left on your own, with periodic follow-up appointments to make sure that you are progressing on the right track. If you are not progressing well, then it becomes a lifelong struggle between Western medicine and the disease process.

What can Eastern medicine offer you?

Once again, there are a myriad of Eastern medical disciplines that we can choose from, either alone or in combination, as adjuncts with Western medicine to help us address not only the predisposing factors for a stroke, but also afterwards—or simply to maintain a healthy state.

Acupuncture

When I was an instructor at the University of Alternative and Complementary Medicines in Sri Lanka, a team of Korean Acupuncturists visited our clinic. I had several patients who had suffered a stroke and, as a result, were paralyzed. The Korean Acupuncturists wanted to demonstrate their technique and chose one of my stroke patients.

This patient had complete paralysis of her left arm that I had been treating with Acupuncture...without much improvement. She couldn't even move her fingers due to the paralysis. The Korean Acupuncturists did not speak much English, so they just went to work on the woman after I explained to her that they were going to treat her with Acupuncture.

They chose her right arm (the arm opposite the paralyzed arm) for the insertion of the needles. They stimulated the needles quite vigorously compared to what we had been doing and—all of a sudden—the woman was able to briefly lift her left arm. It was like magic. At the time I was a third-year medical student—and I didn't believe in magic.

What I witnessed that day gave me full confidence that there is merit to Acupuncture and its underlying energy theory. After the demonstration, the Korean physicians left and my patient went back to having a paralyzed left arm. And I learned an important lesson: Failure of therapy may have nothing to do with the discipline, but with the *practitioner*. The concept of using the right side of the body to treat problems on the left side (and vice versa) is one of the recommendations in Acupuncture philosophy.

Current recommendations suggest that there is benefit in using Acupuncture with electrical stimulation to help recover the strength of a paralyzed limb[7]. As a result, Acupuncture can help during the recovery period after a stroke. It is recommended that you start Acupuncture therapy one week or so after the stroke in the case of what is called *ischemic stroke* (stroke due to a clot in the blood vessels to the brain). In the case of a stroke due to bleeding in the brain, a longer waiting period of several weeks is recommended.

Massage

Massage is another good addition to the post-stroke care of a patient. Whole body massage stimulates the nerves and muscles of the affected limb and helps restore and maintain muscle tone and the integrity of the tendons, fascia, and the energy flow in the space between muscles and tendons. It also helps remove toxins from the affected limb where the normal mechanisms that help in this process are lost, due to the lack of robust nerve supply and muscle tone.

Homeopathy

Homeopathy can be used successfully with stoke patients as an adjunct. However, most frequently Homeopathy and other Eastern modalities are used only after Western medicine gives up on the condition of a patient. By that time it may be too late to see any meaningful recovery or change in the condition of the patient.

The diagnosis is made as a weakness, depending on the underlying constitutional make-up (called *miasm*) that you are categorized into as determined by the practitioner after he or she completes the evaluation. There are two types of remedies that will be prescribed. A constitutional remedy is often prescribed to treat the underlying constitutional make-up and strengthen it. Treating the constitution means addressing the entire person at a deeper level of their being, and not just the symptoms. In Homeopathy, it is called treating the underlying *miasm* of the patient. This is then followed by or accompanied by specific remedies that are tailored to the symptoms of the patient.

Chiropractic Care

The principles of treatment with Chiropractic therapy remain the same. It is used to invigorate the nerve supply. In the case of stroke, it is quite beneficial to stimulate and relieve pressure on what we call *peripheral nerves*, the nerves that come out of the spinal cord to supply various organs. Chiropractic care helps keep the peripheral nerves in optimal condition while we are addressing the brain and its functions with other modalities. Chiropractic therapy therefore will be a great adjunct, a great complement to the use of other modalities.

There is often a concern about expenses when we start adding additional therapy. Even though there is extra expense at the beginning, these expenses are often offset when the patient is able to perform his or her activities of daily living with minimal caregiver support. In the long run, there is a good chance of saving money due to fewer caregiver requirements for the patient.

If a patient can afford it, I usually do not like to allow finances to come into the question of health and disease. If you are not in good health, you cannot enjoy your wealth. Some insurance companies are beginning to understand the value of Eastern therapies and are providing coverage and covering claims. However, it is not yet a widespread practice among all the companies that provide medical insurance. Check with your insurance provider to determine if the services you are considering are covered.

Herbs

Traditional Chinese practitioners, Naturopaths, Chiropractors and even several Western medical practitioners use herbs either as primary treatment or as adjunct for various illnesses. In fact, several formulas are available to help patients with either a speedy recovery or to help facilitate a gradual one. At the end of the day, the concern is about the best interest of the patient. Any modality that helps and does not cause harm can be used and it is always the patient's choice.

However, make sure that you inform your Western medical practitioner of the efforts you take to facilitate your recovery. Do not just discontinue Western physical therapy, or medications, without the agreement and consent of your Western medical practitioner. Take care to ensure that the herbs that have been recommended have no interaction with blood thinning medications that your Western medical practitioner may have prescribed.

Yoga and Meditation

Yoga exercises are excellent for the overall health of anyone. Yoga is my favorite when it comes to both health and disease. Not because it treats disease successfully, but because Yoga and meditation are perhaps the best ways to influence your You Power. I believe that your You Power plays a more significant role in health and disease than either Western medicine or Eastern medicine. In fact, Eastern medicine helps you to optimize your You Power, because it treats the person as a whole. Western medicine, on the other hand, does not have any influence on the Power of You unless therapy with a counselor is recommended and sought. Unless you are diagnosed with the psychological problem, most Western physicians do not have counseling on their radar screen as a recommendation for their patients.

Using Yoga and meditation to your advantage can play a role in your health well before you suffer a stroke. They can help tremendously in addressing high blood pressure (which has a big connection with stress), diabetes, obesity, and cholesterol levels (which have a big connection with emotional eating) and with regard to smoking by strengthening your ability to sustain extremes in emotional fluctuations without resorting to addictive behavior.

Finally, Yoga and meditation can help you deal with post-stroke depression or melancholy, as well as to help train paralyzed limbs. They can also help you to prevent the recurrence of a stroke. Obviously, a Western medical doctor may claim that there is no evidence that Yoga helps patients with stroke. I would argue the opposite, and ask the question, *What is the downside to Yoga in stroke patients?* And... *What if it really can help you prevent—or deal well with the effects of—a stroke?*

In the example of the first stroke patient, he was having a hard time embracing the mind-body therapy to influence his You Power. Although this intervention was recommended, he did not pursue it because of his personality. Sitting in meditation or slow-motion exercises like Yoga or Tai Chi were not the type of interventions he was used to in solving his problems as a businessman. What he did not realize was that different circumstances and environments require different coping mechanisms. In this case, one size does not fit all.

Ayurveda

As I've explained, Ayurveda uses a system of healthy living to promote the health and well-being of a person. This system utilizes various cleansing methods to purify the body of its toxins, and unwanted substances on a regular basis. As such, it is a very helpful adjunct to help keep our bodies free of impurities which will, in turn, allow optimal function of the organs.

When it comes to post-stroke care, Ayurveda can help with remedies that counter-balance the VATA energy regulatory system. Again, and unlike with kidney or liver disease, there is no extra caution that needs to be used with the oral intake of remedies. But, as always, make sure to share your medications with both your practitioners to eliminate the risk of drug interaction.

My favorite treatment when it comes to Ayurveda is the cleansing practices that help remove toxins and impurities that enter our bodies from food, drinks, lack of exercise, etc. Did you know that the cells in our body make toxins as part of the process of living, as it assimilates and utilizes food and nutrition as part of the normal function? These toxins are usually excreted by the kidneys as urine, the lungs as expired air, the skin as sweat, and bowels. If the function of these organs is not optimal, the toxins will not be eliminated properly and will continue to accumulate in the body. On the other hand, if we put more toxins into our bodies than can be excreted through these organs, toxins will accumulate in our body. These accumulated toxins, the result of unhealthy living, will begin to impair the optimal function of the cells and can result in disease. Therefore, it makes sense, in my opinion, to utilize periodic cleansing methods to keep up with the polluting effect of modern life.

Here's an easy way to look at the need for cleaning. Consider that your body is the house you live in. In a house, dust and dirt accumulate from various activities and the environment. Even if you are someone who is obsessive-compulsive about cleaning your house daily, how many times do you find dirt and grit in places that you thought would not get dirty? As a result, we do major cleanings of our house from time to time... think "Spring Cleaning." It is the same with our bodies. We cannot accurately keep track of how, when, and where toxins accumulate in our bodies but we can perform periodic cleanses.

There are several other modalities that can be successfully used to cope with chronic diseases such as high blood pressure, diabetes, obesity, and cholesterol, as well as addictive habits such as smoking. These modalities include (but are not limited to) aromatherapy, music therapy, spiritual therapy, pet therapy, reflexology, and biofeedback. I have only selected the most predominant disciplines that I am most familiar with to comment on in this book.

Handling your You Power

You Power plays a major role in your ability to reap the benefits of whatever tools you use from both modalities once you have an imbalance. It also helps you to maintain wellness, and avoid getting into a situation of an imbalance. The emotional and psychological characteristics described in this chapter with regard to patients who suffered a stroke play a significant role in the way the disease progresses.

To have the best chance at preventing stroke, it is important to recognize the underlying psychological characteristics for predisposing conditions like high blood pressure, diabetes, and other conditions. Many of these have been referenced and you will find entire chapters dedicated to them in this book.

Internal dialogue or Primal being

When it came to the first patient referenced in this chapter, it was obvious that he was going through a turbulent time due to the feeling of having lost the sense of purpose in life that was tied to his work and feeling trapped in whatever he was doing at that time. Losing a sense of purpose is a slow, insidious process that affects us over a long period of time. However, feeling trapped kicks in our fight or flight mechanism and can lead to acute events or actions to get out of the trap. Therefore, if a person does not have a practical solution for the release of any distress then a disease may become a "solution" as an unintended consequence.

The second patient described in this chapter had the personality type that fits with patients who have an increased risk of dying from stroke. His internal dialogue was not evident to me, due to my limited interactions with him.

I provide these examples not as concrete evidence of cause and effect for diseases, but as stimulating thoughts for you to start looking within yourself to identify emotions, internal dialogues, and other conflicts that propel you on a path that may lead to the development of disease. Current ongoing research seems to be aligned with this thought process, although no concrete evidence is available at this time.

Personality or Social being

Personality refers to an individual's characteristic patterns of behavior *driven* by their deeper thought and emotions. This is modified by their rules of conduct created to suit the outside world. In other words: It is the primal self modified to suit the outside world and society in order to be accepted.

The two patients described in this chapter fit into what we call *Type A* personalities and *Type D* personalities. Both of these personality types have been shown to have a relationship with stroke. A Type A personality is a person who is driven, hostile, impatient, and competitive, has difficulty expressing emotions, and has an unhealthy dependence on external rewards such as wealth, status, and power. The Type D personality is what we call a *distressed personality*. These people tend to be worried, irritable, and have a tendency to express negative emotions to events (like in the case of the first patient). A Type D personality is said to be indicative of a person who is disease-prone. Learning ways to cope with and work through what is called *stress-filled* or *conflict-ridden* life relationships will help you to stave off these diseases. Several of the Eastern medical modalities can help you achieve this goal. Therefore, incorporating Eastern medicine as a method to optimize your You Power for disease prevention is a choice that is available to us all.

Chapter Five

Kidney

The Toxic Killer

I am afraid...take care of me.

Our kidneys are a pair of organs that function to eliminate toxin waste produced by the living cells of our body. They produce urine that contains waste products. It takes the kidneys only 30 minutes to filter all the blood that is in our body. If a person's kidneys are in an extreme state of dysfunction, harmful toxins will accumulate within his or her body, which will lead to the death of the individual. Although we have two kidneys, it is possible to live with one.

The United States Renal Data System reports that, in 2010, the annual overall Medicare costs for patients living with chronic kidney disease was in excess of $40 billion[1]. In the United States, one out of three adults has the potential to develop kidney disease[2,3]. Most Americans who have kidney disease don't even realize it, and that burden is currently estimated at $26 million[2,4]. Kidney disease is the 9th leading cause of death in the United States[2,5] and every day 12 people die waiting for a kidney transplant[2,6].

As chronic kidney disease progresses, it leads to what we call end-stage kidney disease which results in premature death. This is also true if the chronic kidney disease is associated with other diseases such as heart disease, diabetes, or cancer. When a patient has kidney disease and progresses to end stage, he or she needs either dialysis—to artificially clear the body of the toxins and fluids it produces on a daily basis via a dialysis machine—or a kidney transplant.

Most patients with kidney disease tend to have other diseases as well, such as heart disease, high blood pressure, diabetes, and obesity. Later in this chapter, I will explain why some of these related diseases are considered to be risk factors for developing kidney disease.

Interestingly, Eastern and Western medicines describe the function of the kidneys very differently, as the following story illustrates.

A 37-year-old man had come in for a follow-up visit and sat across the desk from me. He was very angry with our medical program and me because he claimed that, for the past four months, *we* did not contact him to make a follow-up appointment.

He had been referred to my office by the kidney transplant team for cardiac clearance before undergoing a kidney transplant. Four months prior to this meeting, he had his first consultation with me. At that time, I had recommended pertinent health investigations that included blood tests and imaging studies of the heart—and asked him to follow-up with us in six weeks.

He did not contact us for a follow-up appointment and many weeks passed. Finally my office called him to ask why he hadn't scheduled a follow-up appointment. I asked him where we were related to the investigations I had recommended and why *he* did not follow-up with us in six weeks as instructed. He told me that he was not called to schedule an appointment for follow-up or to schedule the blood tests and investigative imaging I recommended. I asked him why he did not even call us to tell us that he did not have any appointments scheduled. He said that he was waiting for us to call him. This may seem like a minor point or simply a case of miscommunication. In truth, it points to a deeper issue... one that related to the disease itself.

This patient developed kidney failure because his own body was attacking his kidneys. Western medicine calls this condition an *autoimmune disease*. The cells in his body had attacked and destroyed his own kidneys and as a result he developed end-stage kidney disease. The entire process started when he was 34 years old.

One day, three years earlier, he had gone to the Emergency Room because he had a nosebleed. In the ER, the doctors found that he had very high blood pressure. He was treated for his high blood pressure and subsequent investigations into its cause led to the identification of the underlying kidney disease. Since that day, his kidney function had continued to deteriorate and, at the time of our meeting, he was being treated with dialysis.

Finally, after all the investigations were completed at our institution, he was accepted for kidney transplant and was placed on the waiting list.

During the next few years, he was admitted to the hospital frequently because he had failed to go for his dialysis treatment on the days that he was supposed to. He would arrive at the ER with symptoms of fluid overload and would be admitted for emergent dialysis. Every time he was admitted, I was consulted to evaluate him from a cardiac perspective— because by this time he had developed an abnormal rhythm of the heart called *atrial fibrillation*. This is an abnormal rhythm of the top two chambers of the heart. This condition, typically, does not kill a person, but it can cause light-headedness or fainting if the heart rate is too fast. This rhythm does, however, place the patient at high risk for stroke. With every hospitalization, he would get treated with dialysis and be discharged with repeated instructions to not miss his dialysis treatments.

Unfortunately, one of those admissions was his last. During his final admission—because he had missed a regular dialysis session yet again— his blood toxin levels were so high that he was mentally altered and semi-conscious. The level of potassium in his blood was very high because of the missed dialysis appointments. We rely on our kidneys to help regulate the level of potassium in the blood. And as a result of the high potassium level, he had a cardiac arrest and died from the toxins in his body. He was 44 years old at the time of his death. His was a life taken prematurely and, quite likely, unnecessarily.

After he passed, my memory of him remained vivid in my mind. I struggled to find an answer to why he behaved in such a fashion that was so detrimental that it led to his eventual death. Did he wish to die? Did he not know that his behavior would result in death? What was it that prompted or kept pushing him to miss his dialysis? Why did he behave so angrily during appointments? Did his personality have anything to do with the end result? Obviously, this case is extreme, but I have come across so many patients who have raised similar questions in my mind. The fact is that all these questions relate to the behavior of the patient.

The Western side of the kidney disease coin

So how does Western medicine manage this patient? We go through the process of looking for the underlying causes and then confirming the presence or absence of disease. Western doctors measure the function of the kidneys by performing a blood test. They measure two substances in the blood called *blood urea nitrogen* or BUN, and *creatinine*. These two substances serve as screening markers in the blood to assess toxic accumulation in the body. The BUN and creatinine levels tell us the ability of the kidneys to eliminate waste products. In other words, chronically elevated levels of BUN and creatinine in the blood indicate an impaired ability of the kidneys to eliminate these substances in the urine. An elevated level of these substances means abnormal kidney function. An obvious fact is that kidneys also get rid of fluids (water) from our body. If the kidneys do not function well, we would accumulate fluids in the body and swell up. Western medicine recognizes several factors as either causing or pre-disposing a person to kidney disease[2]. These are:

- Diabetes (#1 cause)

- High blood pressure (#2 cause)
- Glomerulonephritis – a condition in which the kidney filtering system is damaged. No specific reason for this has been identified as yet, but certain infections are thought to trigger this damage. (#3 cause)
- Infections
- Familial or genetic predisposition
- Kidney stones
- Excessive use of medications such as pain killers that belong to the class of ibuprofen (NSAIDS)
- Use of recreational drugs such as heroin

My patient had glomerulonephritis, the third leading cause of kidney disease. I should emphasize that the above list of causes does not include all of the causes for kidney disease that Western medicine recognizes. The list I provided is only an example to illustrate how Western medicine looks at the development of kidney disease. According to Western medicine, the symptoms associated with kidney disease initially include weakness, fatigue, difficulty concentrating, and reduced appetite. Then, as the disease progresses, nausea, vomiting, mental confusion, abnormal rhythms of the heart, and even coma can result. One of the other ways kidney disease can present is with high blood pressure. Just as high blood pressure can give rise to kidney disease, it can also be the other way around. Kidney disease is thought to be one of the secondary causes of high blood pressure.

Once a diagnosis is made, the treatment is aimed at using medications that promote more urine production by the kidneys. These pills are called *water pills* or *diuretics*. These water pills increase urine production by the kidneys. The intention is that this medication will help get rid of the excess water in the body and, along with it, the toxins. Additionally, Western medicine recommends tighter control of diabetes and high blood pressure, and stopping the use of medications and drugs that are known to cause kidney problems. If infection is the cause of kidney damage, it is treated with appropriate antibiotics. If blockage by kidney stones is the cause, it is treated with surgery.

Overall, most of the treatment for kidney failure tends to focus on managing the failing kidney, rather than curative measures. When patients reach end-stage kidney failure, they are placed on dialysis. Usually this procedure is carried out three times a week for the life of the patient. Alternatively, a kidney transplant can be an option.

The functions of the kidneys from Western medical perspective are as follows:

- Elimination of water (as urine) and unwanted toxins along with it. These unwanted toxins can include broken-down products of food, medications, supplements, and any other substances that we put into our body either via the mouth, veins, skin—or simply by breathing.

- Secretion of a hormone that stimulates the bone marrow to produce red blood cells.

- Maintenance of optimal blood pressure levels.

- Maintenance of healthy bones by activating Vitamin D.

- Regulation of minerals (like potassium, sodium, and phosphorus) in the blood.

Eastern side of the kidney disease coin

In traditional medicine, organ systems are rarely looked at individually. Eastern medical practitioners will look at the condition differently than their Western counterparts will—and from an energetic (or energy-related) point of view. One way or another, kidneys are energetically connected to the vitality and life of the person. This is in contrast to Western medical concepts, which are far removed from this idea.

Although Chinese medicine has names for these energetic circuitry (such as the *kidney meridian, lung meridian, heart meridian*, etc.), the underlying meanings of these names are not the same as in Western medicine. As such, the functions comprised under the label *kidney* in Chinese medicine are quite different. In Western medicine, we only consider the disease of the organ itself, in this case the kidneys. In Chinese medicine, both the functions of the organ kidney, as well as that of adrenals and the effects of adrenal hormones, are taken into consideration. One of the hormones secreted by the adrenals is *cortisol*—a stress hormone secreted in response to perceived stress. In situations of chronic anxiety, for example, the level of this hormone is elevated in our system. Elevated levels of this hormone have been associated with the development of several diseases such as cardiovascular diseases, high blood pressure, obesity, and diabetes. As a result, according to Acupuncture philosophy, an abnormal kidney function can underlie the development of diseases such as cardiovascular conditions, high blood pressure, obesity, and diabetes.

In Eastern medical traditions, the kidney is considered to be the reservoir of the life essence (*Jing*) or Ancestral energy in every human being. This is the energy that is given to us at birth and is formed by a combination of both parents' *essence* or *Jing* at the time of conception. This energy is also called *original energy* and in Chinese it is called *Yuan Qi*. When this energy is spent, life comes to an end. In other words, according to Acupuncture, this energy is directly related to the length of our lifespan.

Related to this philosophy, traditional Chinese medicine considers several factors that deplete our life essences and often lead to kidney disease. They are as follows:

- Aging – Aging is accompanied by slow depletion of our original energy and thus kidney function declines with age.

- Emotions such as fear – The emotion fear is associated with the organ kidney in Acupuncture philosophy. Fear is closely associated with anxiety and shock, therefore these emotions too can deplete kidney energy.

- Genetics – Kidney disease can be genetically inherited.

- Excessive sexual activity – Since kidneys store the original energy of the human being and this energy is transmitted via procreation to the offspring, sexual activity is closely related to kidney function. Traditional Chinese medicine recognizes excessive sexual activity as one of the causes of kidney dysfunction.

- Overwork – Both mental and physical. Since original energy cannot be increased from what has been given to us, any activity that rapidly depletes this energy will affect the function of the kidneys. From an Acupuncture perspective, this is considered to be one of the common causes of kidney disease.

It is interesting to note that high blood pressure is the leading cause of kidney disease according to Western medical thought. Western medicine also considers those with an anxious personality to have a greater tendency to develop high blood pressure. Acupuncture associates anxiety with the emotion fear, which, as we've covered, affects the kidneys. I believe that both Western medicine and Eastern medicine are not far from each other when it comes to the most common cause of kidney dysfunction: high blood pressure.

As you may recall, my young patient had high blood pressure. In fact, his first presentation to the ER that led to the diagnosis of kidney disease was a nosebleed caused by very high blood pressure.

In Acupuncture, the kidney organs and adrenals are defined by their functions as described below:

- The kidneys govern the marrow and bones. In Acupuncture, the brain is considered marrow.

- They govern birth, growth, reproduction, and development.

- The ears and hearing are associated with the organ kidney.

- The vigor of the kidneys manifests in the hair.
- The kidneys govern water in the body.
- They house the willpower and determination of a person.

What I find intriguing is that although these Eastern functions were described thousands of years ago before we had even the origins of Western medicine, the functions are not dissimilar to what I learned in my Western medicine training. The bone marrow makes blood cells. Almost all the patients with end-stage kidney disease need a hormone (normally secreted by healthy kidneys) replacement to stimulate the production of more red blood cells. If that doesn't happen, they will develop what is called *anemia,* or a low blood count.

Consider the other similarities. In Acupuncture the kidneys govern bone marrow, which makes the red blood cells. In Western medicine kidney patients develop low blood cell counts. Most patients with kidney disease also have some degree of hearing difficulty. It is interesting to note that the kidneys develop in the uterus at the same time as the ears. Acupuncture states that the kidneys influence the ears and hearing. Another interesting parallel: The kidneys are shaped just like our ears.

Patients with kidney disease have problems with determination and willpower. Premature greying of hair is often indicative of the depletion of kidney energy or a kidney imbalance, according to traditional Chinese medicine. In Acupuncture, the kidney governs the water, and in Western medicine we know that kidneys eliminate water in the form of urine. It appears that there are only small differences between these two disciplines from a functional perspective.

In Ayurveda, although similar concepts of energy imbalance are described, the association of kidneys as the reservoir of life essences is not evident. In chronic kidney disease, Ayurveda proposes a predominant imbalance in two of the three energy regulatory systems, called Vata and Kapha[7]. As with Acupuncture, Ayurvedic tradition recognizes causative factors such as excessive sexual activities, exposure to noise pollution (interesting since in Acupuncture, ears are associated with kidneys), lack of sleep, consumption of junk food, mental or physical overwork, and too much exposure to sun or heat. As we can see, both traditions recognize energy imbalance as the initial event that triggers the development of organic disease at the organ level.

Traditional Chinese medicine delves into greater details about the functions of the kidneys. The Acupuncture practitioner may utilize some or all of the above distinctive characteristics prior to diagnosing an abnormality of the function of kidneys. For example, people who strongly manifest the kidney energy prefer the color black and the taste salty. They like the cold climate. The practitioner may ask questions regarding these preferences to make a diagnosis. Based on these questions, a diagnosis of existing kidney weakness can be made—even if the blood tests are normal. This allows for the prevention or delay of disease development due to an earlier diagnosis at an energetic level by Eastern medicine.

You Power • The third side of the kidney disease coin

As a heart transplant cardiologist, I see many kidney transplant patients in consultation when they need cardiac clearance to undergo the transplant. That is how I crossed paths with the patient described earlier in this chapter. I recognized a pattern in these patients. The kidney failure patients I have seen exhibited a common and consistent emotional or personality undertone. The following are the tendencies I have observed:

- They expected other people to do everything for them. They had a childlike expectation of everything being done for them. If it is not done, they will not do it or are reluctant to do it themselves. This is related to being less self-efficacious.

- When things were not done, there was a tendency to criticize everyone else—and expect others to pick up the ball and complete the task. In other words, a tendency to displace responsibility.

- There was a tendency to blame external factors (everything else in the world) for having acquired the kidney problem and the consequences of it. Actually, we all tend to have this characteristic to some degree, but it was more prominent in patients who had end stage kidney disease.

- A tendency to feel depressed and exhibit it outwardly. (Feeling depressed is not abnormal unless it becomes a disease.) For most people, when they feel depressed, they may not exhibit it to the outside world and simply behave in a way that is opposite of how they're feeling. In other words: present themselves as if they are not depressed at all.

Among these patients, I have seen both aggressive adult-children and shy adult–children. In both cases, they exhibited similar characteristics. For example, the patient mentioned earlier would fall into the category of aggressive adult-children whereas, my brother—whose story I shared with you earlier in this book and who died from kidney failure—would fall into the shy adult-children category. My brother was not aggressive. He was passive. My brother did not miss any dialysis sessions, but he handed over the power of healing to the practitioners of Western medicine and relied on them solely and completely. He did not survive.

The patient I've described in this chapter was aggressive and angry, and protested that others were not helping him. In most cases, these characteristics work in favor of a patient. The problems with the patient I've used as an example were that he failed to take any responsibility or initiative in his own self-care and he did not know how to cope with everything that was going on in his life. And as a result he did not survive. These attributes have been identified in the Western medical literature as being prominent in patients with end-stage kidney failure.

I must admit that I was astounded when my patient told me (during that delayed follow-up visit) that he had not come to see me earlier because he was expecting *us* to call him and make an appointment. What bothered me more was that he was very angry and accusatory.

When someone expresses anger, what they are really saying is that we are not hearing them or they are not being recognized. They are frustrated that their point of view is not being heard or accepted. Anger is also very closely associated with fear. And, most often, it is fear that leads to anger. Therefore, when someone is angry, the question to ask is: What are you afraid of? There is no point in getting angry with them, since it won't lead to a meaningful solution.

I asked my patient what he was afraid of. He told me that he was fearful that he was losing his life and that he was going to die unless he got help. He said that he was not being helped enough by the people who were supposed to help him. As you can see, this internal dialogue—"I am going to die if I am not helped by someone else and I need to be helped."—was the underlying motivator and his form of acceptance or justification for his actions. He did not acknowledge that, to some extent, he needed to help himself. He relied on the outside world to help him, just as a helpless child would. Children usually look to their parents or other adults for help in high-stress situations. In looking back on my patient's situation, I see that he became depressed in the years between our first encounter and his death. He lost the willpower to live.

What can you do?

At the risk of being repetitive, I will stress this point yet again: The first step is to understand that there are three sides that need to be considered. These are Western medicine (a teammate), Eastern medicine (a teammate), and You Power (you... as captain of your team and your life).

In the case of my patient, Western medicine only offered him partial help. He did not reap the benefit of Eastern medicine—and his You Power was not addressed at all. When he developed depression, he was sent to a psychiatrist and was prescribed antidepressants, medications to treat his depression. A better treatment might have been to identify the underlying cause of his depression. Better yet, it would have been more effective to identify the underlying cause of his fear and subsequent anger. This may have been achieved if the recommendation had been for him to see a psychologist or a counselor rather than a psychiatrist. What he needed was a counselor to help him learn how to cope with the psychological stress he was under. If he had been taught better coping mechanisms, he may not have missed his dialysis sessions. He might have enjoyed better psychological health, motivation, determination, and willpower. As a result, he might still be alive today.

As I write this chapter, I recall an encounter with another patient who came to the clinic for cardiac evaluation for a kidney transplant. He was in his mid-fifties...a well-mannered, well-spoken individual, and an academician. As I was talking with him, I found him to be well adjusted to his illness and I started doubting my impression of the internal dialogue that most kidney patients have. He did not appear to fit the profile. I asked him if he knew the medications he was taking. He said he did—and then he asked me to pick up and hand him his briefcase while he sat and watched me. He opened the briefcase and pulled out a list and handed it to me. He said, "My daughter wrote this list for me." I asked him if his daughter helped him a lot. He told me that his entire family helped him a lot and that he, in turn, helped them.

If I did not have this detailed conversation, I would not have found in him the presence of personality similarities that exist among kidney patients. This patient described relying, repeatedly, on other people to help him. What initially perplexed me was the fact that he was coping well with his disease and had been able to adjust. Therefore, the manifestation of his internal dialogue was not apparent. When I asked him how he was coping, he said that after having kidney disease for 11 years, one learns to cope with it better every day. It appeared that he was working with his You Power better than most of my patients—and certainly better than the patient who suffered a death that might have been prevented. This was the kind of realization and level of understanding that my other patient needed. But he did not utilize the opportunities to extend his life because he played the game with only one teammate, looking only at one side of the coin. And, very possibly, he never even realized there are two other sides, two other points of view and related treatments, to his situation. Both the first patient I described and my brother suffered the fatal consequences of playing with one teammate—and not being good captains of the game.

It is important to recognize that there are several levels of dependence that result from internal dialogue. If some of these patients had learned to cope better, they may not have manifested apparent dependability. Lack of manifestation does not mean that the internal dialogue is not there. It means that more attention needs to be given to explore and address it.

What can Western medicine offer you?

How would a Western medical practitioner address the first patient example in this chapter? Once symptoms develop, you and I both know that functional and structural changes have already occurred in the related organ. The practitioner will go through the same process that is taught in medical school and subsequent specialty training: identify the disease, look for the underlying cause, and institute appropriate treatment. Once again, treating the *disease* is the main focus. The patient, as a person, is not even on the Western medicine practitioner's radar screen.

Medications

Unless the kidney disease is caused by an infection or your own body attacking itself (what we call *autoimmune disease*), the medications prescribed are to support and preserve the kidney function, not to cure the kidney disease. For example, a hormone could be prescribed to stimulate bone marrow to produce more red blood cells, because the failing kidneys cannot secrete this hormone themselves. Other than that, treatment involves monitoring the kidneys to try to preserve their function and to avoid dialysis for as long as possible. The progression of kidney disease is usually divided into five stages: From stage one, which begins with mild kidney imbalance, through progression to stage five, which is where dialysis and/or a kidney transplant is warranted. The main point here is that most of the medications for chronic kidney disease are prescribed, not to cure the disease, but to support the function of the organ and the body.

Because the focus is not curative, Western medicine focuses on controlling the other diseases that lead to or worsen kidney disease. Your practitioner will give you new medications or optimize existing medications to treat these other diseases, such as high blood pressure and diabetes, so that their adverse effects on the kidneys are minimized.

Diet

There is controversy around the belief that a diet very high in protein for a prolonged period of time may result in abnormal kidney function. A high protein diet places a lot of demand on the kidneys. That said, there has been no confirmation to date of this theory by robust research. Kidneys eliminate the waste products that are created when protein is broken down for normal utilization in the body. When one consumes very high amounts of protein on a regular basis, the kidneys may react and adapt.

A diet high in sodium for a prolonged period of time can decrease kidney function by causing high blood pressure. There has been a lot of hype in medical circles and in the media in New York City around sodium intake and its effects on health. The New York City Board of Health recently (September 2015) approved a mandate requiring all NYC chain restaurants to post a warning related to salt content in their menu items if any of them contain more than 2,300 mg of sodium. This amount is the maximum daily sodium intake level recommended by many nutritionists. The African-American population, specifically, is at higher risk because this demographic has what is called *salt sensitivity*. But wait—that's not the whole story! This salt sensitivity is not limited to the African-American population. Salt sensitivity increases in *everyone* as they grow older, especially after age 45. This same tendency has also been documented in Caucasian adolescents who are overweight.

From a Western perspective, diet becomes more important after kidney disease develops. When kidney function is impaired, the kidneys lose the ability to excrete waste products from the breakdown of protein. This is why a high-protein diet for a prolonged time may influence kidney function. Additionally, impaired kidneys fail to maintain optimum levels of phosphorus (a mineral in our body) and potassium (an electrolyte) in our bodies. Patients with kidney disease are therefore advised to limit their consumption of foods that contain high potassium, protein, and phosphorus. I suggest that you consult a nutritionist to get recommendations about what foods you can eat and which foods should be avoided.

The patient I described in my first example died in the ER from a high potassium level that led to cardiac arrest. High or low potassium levels can lead to abnormal cardiac rhythms and can potentially lead to death. A related note: Over-the-counter supplements, vitamins, and medications should always be taken with caution and under the supervision of a health practitioner. The semi-consciousness that occurred in my patient was related to the level of toxins that had build up in his blood from protein breakdown, as these toxins were not promptly eliminated from the body through dialysis... in the case of my patient, the *lack* of dialysis.

Exercise

Regular moderate exercise is one of the best ways to improve your overall health. The benefit of exercise with regard to kidney function relies on improving the underlying causes of the kidney abnormality. Regular exercise has been deemed beneficial in conditions like diabetes, high blood pressure, and obesity—all of which can potentially lead to kidney failure. A regular exercise program not only helps improve these associated conditions, but also improves your overall sense of well-being, that in turn allows you to handle life's stressors better.

Medications that are detrimental to your kidneys

Most all medications that we take are broken down by the liver and are excreted in the urine by our kidneys and via the intestines in the stool. There are medications that can potentially lead to kidney dysfunction and can even damage the kidneys permanently. As I have mentioned, the most common medications that fall into this category are pain relievers. Specifically, medications that contain *ibuprofen* as the main ingredient. This category of medications is known as NSAID. Some antibiotics that are used to treat infections are also very destructive to the kidneys. These are only a few examples and this is by no means an exhaustive list.

The risk of kidney damage with these medications increases if you already have predisposing factors, such as high blood pressure or diabetes. Additionally, if you already have mild kidney disease, excessive use of these medications can accelerate the progression of the disease. There are other medications that can lead to abnormal kidney function, but those specifics and detailed descriptions are beyond the scope of this book. I encourage you to be mindful of excessive vitamins, supplements, and the like. The list of medications that are harmful when you have kidney disease is also something to consider and should be discussed with your Western medical practitioner.

What can Eastern medicine offer you?

There are a myriad of Eastern medical disciplines that one can choose to use either alone or in combination as a complement to Western medicine to help you to continue to address your kidney disease, or simply to maintain a healthy state.

Acupuncture

As I've mentioned, an Acupuncturist understands the kidney from its function. He or she will examine you based on Acupuncture philosophy and may ask questions such as your favorite color, taste, season, etc. These are efforts to identify whether the kidneys are the main culprits or whether other organ imbalances are affecting the kidneys. In Acupuncture, all organs work as a unit and an imbalance of one can affect the others. Because of this, a complete evaluation of *you* as a person is carried out. An important role that the kidneys play in Acupuncture is through their associated channel. The associated channel for the kidney in Acupuncture is the urinary bladder channel. The bladder channel runs from your foot all the way to your head and face. It covers most of the back of the body and is very useful in treating several conditions. Therefore, if the kidney is at the root of imbalance, the Acupuncturist may place needles along the channels pertaining to the kidney and urinary bladder, and not necessarily at the exact physical location of the kidney.

A claim by an Acupuncturist to treat a particular disease has no basis, except in the case of pain relief for musculoskeletal problems. This is because, fundamentally, Acupuncture does not treat diseases. It treats patients...the You Power in patients. Therefore, if your practitioner claims to treat a particular disease, it is time to change to a different practitioner.

While Acupuncture or any other Eastern medicines cannot claim to "cure" disease to meet the standards set by the Western medicine, they can be used to improve your general well-being and support Western medical therapies. This combination of treatment has been documented to work well. For example, Acupuncture has been shown to be effective in reducing post-operative pain and nausea in patients that undergo major surgeries—and does so without major side effects[8].

A good friend of mine needed major abdominal surgery for cancer treatment. Without surgery, he was looking at less than six months of survival. His kidney function was abnormal, with elevated creatinine levels, which indicated dysfunction. When he was evaluated for surgery at one of the premier medical centers in the United States, and was declined because of his abnormal kidney function and advanced age, I had him undergo Acupuncture therapy. I recommended Acupuncture therapy not only for kidney improvement but also for improved general health. After three months of Acupuncture treatment, his kidney function normalized. The only intervention during that three month period was Acupuncture. His primary care physician, a Western medical practitioner, was astonished at the results— he did not expect improvement in the kidney function of his 90-year-old patient.

The patient went back to the surgeons and was accepted for the abdominal surgery because of the improvement in his kidney function, despite his advanced age. In fact, he was the oldest person ever to undergo such surgery in that hospital. He was treated with Acupuncture in the days preceding the surgery to improve his chances of recovery from surgery and to minimize complications. After this major surgery, he spent only 10 days in the hospital and did not have any complications. I do not often see a 90-year-old have a major surgery without any complications and then walk out of the hospital in 10 days. And he walked out of the hospital on his own. Sidebar to this story: This was the man I mentioned in Chapter 2 on Liver disease... who, with Chiropractic manipulation, was able to get rid of his walker.

I hope that you are beginning to recognize that while Eastern modalities may not be able to claim victory by the standards set by the Western medical system, they can claim victory on their own merit. They can have significant impact on your health and disease and even save your life, as they did for my friend. He lived, quite happily, another year and a half after his surgery.

Massage

Massage on a regular basis can influence your stress and aid in handling emotions better—emotions like fear and anxiety, that are commonly associated with the kidneys. As mentioned under Acupuncture, an associated channel with the kidneys—the bladder channel—runs on the back of our body along either side of the vertebral column to reach the neck and head. A massage therapist can use these channels and the points along these channels to help relieve blockages and stimulate the energy flow along the channel to harmonize the entire body. Stimulating the kidneys and bladder channel tend to improve a person's overall energy status because the kidneys function as the supplier of energy to the rest of the organ systems. In addition, the general effect of massage in reducing stress and stress-related tension may help reduce surges in the hormone *cortisol*, a stress-related hormone in our body.

Homeopathy

Homeopathy can be used at stages of kidney abnormality when detected very early by Eastern medical practitioners. This diagnosis is called a weakness, based upon the degree of energetic imbalance. At this point, Homeopathic remedies can be used alone to treat the condition. However, if you have developed structural abnormalities and have a Western medical diagnosis of kidney disease, Homeopathy can be a great adjunct—as long as it is prescribed by an experienced practitioner.

Several practitioners claim various responses to the treatment with Homeopathic remedies. As I always emphasize, make sure to inform both your teammates about the assessment of the severity of the condition, as well as the other medications that you are taking. Homeopathy has been useful in helping alleviate some of the symptoms resulting from kidney failure, although a cure is not possible if the disease has already taken hold in the body. For that matter, a cure is not possible even in Western medicine. Again, in Western medicine, curing the disease is not the focus in most cases. Prevention is a better avenue than trying to cure a disease that has already affected your organs. Therefore, a healthy lifestyle where you proactively engage with both disciplines is the best approach. It should be emphasized that Homeopathy is not regulated in the United States. Nevertheless, several Western medical doctors also practice Homeopathy.

Chiropractic Care

The principles of treatment with Chiropractic therapy remain the same. It is used to invigorate the nerve supply to the kidneys. Experienced chiropractors can perform necessary manipulation without much discomfort and are cautious depending on the severity of your illness. The manipulation of the entire vertebral column helps relieve the tension on the nerves that supply the kidneys, as well as the urinary bladder and other abdominal and thoracic organs.

Herbs

Traditional Chines practitioners, naturopaths, chiropractors, and even several Western medical practitioners use herbs either as primary treatment or as adjunct for various illnesses. Consumed substances are usually degraded by the liver and excreted in the urine and stool. Bear in mind that some herbs can be harmful if you have kidney disease. Make sure that both your Western and Eastern practitioners are aware of the medications and the herbs you are taking.

Again, herbs can sometimes be used to support or aid in the prevention of kidney imbalance if you are healthy and are diagnosed by an experienced Eastern practitioner to have a weakness in the area of kidney—even if the biochemical tests by a Western practitioner are normal. Even if you are healthy and want to use herbs, make sure to ask your Eastern practitioner about their effect on the kidneys.

Once kidney disease has been confirmed by tests that are done by Western medical practitioners, it is not advisable to use herbs. This is because herbs can worsen the dysfunctional kidney. Additionally, herbs can contain the very substances that you are supposed to avoid in cases of kidney disease, such as potassium and phosphorus. If you need more information on this area, please visit The National Kidney Foundations website[9] to learn more. The good news is that there are other Eastern therapies that you can use.

Yoga and Meditation

Yoga exercises are excellent for the overall healthy status of anyone. When it comes to kidneys, the way Yoga can help is by using exercises that stimulate the kidneys. There are two ways Yoga can help prevent kidney disease. The first is by reducing your stress level and improving your response to stress. This, in turn, reduces your anxiety response and can help minimize elevated blood pressure that can result from stressful situations. Since high blood pressure is the number one cause associated with the development of kidney disease, Yoga can help prevent such a **disease from developing.**

Secondly, Yoga exercises such as "shoulder stand" and "half shoulder stand" help massage the kidneys and adrenals by putting pressure from your weight on them. This daily stimulation of the kidneys, in my opinion, helps keep them healthy. These exercises can be safely performed under the guidance of an experienced Yoga teacher, even if you have established kidney disease.

The addition of meditation to your daily practice will help you deal with your internal dialogue with clarity and assist with mindful living.

Ayurveda

Ayurveda uses a system of healthy living to promote the health and well-being of a person. This system utilizes various cleansing methods to purify the body of its toxins and unwanted substances on a regular basis. As such, it is a very helpful adjunct to help cleanse our body of impurities, which in turn allows optimal function of the organs.

Therefore, Ayurvedic lifestyle and remedies can be very useful when you attempt to prevent the development of kidney disease, if you think that you are predisposed to develop such a disease.

However, the outlook is different once you have established kidney disease. An Ayurvedic physician may recommend a diet that is supposed to pacify the underlying abnormality based on the Ayurvedic evaluation. Make sure to work with your nutritionist to determine the acceptability of such dietary recommendations. Additional remedies may be prescribed. However, just like in the case of liver disease, use of Ayurvedic remedies for kidney disease should be exercised with caution, especially if you have established kidney disease. While lifestyle modifications are harmless with existing kidney disease and may enhance your well-being, oral remedies should be taken with extra caution under the supervision of an experienced practitioner and with the full awareness of the Western practitioner.

There is always an aspect of any Eastern modality that can be very useful in conjunction with Western medical therapy to enhance your chance of winning the game of health and disease. Make sure to explore all your options. And, in doing so, you should also explore the adverse influence of Eastern medications (just like you would want to find out the side effects of Western medications) when you have established disease. Guidance from a practitioner who is well versed in both disciplines is very useful. As a general rule, most Eastern modalities are useful in *acquiring and maintaining health*, while Western therapy is used once a disease is diagnosed to *restore health*. Some aspect of most Eastern modalities can be used even if you have established disease to benefit you as long as you do the due diligence to make sure no harm is done.

There are several other modalities that can be successfully used to cope with chronic diseases. These modalities include (but are not limited to) aromatherapy, music therapy, spiritual therapy, pet therapy, reflexology, and biofeedback.

Handling your You Power

You Power—again—plays a major role in your ability to reap the benefits of whatever tools you choose to use from both modalities. The emotional and psychological characteristics described above, with regard to patients with kidney disease, play a significant role in the way the disease progresses. To prevent kidney disease, it is important to recognize the underlying psychological characteristic for predisposing conditions like high blood pressure and diabetes. Chapters on these topics can be found in this book.

Internal dialogue or Primal being

When it came to the first patient I described in this chapter, he felt afraid and thought he was losing his life as a result of the fact that other people were not helping him—or helping him enough. As a result of this fear, he was being an aggressive adult-child. The internal dialogue in the case of kidney disease appears to be "I am afraid and I need to be taken care of." Or "Take care of me." This internal dialogue leads to abnormal coping mechanisms in patients, resulting in abnormal behavior that leads to adverse outcomes.

What is needed is recognition of the internal dialogue that goes on within ourselves. The next step would be what I call an *emotional cleanse*, accomplished by choosing to seek help from a counselor or psychologist. Most of my patients refuse to seek help of this kind because they consider such action a manifestation of weakness. There is nothing wrong in trying to find out how well you are coping with an illness that threatens to shorten your life.

Personality or Social being

Personality refers to an individual's characteristic pattern of behavior *driven* by their deeper thought and emotions. This is modified by their rules of conduct to suit the outside world. In other words, it is the primal self modified to suit the outside world and society in order to be accepted.

By understanding your personality and recognizing certain tendencies, you may be able to recognize abnormal coping mechanisms. This understanding may help you to either prevent kidney disease or slow its progression. For example, part of the coping mechanism of my first patient was the decision to miss dialysis, whereas the second patient was better adept at coping. Learning about your personality, followed by a good emotional cleanse, and then learning coping mechanisms to deal with external or internal stressors, will help you avoid conflicts.

Your partner in identifying conflicts and changing your coping mechanisms to such conflicts is a counselor or a psychologist. Mindfulness, meditation, and Yoga exercises can also aid with clarity of thinking, which will make it easier to identify your internal conflicts and emotional imbalances. Unresolved conflicts and emotional imbalances often lead to illnesses down the road by changing the way you behave. It's well documented that abnormal behaviors can lead to predisposing people to different diseases.

Chapter Six

Obesity/Diabetes

The Masked Killer

I need protection. I need to control.

O besity and diabetes are two major health concerns across the world. The incidence of these destructive diseases is steadily on the rise. They contribute significantly to health care expenses and impaired quality of life, and in many cases lead to the increased chance of death at an early age. Unfortunately, these two diseases present two major problems: First, their effects begin and progress very slowly, and second, these conditions are grossly under-diagnosed and, therefore, under-treated. What is devastating is that Type II diabetes is one of the few REVERSIBLE diseases, yet the incidence still continues to rise.

Obesity

Worldwide, in 2014, the estimated number of overweight adults over the age of 18 was 39 percent[1] of the entire global population (that is more than one in three of us), and another 13 percent were considered obese[1]. In the United States, one in three Americans is considered obese. The Centers for Disease Control and Prevention (CDC) reports that 35.1 percent of U.S. adults over age 20 are obese and 69 percent are overweight. It is projected that 42 percent of Americans will be obese by the year 2030. Approximately $147 billion is currently spent—

annually—on obesity-related expenses in the United States, according to the CDC (in comparison we spend about $200 billion annually on cancer). These numbers are devastating and I believe that many people do not understand the effects of excess weight on our overall heath. More importantly, I believe that most people don't realize that the negative effects of excess weight are avoidable!

Obesity is defined as abnormal fat accumulation that may impair health. Fat storage is responsible for obesity. We categorize obesity at different levels based on a global measure of obesity called *body mass index* (BMI), or a central measure of obesity called waist-to-hip ratio. BMI is calculated based upon your height and weight and I will supply more details on BMI and the distinction between obesity and morbid obesity in this chapter.

If you don't care what your BMI is... you may want to think again! Insurance companies and the government may be watching and "weighing" your premiums and coverage based on this index measurement. Now that obesity is a diagnosable disease in America, it is an important factor when you are considering purchasing life insurance.

I have several patients who would meet the criteria for a diagnosis of obesity. In fact, we tend to turn down heart transplant requests for people who meet the criteria for morbid obesity. This is due to the fact that obese people develop more complications during and after surgery and are therefore considered high-risk candidates for heart transplants.

What most people do not realize is that obesity can kill people prematurely if the right attitude and actions are not maintained. Obesity can either put you at risk of developing other diseases such as high blood pressure, stroke, heart attack, diabetes, and cancer or, in and of itself, can lead to premature death. I have had patients hospitalized because they could not breathe due to their excessive weight, a condition Western medicine calls *obesity hypoventilation syndrome.*

There are several websites that offer free BMI calculators, so you won't have to do the formula calculation manually. You can find a BMI calculator on the CDC website: www.cdc.gov/healthyweight/assessing/bmi/adult_BMI/english_bmi_calculator/bmi_calculator.html

Once you arrive at your BMI, you can determine where you fall on the scale based on the fluid ranges that extend from undernourished to morbidly obese.

BMI <18.5 = Underweight

BMI 18.5 – 25 = Healthy

BMI 25 – 30 = Overweight

BMI >30 = Obese

BMI >40 = Morbidly obese

In my practice, I have seen obese people who live a long life well into their late eighties without any other obesity-related diseases. I will admit that it makes me wonder why—and what in their makeup supports such longevity. I have seen lean people who develop disease and die young. In an age when man had to work hard, farming and hunting for food to survive, obesity was considered an indicator of affluence and wealth. This was because obesity indicated an abundance of food and therefore health and good nutrition. In certain cultures in Africa, being overweight is a sign of health, not ill health. However, in the era where food can be delivered to your doorstep, obesity has reached epidemic proportions. And, with it, a growing propensity toward disease.

Diabetes

Diabetes is the 7th leading cause of death in the United States[2].

In the year 2012, 29.1 million Americans were found to be diabetics. This represents 9.3 percent of our population[2]. Of those 29.1 million Americans with diabetes, 8.1 million were undiagnosed[2]. As you age, the chance of developing diabetes increases. One in four seniors, age 65 or older, has diabetes, either diagnosed or undiagnosed[2]. That 25.9 percent translates to 11.8 million American seniors. These are devastating statistics. In the year 2012 alone, 1.7 million new cases of diabetes were identified[2].

It is interesting to note that diabetes is thought to be associated with a high intake of sugar and sweets. This is one of the reasons for the increased incidence of diabetes among both adults and children in the United States. However, carbohydrate intake also influences the onset of diabetes. And this includes alcohol.

Further complicating the issues surrounding this disease is the lack of regulation related to the amount of diabetes-promoting ingredients that are packed into the foods and drinks we consume on a daily basis. Sadly, many of the foods in restaurants and grocery stores that are advertised as "healthy" are in fact (upon close scrutiny) far from healthy. Interestingly, there is emerging evidence that cancer is also associated with a high intake of sweets and sugary food.

There are two type of diabetes: Type I and Type II. Type I is caused when the pancreas secretes insufficient amounts of the insulin that the body needs to handle the glucose in the blood stream. Often, Type I diabetes is diagnosed during childhood. Type II diabetes is a situation where the pancreas secretes adequate amounts of insulin, but the cells in our body have lost their sensitivity to the insulin, and it cannot, therefore, enter our cells so that the body can use it appropriately. Think of it like this: A cell is like a house, and the glucose needs to get in through the front door...but it cannot do that without a key. And the key is insulin. In cases of Type II diabetes, the keyhole on the lock has changed its shape. The key doesn't fit the door so it can't open it, and as a result the insulin cannot get into the cell. But your pancreas does not know this.

Initially, the pancreas compensates by producing greater amounts of insulin—like producing more keys, hoping that one will eventually open the door. For a while, this compensation works to get the insulin inside the cell that still responded to insulin, but eventually this compensation process fails. At that point, the glucose just floats around in the bloodstream with nowhere to go. In both situations, the problem is abnormal handling of glucose in the bloodstream, but the reason for failure is different. As a result of this abnormal handling of blood glucose, the glucose level in the blood tends to be high.

Interestingly, you may hear of Alzheimer's disease referred to as Type III diabetes. This is not a true diagnosis, but because of the havoc that diabetes wreaks within your body, some evidence has been found that it may be a cause of Alzheimer's!

I will discuss diabetes and obesity together because as someone's weight increases, it puts them at higher risk of developing diabetes. The more sugar and carbohydrates that are ingested (and which turn into glucose), the more insulin that needs to be produced to make the glucose work as it should. The body's failure to produce insulin increases the workload on your body.

Years ago, when I was in London working as an Acupuncturist, I met two sisters. They came to the clinic for treatment for different conditions. And I got to know them well over a period of two years.

One sister had an ideal BMI, while the other's BMI fell into what we would consider morbid obesity. As sisters, they had the same upbringing, the same family circle with the same kind of eating habits. The sister with high BMI is pre-diabetic and the sister with ideal BMI is not. As we have seen, obesity predisposes you to diabetes. Both of the sisters admitted that they loved food and ate a lot. The sister with the ideal BMI ate constantly. I asked her why she ate all the time and she said, "I eat when I'm anxious, nervous, or bored." She added: "These emotions make me feel negative and I want to distract myself from the negative effect of these emotions." I was impressed that she was aware that her emotions led her to eating.

This story begs two questions. First, *What prompts both these sisters to eat so much?* Is it a habit of the family? Is it their way of coping with uncomfortable internal emotions, as described by the sister with ideal BMI? The second question is, *Why is there such a big discrepancy in the weight between one sister and the other?*

Let us explore the first question. Obviously we all eat differently and change our eating habits based on our mood. For example, how many times before going out to dinner do you ask yourself, *What am I in the mood for?* We all do this. So it is no wonder that our mood is associated with our eating. Moods arise out of the emotions that we feel. Therefore, emotions have an influence on the habit of eating. So it's not surprising that the sister with ideal BMI ate in response to her emotions, as she described, to "distract" herself. In other words, what she was telling me was that the best she could do under the circumstances was to distract herself with food rather than addressing the emotions and dealing with them. Eating was her coping mechanism when she felt negative emotions.

As to the second question, we will find ourselves addressing the *being* of each of the sisters. Why was there a big weight discrepancy between these two sisters? Because it depended on who they were being. These two sisters were very outgoing and loved to be the center of attention. They tended to seek approval of others and liked the limelight. In that regard, they were very similar. They also both reacted negatively to fluctuations of emotions. I had a hard time understanding and explaining this weight discrepancy. Although the sister with obesity was on a diet program and worked with a trainer on a regular basis, she was not making any progress with regard to losing weight. The sister with ideal BMI had her own "diet plan" but was not on a prescribed program, was exercising on her own, and did not need a trainer. I had a hard time understanding the situation and it stayed with me for many years after I left London. The person on a structured diet program and who had a trainer was obese, unable to lose weight, but the person implementing her own programs was not obese. One would expect the opposite results. The answer lies in the fact that the sister with the ideal BMI never got to the level of being obese.

I have had long discussions with the sister with high BMI about her failure to make progress with weight loss. She told me, "I just love food and cannot control my eating. But I eat healthy."

I hear this a lot from my patients. "Eating healthy" is defined differently by different people. For example, many of my patients will say they choose to eat salad in order to be healthy, but will go on to admit that they add a lot of salad dressing to make it palatable. Here is an example of taking clean, healthy food like vegetables and making it unhealthy with unhealthy salad dressing. And all the while you think you are eating healthy. To take it a step further, maybe they are trying to be mindful and order the fat-free dressing. Unbeknownst to them, *that* dressing is loaded with sugar instead! The same is true with regard to many other food products on the market. I get reports such as "I only buy low-caloric, organic food" from patients regularly. Yes, it may be low calorie and organic...but how many chemicals and additives were used to increase its shelf life? Another comment I hear often is this: "I only buy gluten free products." I can't tell you how often my jaw hits the floor when I look at the ingredients and nutritional value (or lack of) in these seemingly "healthy" foods. Do you know that the chemicals added to food to make them last longer on grocery store shelves can alter how your body handles that food? This reaction can be different for different people.

Now... let's talk about portions. People seem to have no clue what a true portion size is because it is the norm today to expect huge servings. No wonder people who think they are eating healthy to lose weight and be healthy do not actually lose weight or get healthy because of hidden (and unhealthy) substances and calories in the food that they consume in today's world.

Now... back to the sister with the higher BMI. She was on the wrong path with all of the habits that I have mentioned. She would eat salad, but order unhealthy dressing and then finish the meal with a sweet, calorie-loaded flourless ("healthy!") cake. She justified the dessert by saying she had eaten a healthy dinner and it was a "cheat day." Cheat days are days when you allow yourself to "cheat" with foods that aren't allowed on your weight loss program. She also did not pay attention to the ingredients of what she was buying and she only exercised when she worked with her trainer.

Her sister, on the other hand, was more consistent in every aspect of her lifestyle. Like her sister, she "ate all the time," but she exercised regularly, was conscious of portion control, and paid attention to the ingredients in the foods she ate—primarily natural, healthy, and nutritious foods with the least amount of chemical in them.

The Western medical side of the obesity and diabetes coin

Obesity

Recently, the American Medical Association identified obesity as a disease[3].

It has become a worldwide problem, and here are a few reasons why. According to the World Health Organization (WHO), the following global observations have resulted in obesity being considered a disease[1]:

- There is a significant association between obesity and cardiovascular disease, mainly heart disease and stroke, which continues to be the leading cause of death in the United States and several other countries around the world.

- There is a significant association between obesity and diabetes.

- There is a significant association between the development of musculoskeletal disorders (such as osteoarthritis) and obesity.

- There is an association between at least some cancers (colon, breast, and endometrial cancers) and obesity.

- There are other conditions that are associated with obesity such as sleep apnea and hypertension.

- Increased BMI is associated with an increase in the number of days a patient stays in the hospital and the number of consultations needed from other specialists[2].

- Increased BMI is associated with an increase in the number of medications a person takes[2].

Medically, obesity is the result of the consumption of more calories than a body needs, or burning fewer calories than we consume, resulting in fat deposits in the body. There are other theories, such as decreased metabolism in some patients, which can lead to the under utilization of the calories consumed, and genetic mutations that lead to overeating. Nevertheless, the predominant mechanism that leads to obesity seems to be excess calorie intake compared to the utilization of calories. Biomedicine or Western medical disciplines recommend the following to combat obesity[1].

Lifestyle modifications:

- Reduce caloric intake of sugar and fat.

- Engage in regular physical activity. The WHO recommends 480 minutes a week (60 minutes a day) for children and 150 minutes a week for adults.

- Increase consumption of fresh vegetables and fruits. One may also consider nuts and legumes, however, there is a need to monitor caloric intake as nuts and legumes can pack in a lot of calories.

And while we might all agree that these three modifications to our lifestyle are pretty straightforward and require only awareness and discipline...changing your lifestyle when it comes to food is easier said than done! It is difficult to monitor our food and calorie intake when dining out and if we're not mindful of our choices, it's possible to consume an entire day's allotment of calories in one meal. To further complicate this process, food labels are misleading, and multiple choices of unhealthy foods are readily available.

There are many weight loss programs that, while not part of the medical community, are marketed for the purpose of losing weight. They don't fall into the disciplines of either Western medicine or Eastern medicine, but would be considered behavioral modification programs. There are several weight loss pharmacological medications on the market as well. Some of these pharmaceutical medications have resulted in illness and other serious medical conditions. Additionally, there are surgical procedures that can be recommended by the biomedical community for the treatment of obesity. These include *gastric bypass surgery* (also called *bariatric surgery*) and surgical *liposuction* (a procedure considered cosmetic surgery where fat tissue is surgically removed from unwanted areas of the body). Liposuction is not only performed on obese patients. It is also performed on non-obese people to modify their physical appearance.

Diabetes

In Western medicine, diabetes is considered a chronic disease. Once you have this diagnosis, each time you visit a Western physician he or she will address your disease—and not you. As I have maintained throughout this book, we Western medical practitioners will treat your disease but will not delve deeply into why you developed the disease. We will look for what we know to be predisposing factors for diabetes when we take a history from you. Risk factors for Type I diabetes include a family history of diabetes among other factors, but this is an area of intense research because Type I is the number 8 killer in the world, according to the WHO. There are several risk factors for Type II diabetes that have been recognized. These predisposing factors are divided into modifiable and non-modifiable risk factors[4].

Non-modifiable risk factors include:

- Family history

  Your risk of developing diabetes is high if you have a blood relative who has diabetes.

- Race or ethnic background

  You have a greater likelihood of developing diabetes if you are of Pacific-Islander, African-American, Native-American, Asian-American or Latino/Hispanic American descent.

- Age

  As I have mentioned before, as you grow older, your chances of being diagnosed with diabetes increases.

- Diagnosis of transient diabetes during pregnancy

  If you had diabetes while pregnant, your chance of developing diabetes later in life is increased.

Modifiable risk factors include:

- Obesity

  About 70 percent of women and 50 percent of men who have diabetes are obese[4].

- Physical inactivity

  A sedentary lifestyle has been associated with an increased chance of developing diabetes.

- High blood pressure

  High blood pressure that goes untreated has been linked to the development of diabetes.

- Cholesterol levels

  Abnormal cholesterol levels have also been linked to the development of diabetes.

Diabetes is a disease that is remarkably under-diagnosed. Most people who have diabetes, do not even know that they have the disease. Therefore, it is important to have screening tests if you have any of the risk factors that I have mentioned.

Additionally, an awareness of the symptoms of diabetes may alert you to the possibility of developing this disease and drive you to request testing early. Remember, you do not want to be an undiagnosed diabetic. I have seen several patients who had diabetes and by the time they were diagnosed, the diabetes had already affected their heart, kidneys, and the blood vessels in their legs, causing the blood vessels to narrow and cause pain while walking.

Diabetes can lead to blindness, numbness and tingling in your extremities, increased risks of infections, and longer healing time after an injury. You will want to talk with your Western medical practitioner if you experience any of the following symptoms:

- If you find you have become more thirsty than usual, without an identifiable cause
- If you have become more hungry than usual
- If you feel increased fatigued for long periods of time
- If you notice unusual weight loss
- If you develop blurred vision
- If you find that sores or wounds take a long time to heal, or do not heal
- Finally, even if you feel no symptoms...do your annual physical exam and a diabetes screening test because this disease does not always produce symptoms in its early stages.

Being vigilant and proactive related to these silent conditions is advised and encouraged. Early detection and diagnosis can lead to possible cures when it comes to Type II diabetes and the prevention of complications of diabetes for both types.

Eastern medical side of the obesity and diabetes coin

From an Eastern medical perspective, diabetes and obesity share similar patterns and, as a result, they are described together in this book.

Widely practiced Eastern disciplines, Traditional Chinese Acupuncture and Ayurveda, both recognize and treat obesity. Mechanisms of obesity described in both disciplines tend to be similar, although they take on characteristics from the country in which they are practiced most widely.

In Acupuncture, fat is considered a form of congealed phlegm (turbid, thick, and cloudy fluid) that is later transformed and stored as fat. Chinese medicine considers phlegm as originating from the abnormal handling of body fluids in general. Such phlegm results in dampness in the body, and this causes interruptions in energy flow. Chinese medical theories describe the development of fat as occurring when body fluids, via abnormal processing, become turbid and convert into fat that the body stores. Have you ever left a frying pan you've used for cooking out overnight? The next day, the oil or butter (*phlegm* in Chinese medicine) has thickened and hardened into a stagnant mass (fat). That is an example of a liquid (melted butter) turning to fat.

Obesity is not considered a disease in Acupuncture, but instead a manifestation of an underlying abnormality of the person. Acupuncture points to the overeating of foods that are high in phlegm as a cause of diabetes. Foods high in phlegm are greasy, fatty foods and sweets.

The spleen's role in processing food is described as warming, fermentation, and distillation—or *cooking*. We could liken this ancient description to a modern term like *digesting*. Therefore, in actuality, the function described for the spleen in Eastern medicine is the same functions ascribed to the pancreas by Western medicine. Once we make the connection between the function of the spleen to that of the pancreas (which is involved in digesting food), it is easy to understand Acupuncture's association with the increased incidence of diabetes in obese patients. This connection was made thousands of years ago by early practitioners of Acupuncture.

In other words, in Acupuncture, abnormal function of the pancreas plays a role in obesity and, per Western medicine, there is higher incidence of diabetes in patients with obesity. Diabetic patients often develop kidney disease related to diabetes, which was also described as kidney deficiency in Chinese medicine many years ago. The obvious treatment of diabetes is aimed at eliminating the abnormal phlegm and invigorating the spleen and kidneys via Acupuncture and herbals.

Ayurvedic medicine describes the development of obesity in a fashion similar to Acupuncture and both philosophies share common mechanisms in describing obesity. One of the basic differences between the two is that Ayurveda considers fat as one of the seven tissues of the body. Under normal conditions, the fat channels are well nourished and lubricated, or energized. Under conditions of imbalance (believed to be caused by overeating fatty, greasy food and sweets) toxins accumulate in the channels of fatty tissue and result in the excessive production of fat, which is then stored—with subsequent weight gain. Ayurveda recommends increased activity, avoidance of fatty food, and additional natural home remedies as treatment.

You Power • The third side of the obesity and diabetes coin

What has been described so far is the attempt of both Eastern and Western medicine to explain the problems of obesity and diabetes at the physical level. Eastern medicines also view the development of disease, such as the manifestation of weight gain or obesity, as having originated well ahead of physical manifestations. In this regard, the imbalance starts at a deeper level than the physical level. This is what is considered the constitutional make-up of the individual...what I call You Power. Emotions are an intricate part of your You Power. **And how *you* handle emotional imbalances at**

the mental, emotional, and spiritual level determines the degree of imbalance that is created within you.

The more internally unbalanced you are, the more disease prone you will tend to be. The abnormal handling of emotional imbalance can lead to emotional eating and the development of obesity, if you are predisposed to it. And long before the mechanisms proposed by Western medicine or Eastern medicine begins at the physical level, there is an imbalance that occurs and is perpetuated at the mental emotional level.

The Impact of You Power on Obesity

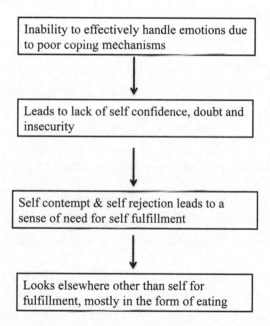

Figure 1: An illustration of the process leading to emotional eating.

It is obvious that these emotional characteristics pervade the individual prior to developing the habit of overeating and seeking comfort foods that are greasy, fatty, high in sugar, and dense in calories. These very emotional characteristics also predispose the individual to avoid physical activity, resulting in inertia, and thus further contributing to the development of obesity. You actually get a double whammy (overeating *and* a lack of physical activity) from this imbalance. Most people eat as a distraction from a mental conflict. Remember the two sisters that I mentioned? They both ate to avoid dealing with conflicts in their minds. The difference between the two sisters was that one was actually aware of the role emotions played in causing her to eat all the time.

It is important to ask yourself, *What am I feeling?* Am I feeling...

- Insecure
- Out of control over my life
- Anxious about something
- Fearful of something
- Bored... which, by some definitions means not feeling comfortable in your own skin
- An inability to sit still
- As if I do not want to deal with something on my mind

This simple step toward self-awareness is a great stride forward in combating obesity. This will help you identify the internal dialogue that is making you behave in ways that cause you to gain weight.

The personality characteristics that are often used in differentiating obese individuals from leaner ones have been described[3]. The most prevalent characteristic of people who tend to become obese is described as *overtly emotional*. These people tend to be:

1. **Prone to stress and worry:** These individuals tend to be anxious people who are apprehensive and worry a lot. They can get frustrated easily, feel irritable, and are quick to get angry with others. They are prone to feel lonely, sad, and rejected. They tend to have difficulty controlling their impulses, wants,

and wishes, but have no problem handling normal stress.

2. **Outgoing interpersonal attitude:** In contrast to what is described in point #1 above, these people are affectionate, with warmth towards others and who enjoy being the center of attention. In fact, they may dislike a situation if they are not the center of attention. They have a tendency to please others and seek approval from others. The stimulation of thrills and excitement has little appeal to these people and, as a result, they tend to not experience feelings of joy and happiness.

Just because you have these characteristics does not mean you will become obese. It appears that the above two characteristics need to combine with another characteristic (number 3 below) for a person to develop obesity. This characteristic is related to poor performance in goal-directed behavior.

3. **Spontaneous and careless:** These people tend to have poor organizational capacities, are not efficient in making rational decisions, tend to not meet their obligations, and lack self-discipline and motivation.

Sound familiar? My patients—the sisters—fit perfectly into what I have outlined in the three points above. In my practice, patients who are not successful in losing weight are those who come up with an excuse to take action tomorrow instead of today; they're *easy going* and *careless,* just like one of the sisters that I have described. She was always going to get serious about her weight loss "tomorrow" or "next week."

I hope you can now see the answer related to the difference in weight between the two sisters. Both of them shared the characteristics described in #1 and #2. But where they differed was in the characteristic #3. The sister with ideal BMI is someone I would describe as the exact opposite of characteristic #3. She was rational in making decisions, well organized, dependable and reliable in meeting obligations, had a high need for achievement but could take time to relax and enjoy life, thought things through before acting, and finished what she started. The sister with the high BMI was the opposite. That was the only difference between the two.

They were both born to the same parents, but because of these characteristics, the sister with the ideal BMI had succeeded in managing her weight even without a trainer or weight-loss program, while the other sister still continues to struggle.

Isn't it true that most people who are successful with any weight-loss program are successful because of the discipline they exercise with the program rather than the food they eat? This is why mastering the *discipline* of weight loss or weight management is so important. If you don't have discipline you are likely to gain back the weight you've lost.

How about patients who develop diabetes?

Diabetes was found to be a frequent diagnosis among people who exhibited spontaneous and careless behavior (#3 on the previous page) and had a tendency to be uncooperative with hostile internal thoughts. In addition to being spontaneous and careless, they also have a tendency to be **uncooperative and hostile**. They seldom see the best in other people and are often unwilling to "forgive and forget." They tend to be hard-headed or tough-minded, and have a tendency to be manipulative. Remember, these are internal feelings and may not be obvious to people who routinely interact with these kinds of people on a daily basis. My sense is that the patients themselves are not aware that they have these tendencies.

The sister with high BMI and who was diagnosed as pre-diabetic also shared the characteristics described above. I now have a more complete understanding of what went on in the minds of these two sisters and am no longer confused by the discrepancies in their weight. And while we can point to the traits and characteristics that helped one sister maintain ideal body weight, what would be more effective would be to explore and get rid of the internal dialogue. In other words, what would be more beneficial for the sister with ideal BMI would be to find out why she felt that she needed to be distracted when she felt anxious or nervous instead of facing these emotions. If you can do that—and even if you did not have a lot of motivation and drive—you are less likely to become obese.

How would I advise these two sisters?

I would suggest that the sister with ideal body weight attempt an emotional cleanse to deal with the emotions that drive her to eat all the time—so that she does not have to waste a lot of her energy in counterbalancing measures. She can then direct this energy to other achievements in her life.

I would suggest to the sister with the higher BMI to consider both an emotional cleanse *and* a program to train herself to be more efficient, organized, and motivated.

Keep in mind that these behavioral conclusions and recommendations are not absolute. Behavioral characteristics give us a general impression of what our tendencies are in reaction to what life sends our way. And, as you can see, this helped in giving specific recommendations to two sisters.

I also encourage you to keep this in mind: There is no such thing as one personality being better than another, or an assessment that a certain personality type is bad. Tendencies are identified by analyzing several different characteristics and conclusions that are drawn to measure the general direction and propensities of the person with regard to their style of handling life.

I have noted that not everyone who exhibits certain tendencies develops a certain type of disease. Many factors come into play in the development and outcome of health and disease. On the other hand, what I have noted is that regardless of a person's personality—or how well he or she handles their internal You Power and the internal dialogue and personality traits—personality seems to play a significant role in a person's health and predisposition toward disease.

What can you do?

As with other diseases, it is important to understand that there are three sides that need to be considered. Remember the 30/30/30 Rule that I have coined as a guide to better understanding and navigation of the complex nature of health and disease. We have seen the Western medical aspect, Eastern medical aspect, and the Power of You *all* contributing to health and disease. There is a lot you can choose to do if you decide to utilize both your Western and Eastern team members along with your power as the captain.

What can Western medicine offer you?

How would a Western medical practitioner address the health issues of these two sisters? First of all, a Western medical practitioner won't even consider addressing any issue unless a disease is confirmed by biochemical tests. While this is true for diabetes, obesity requires only a scale and a BMI calculator to make a diagnosis. In the management of diabetes, a simple laboratory test can monitor the progress of treatment by measuring the level of a biomarker (a chemical substance in the blood that identifies a specific problem) called *Hemoglobin A1C*. The level of this biomarker usually tells the story of how well a person's diabetes has been managed during the three months preceding the test. If the biomarker level is high, then the medications you are taking to control your blood sugar (and your diabetes) aren't working very well.

Hemoglobin A1C is also currently used as one type of lab measurement to diagnose diabetes and pre-diabetes, in addition to being used to monitor how well the diabetes is controlled with therapy. Normal A1C is below 5.7 percent. Levels between 5.7 percent and 6.4 percent indicate what we call pre-diabetes[5]. A reading of more than 6.5 percent would lead to a diagnosis of diabetes[5]. If you are on medications for diabetes, you should aim to keep your A1C levels below 7 percent to avoid developing complications from diabetes[5].

The target for your BMI to manage obesity is between 18 and 24. Western medicine can offer only a limited number of therapies for both obesity and diabetes. For obesity, the recommendations are related to diet and exercise. If these measures fail or if you are morbidly obese, bariatric surgery can be considered. For diabetes, Western medicine recommendations are related to medications, diet, weight loss, and exercise.

Medications

Obesity is typically not treated with medications. A Western medical practitioner will prescribe medications to treat diabetes. The medications are most often taken by mouth while monitoring A1C levels to a target of 7 percent or less. There are about seven different oral medications to treat diabetes. If oral medications are not enough to control your diabetes, the practitioner may prescribe insulin that is injected with a needle.

Diet

Diet is a very important part in the management of obesity and diabetes. Remember my patient, one of the sisters, who had both pre-diabetes and obesity? From a diabetic perspective, she should be advised to include fruits, vegetables, and whole grains in her diet. She would be advised to eat fewer animal products, sweets, and refined carbohydrates. Food recommendations for a diabetic are divided into high glycemic-index foods (foods that raise blood glucose levels quickly) and low glycemic foods (foods that help stabilize blood glucose levels). Usually, foods that are high in fiber content are lower on the glycemic index scale. Low glycemic foods are not only good for a diabetic but are also healthy options for people like you and me who do not have diabetes but want to eat well. A consultation with a dietitian would be recommended for my patient to teach her about controlling the intake of carbohydrates in her food choices. Additionally, a vegetarian diet could be recommended as it has been shown to provide better glycemic control in diabetic patients[6] than diets that include meat and dairy.

When it comes to obesity, a low calorie diet in combination with regular exercise will be recommended.

A word about losing weight...

There are a multitude of diet recommendations and weight-loss commercials that are either misleading or miss the point completely related to weight loss. They promote their own "diet"—packaged in one way or another. Sometimes I don't even know what they are promoting, because it is not addressing weight loss at all!

Even in Western medical practice, I refer a patient to a dietitian and ask them to follow the dietitian's recommendation. In reality, success in weight loss can be achieved without the help of any of these services. I believe that there are a few general steps that need to be taken for a successful weight loss:

The **first step** is a "house cleaning." What I mean by this is cleansing yourself. There are two types of cleansing that you need to do. First, is a physical cleanse. There are sound programs available that allow your body to naturally eliminate toxins over a period of a few days. This will also get rid of cravings and allow you to gain more energy.

Once you have achieved this, the **second step** is to pick a style of eating and nutritional habits that appeal to your wants and that you can realistically follow. For example, a clean-eating type diet (in which all processed foods are eliminated), or a low-carb diet. I advocate this because eating low-carb one day and vegetarian the next, followed by a cheat day, is only cheating you!

The **next step** is to set realistic goals. Give yourself a long enough time to achieve your goal, depending on the degree of obesity you are addressing. Remember, you did not accumulate the excess fat over days or weeks. It happened over many years. Getting rid of excess weight can take years as well. Your realistic goals should be in years.

Then find a motivational tool. It could be as simple as your daily or weekly weigh-in. Keep in mind that this tool doesn't work for everyone. Because fluctuations in weight can be due to hormonal changes or other factors, weigh-ins alone may not give you the steady motivation you need and may, in fact, discourage you. Find something else, like the way you feel or the increased energy you gain with the program, or find a buddy and commit to supporting each other though the process.

The most important step is not the fact that you are doing a program to address your weight. The power is in the first two steps and it's those two steps that will make you successful. The first two steps are the hard part for most people.

Most people jump right into a program—and fail. When they fail, they wonder what happened and usually blame the program. Then they move from program to program, searching for one that "works." Eventually, everyone gets around to doing steps one and two, often in a very circuitous way, unless they simply give up on losing weight.

One final point to keep in mind is that every one of us loses weight in our own unique way. Don't look at TV commercials that portray trim and toned bodies—according to TV standards—and aim to look like that. You have your own beautiful body structure, shape, and appearance. That's what you want to strive for—*your* optimum and healthy body, not someone else's.

Keep in mind that fat is lost from different areas in the body for different people at different rates. I encourage you to understand your unique way of losing weight—and embrace it. Some lose first from arms and legs, others from the abdomen, and still others' weight loss begins with the face and neck. Most often, abdominal fat is the last to disappear. Have patience, especially if you are looking at your abdomen as a way to evaluate the results of your efforts.

Additionally, abdominal obesity can be a sign of increased stress. Work with a health practitioner who can help you understand your internal functioning, genetics, and habits to optimize your diet results. I believe that this series of steps is essential, not just for losing weight, but for achieving health and living free of disease.

Nutrition can be quite complicated, and with all of the misleading information that can be found related to diet and nutrition, advice from a qualified health practitioner is a good investment. Remember, losing weight is 90 percent diet and 10 percent exercise.

Exercise

Regular exercise is perhaps the best secret of the successful management of both diabetes and obesity. With regard to obesity, it is clear why regular exercise helps. It helps to burn calories and curb appetite. When exercise is combined with a low glycemic diet—one that curbs those intense feelings of hunger—your success in losing weight improves. Additionally, regular exercise also helps to maintain a positive attitude, which helps you handle everyday stressors better, and leads to better eating habits. From an obesity perspective, the WHO recommends 480 minutes (60 minutes a day) of exercise for children each week and 180 minutes (or approximately 26 minutes a day) of exercise a week for adults. If you are an adult, aim for 30 minutes of aerobic exercise each day.

With regard to diabetes, it's sound advice to make regular exercise as routine as brushing your teeth. It should be part of your everyday life. In fact, it should be part of everyone's life whether you have a disease or not. A diabetic (and everybody else) should aim for a variety of exercise most days of the week. The combination of exercises should include aerobic exercises, resistance training or Yoga, and stretching. Remember, exercise reduces blood glucose levels. Therefore, if you take medications for diabetes make sure to have a snack before you exercise. Additionally, exercise has been shown to re-sensitize those cells that I described earlier— the "house" into which the glucose needs to gain entry. Knowing that diabetes is a disease that can be reversed should be a huge motivation to exercise!

Sometimes patients are not successful with either their weight loss or diabetes control because they have gotten to the point where they cannot exercise. This is due to other medical conditions that they have developed as a complication of diabetes and obesity. This is a difficult situation because once you get to this level, a downward spiral often begins and you lose your ability to influence the disease process. The key is to not allow yourself to get to that point. But, if you are at that point, don't feel discouraged. There are ways of getting around this situation.

I want to reemphasize that obesity and Type II diabetes can be reversible. You don't need to watch it take over your life and leave you with torturous complications. My belief is that exercise is one of the most important actions that you can take in managing diabetes and obesity. And when it comes to weight loss, remember that success results 90 percent from your diet and 10% from exercise. When patients tell me that they are exercising but are not losing weight, I tell them it's time to take a hard look at their dietary habits.

What can Eastern medicine offer you?

Once again, there are a myriad of Eastern medical disciplines that one can use either alone or in combination to help manage obesity and diabetes. In my opinion, when it comes to diabetes and obesity, these disciplines help more at the level of the person, rather than at the level of the disease. These modalities treat the person—which in turn makes you better equipped to handle disease and adverse influences, including emotional fluctuations, food cravings, insomnia, sensitivity to stress, lack of motivation, and fatigue.

Acupuncture

Acupuncture can be successfully used to improve overall well-being and maintenance of well-being by energy balance. Because Acupuncture is safe, it can be used to curb appetite in an effort to reduce weight. Acupuncturists have used tiny needles embedded in certain points on the ear to curb appetite. Additionally, it can also help reduce extreme fluctuations in emotions and thereby potentially reduce emotional eating. There are also studies underway related to the use of Acupuncture to reduce neuropathic pain associated with diabetes.

An Acupuncturist can help you to balance the energy of your spleen and its paired organ, the stomach, by placing needles along the channel pertaining to these organs. However, remember, Acupuncture does not treat specific disease. It treats the person as a whole to balance the energy in the body. An Acupuncture practitioner may make a specific diagnosis of the underlying energy imbalance that may give rise to diabetes and thus use different organ systems to treat you as well.

Massage

Massage on a regular basis can influence your stress and aid in better handling the emotions associated with emotional eating. A massage therapist can stimulate pertinent Acupuncture channels (if they are trained in this method) to stimulate the spleen and stomach channels to influence better energy flow along those channels. I think that the benefit of massage relies on its ability to rid the body of toxins and achieve a better emotional balance that will help you maintain the motivation to manage your diseases. Additionally, I like to enjoy a massage after a week of vigorous exercise to relax the muscles and invigorate them by eliminating the knots and toxins from them after a week of hard work. This prepares you for the rigors of the next week or two. You can use massage as a reward to yourself for taking on your problem and making changes in your life.

Homeopathy

Homeopathy can be a great adjunct to other therapies you are using for diabetes. There is no replacement for insulin, if you are a diabetic who requires insulin. However, each one of us can strive to work with our own body to improve overall health and then work with our doctor to devise a plan for reducing the need for insulin. Slowly, over time, and by using several natural methods and with discussion with your practitioner, you may have the chance to come off insulin if possible. There is nothing wrong with trying to achieve this, but be cautious and discuss this intention with your Western and Eastern medical practitioners. Homeopathy proposes remedies that can be combined with other medications that are used to treat diabetes.

The process of weaning off of Western medical therapies is possible, but it is a very intense process. Most often you won't be able to accomplish this if the damage to the organ is severe. However, if it is not severe, you can certainly try, but let both practitioners know your intention and recruit their assistance. When I explain this process to my patients, I liken it to retrieving a precious diamond from a drain with a pair of chopsticks—without getting the chopsticks stuck.

Imagine that, by accident, you drop a beautiful diamond into the sink and it goes down the drain! You are terrified to stick your hand down into the drain to get it because it is at the edge and in danger of falling into the abyss. The diamond represents your health...that you have allowed to fall down the drain. You have two choices. One is to avoid turning on the water so the diamond just stays in the drain. You are trying to avoid it from falling deeper and out of sight—so all you can do is watch it. This is what Western medicine does: helps you along the process rather than working from the root to reverse it. The other choice is to try and retrieve the diamond from the drain. To do this you have only a small pair of chopsticks.

Can you imagine trying to pick up a diamond from the drain with a pair of chopsticks? The chopsticks represent Eastern medicine (a delicate process, much like handling a chopstick), and the process of actually picking up the diamond is like reversing the disease process. It will work, but we must know how to use it and pay tremendous attention to what we are doing.

We must also be careful not to get the chopsticks caught in the drain. Getting caught in the drain is similar to what happens when you develop a complication while trying to get off Western medical therapies in the wrong way.

I hope this little story illustrates how tedious it is to correct something naturally, once a disease is allowed to happen. But it is achievable.

Chiropractic Care

Chiropractic and Osteopathic manipulations are very useful adjuncts when it comes to correcting imbalances in energy flow with regard to diabetes and obesity. Management of diabetes and obesity generally fall into the realm of general well-being because they are slow and chronic. Therefore, you can use Eastern medical adjuncts to help you maintain a healthy vitality over the long haul while trying to get rid of these diseases. Chiropractic manipulation helps with invigorating the peripheral nervous system and Osteopathy assists in improving energy flow and joint health.

Herbs

Herbal therapy has long been used as a treatment for diabetes. There have been several studies that support the use of herbal therapy. Most findings suggest that herbs are generally safe (as compared to my recommendations with regard to liver and kidney disease) but data is insufficient to actively recommend the use of herbs for treatment[7]. However, they can be used as adjunct therapy in established diabetes patients and can be considered as main therapy for pre-diabetes with dietary modification and close follow up. Just like homeopathic remedies, you can also use herbs to get your diamond out of the drain. For that matter, all of the Eastern modalities can be used in any combination. Just make sure that you discuss how you are going into the diamond-retrieval-process with both your practitioners.

Yoga and Meditation

Yoga is a very strong discipline that will help you with both diabetes and obesity. The primary way Yoga assists is by helping you achieve a steady emotional state and improved ability to handle your own emotions. It helps with mindful living. Even if you are overweight, you can modify Yoga exercise in order to benefit from these very valuable practices. With time, you will find yourself beginning to reap the benefits. It is a slow process, and therefore, patience is essential. Remember, Yoga really does not address any specific disease, although it can be designed to focus on regions of the body that are related to a disease. The real purpose and value of Yoga is that it is a lifestyle. It should become part of your daily routine. I do not believe in doing Yoga for two or three days a week and expect mind-body union. It does not happen. You are expecting something that is unrealistic. However, if your intention is to get a relaxing stretch every week then at least two or three days of practice each week is better than nothing.

Most of the studies by Western practitioners that have evaluated Yoga are flawed because they typically train the study participants twice a week. Then they ask the participants to do Yoga at home for the rest of the week. One has no idea what happens at home with these study participants. In addition, the studies are conducted for only a very short period of time. So when the results are studied, there is no apparent benefit. I am not surprised that there is no tangible, visible benefit. One does not need a study and the expense to learn this remarkable lesson. In my opinion, the optimal way to evaluate the effectiveness of Yoga is to perform Yoga exercises under supervision for a minimum of five days each week.

Ayurveda

Ayurveda uses a system of healthy living to promote health and the well-being of a person. This system utilizes various cleansing methods to purify the body of its toxins and unwanted substances on a regular basis. As such, it is a very helpful adjunct to help cleanse our body of impurities that in turn allows optimal function of the organs.

I have spoken of cleanse in the weight-loss section of this chapter. Ayurveda is perhaps one of the best modalities that describes various forms of bodily, physical cleanses in addition to dietary cleanses. Previously when I talked about cleanse under weight loss, I was talking about a dietary cleanse to allow your body a chance to naturally eliminate all the chemicals such as heavy metals and toxins that we put into our body on a daily basis. What Ayurveda offers is additional cleanses for various systems in our body. These cleanses can be done periodically or, in some cases, even daily.

Additionally, Ayurvedic remedies can also be either combined or used singularly to retrieve your diamond from the drain. Consult with an Ayurvedic practitioner if you want to adopt this method into your various tools.

Handling your You Power

Your You Power is perhaps the most important aspect to develop and cultivate not only when it comes to health but also when it comes to obesity and diabetes. I have known obese people who did not develop any disease including diabetes, and I have known lean, thin people who develop disease or diabetes. Now, the question is: Why is that? I believe that the answer lies in their You Power. As I have described in different ways throughout this book, the Power of You consists of an internal dialogue that is buried deep down in you (your primal being), and the way you act in the society (personality or the social being). I have also described different personalities that are associated with different diseases throughout this book.

Internal dialogue or Primal being

When it came to my patient described in this chapter, she had both obesity and diabetes to content with.

When it comes to obesity, my experience is that most people who are obese tend to have an internal dialogue that makes them feel as if they need protection. Mostly, this is due to a trigger that is buried so deep that they are not even aware of it. However, in response to this trigger, they feel anxious or fearful and want to be distracted from that feeling. They want to feel protected, just like what was stated by the sister with ideal BMI. This results in resorting to comfort eating to feel that protection.

The tendency to eat in response to negative emotional feelings is not surprising as we were taught to do just that when we were children. We as a society, deal with a crying baby (babies may not always cry due to hunger; it may be the baby is bored and needs loving or simply a diaper change) by feeding and comforting them. If we feed a baby when it cries thinking it is hungry, when in fact it is bored, we have just given the wrong message to the baby: "If you are bored, eat." Children are often consoled by being given candies and treats, in response to unhappiness, unpleasantness, failure, and disappointment. Therefore, it should be no surprise that we tend to do the same as adults (the only coping mechanism we know if we have not been taught or learned any other) in response to negative emotions or when we cannot handle emotions.

What do people do first when they need to prepare in the face of an oncoming natural disaster? We run to the grocery store and stock up on food that will sustain us for many days to come. This is our natural instinct and this same instinct plays a role in the case of obesity. If something scares us, we run to food.

The patient described earlier in this chapter (the sister who was obese) had pre-diabetes. Observation of her and similar patients over the years has led me to get a glimpse of a common underlying drive that is associated with diabetes. This drive appears to be "I need to control." This appears to be the internal dialogue that propels these patients. The trigger that is buried deep down that leads to this internal dialogue is known only to the patient and can only be brought out by an emotional cleanse.

During previous visits to the sister's home (for other conditions that I was helping the obese sister address) I recommended newer interventions that I thought would benefit her. She would try these for a very short time and come back and report that she was not tolerating them. When asked about the side effects or symptoms, she would report effects that I thought were negligible and a small price to pay for the benefit she would gain. However, I was not successful. But she was.

She did what she wanted, regardless of the harm it may have caused her. This illustrated her need for control.

In fact, you need to be in control because you are the captain. I strongly advise you to take control. However, the control should be exercised with rational thinking and sound decision making. This is what will give you the internal peace to effectively gain control of the underlying causes that are triggering you to eat. That rational thinking is what was missing in the obese sister's desire to be in control.

Personality or Social being

Personality refers to an individual's characteristic pattern of behavior *driven* by their deeper thoughts and emotions, but modified by their rules of conduct to suit the outside world. In other words, it is the primal self modified to suit the outside world and society to be acceptable.

Take the time to try to understand what type of person you are. Learn how you handle external stress and internal conflicts. Personality will tell you about your prototype for handling life stressors and conflicts. You can obtain this knowledge by being mindful of your feelings and actions, by seeking help from a counselor or psychologist, or by carrying out a personality test. From there, you can work your way toward better health outcomes. What is important is that your You Power determines how much benefit you will reap from the tools that Western and Eastern medicine can offer you.

Remember, just because you have a certain personality does not mean you will develop a specific disease. There has been no cause-and-effect found by research. However there *is* an association between these specific personalities and obesity or diabetes. What is important to understand is that your personality reflects how you are reacting to an internal dialogue—the software inside you. This is only half the story. You need to identify what that internal dialogue is and then proceed to identify what trigger has resulted in this dialogue.

Another point I want to make is that we all have several internal dialogues going on within us all the time. What matters is the strength of an internal dialogue, its predominance, and the frequency with which it affects us on a daily basis.

When a person does not have the proper coping mechanisms to handle their internal dialogue, they may not know how to handle that emotion in a socially acceptable fashion to achieve fulfillment. As a result, they ignore that primal self and, in the case of obesity, seek fulfillment in the form of overeating and inactivity. Similar mechanisms operate when it comes to diabetes.

Chapter Seven

Cancer

The Invading Killer

I am meaningless, my life is not worth living.

W e all know someone who has had cancer and survived. It's probably just as likely that we all also know someone who has had cancer and died from it.

Cancer is a term that is used to describe diseases that are characterized by uncontrolled proliferation (or replication) of abnormal or disease-ridden cells from any part of the body. This abnormal proliferation of cells results in a growth, or an excess of tissue, that we call a *mass* or *tumor,* as illustrated in Figure 1 on the following page. These cells do not necessarily stay in one area of the body. They can invade other areas of the body, and in medicine this invasion is called *metastasis.* When this invasion occurs, the cancer is categorized as advanced stage. **An important fact about cancer is that the abnormal division and growth continues unabated—even after the inciting stimulus has stopped.** This is an important fact to keep in mind as you read the rest of this chapter.

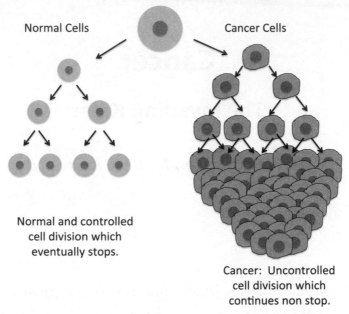

Abnormal cell division and formation of malignant tumor

Normal Cells

Cancer Cells

Normal and controlled
cell division which
eventually stops.

Cancer: Uncontrolled
cell division which
continues non stop.

Figure 1: Illustration of the differences between normal cell division and abnormal cell division of cancer cells. The cancer cells become abnormal due to a genetic mutation which leads to uncontrolled division of these cells that results in the formation of a tumor.

How big is the cancer epidemic in the United States? The National Cancer Institute estimated that there were 1,665,540 new cases of cancer (excluding skin cancers) in 2014 and 585,720 deaths from cancer that same year[1]. More than $200 billion (that's billion with a b...) is spent on cancer-related expenses. Cancer is a deadly disease that often shortens the lives of those diagnosed with it.

Cancer remains a puzzling problem throughout the world. Several factors have been associated with the development of cancer, however no one factor is 100 percent associated with the development of disease. This begs the question as to what actually directs the development of this such a deadly disease for those who come in contact with the associated factors.

At the cellular level, we have identified abnormal activities related to our genes that result in what we call *mutations*. We looked at this type of mutation in Figure 1. The World Heath Organization lists cancer related to the respiratory system (lung and lung-related cancers) as the fifth leading cause of death in the world, taking its place among traffic accidents, infections, and diarrheal diseases, in the past decade[2]. It is a global problem.

There are people who have a strong family history of cancer but do not develop the disease. There are those with cancer who don't have any family history of the disease. There are those who smoke like a chimney and don't develop cancer. And there are those who do everything right in terms of avoiding the known causes of cancer and still get the disease.

Obesity is associated with an increased incidence of cancer. There are obese people who do not develop cancer, and there are thin people who do. The answer to this paradoxical puzzle remains unresolved. The reason for this discrepancy is that there are several factors that work in concert, related to the development of disease in any given individual and no one factor is ever—single-handedly—responsible. The key is in understanding this dynamic interaction that is unique not for a population at large, but for you as an individual.

A 65-year-old friend of mine lost her husband to heart disease. The husband and wife had lived together for many years. She was a very compassionate, self-sacrificing, and patient person. After she lost her husband, she had to move in with one of her children. She confided in me how much she disliked that arrangement. She rented the basement of her daughter's house in order to maintain as much independence as possible.

At the time of her move, she had high blood pressure and was taking medication for it. But apart from that, she was active and healthy. A year or two later she was diagnosed with borderline diabetes. I remember having a conversation with her in which she expressed her feelings of unworthiness and dependence since her move. As time went on, she started feeling neglected, disrespected, and ignored, living in her child's basement. She felt as if she was an inconvenience to everybody and that no one would miss her if she died. She shared several aspects of her innermost thoughts and feelings and I was moved by her candor. By my assessment, it is fair to say that she felt she had become worthless and meaningless to everyone that she cared about. She was deeply hurt, and questioned the meaning and value of her life.

Prior to her husband passing, she was an outgoing and compassionate person who took care of others. She was, in my opinion, emotionally stable and was always willing to sacrifice her own interests to help someone. Even during those years when she was sharing her innermost thoughts and feelings, I found her to be very emotionally balanced. In hindsight, I realized that she did not show her inner feelings to anybody else. She did not act out or lose her calm demeanor. This was a woman who not only lost her husband after many years of marriage, but who also lost her sense of humanity. She buried her sadness and pain deep within herself.

I had advised her to discuss her feelings with her children, but she could not bring herself to do it. I suggested meditation, but she would not do it regularly. She only took on daily prayers. I suggested massage and Acupuncture, but she did not have the means to obtain them. She dismissed my suggestion of counseling and joked with me that she could "teach a thing or two" to the counselor about life.

Seven years after her husband passed, she became functionally disabled. Tests to determine the cause of her functional decline led to the diagnosis (discovered quite by accicdent...) of colon cancer. The cancer had already spread throughout her body and she was terminal. She had no family history of cancer of any kind, going back three generations, and she refused chemotherapy and all other aggressive measures. She preferred to spend her remaining months at home with only comfort measures.

I think about my friend often. My medically-trained mind—in both Eastern and Western philosophies—could not help but explore the possibilities of how her emotions and personality could have played a role in the development of her cancer. Here was a person who went from being outgoing and compassionate, to someone who reacted negatively to life events on a daily basis. Whether it was the loss of her husband or the subsequent changes to her lifestyle, living in her daughter's basement, and the pain of feeling forgotten, is unclear. But what *is* clear is that she did not take action to address this pain immediately. Rather, she ignored it by burying her thoughts and feelings deep within herself. Life, for her, was no longer worth living. It was almost as if she created a death wish for herself, built upon a belief that it did not matter to anyone if she lived or died. I could not help but wonder how much the emotional turbulence she experienced and her personality had to do with the development of the cancer that led to her death.

This is just one example of a person who suffered from cancer. And, obviously, there are many external factors and real-life circumstances that come into play that are often not as straightforward as they were in this example. I have only described what I was able to discern by my medically-trained mind. There are many other people—with different attitudes, behaviors, and expressions—who suffer from cancer. It is not the kind of person you are, but how you handle your emotions and how good you are at recognizing those emotions and dealing with them. The key is not to bury them or ignore them.

The Western side of the cancer coin

In Western medicine, cancer is just a disease. And people get diseases. As I've described, it is considered to result from the abnormal division of damaged cells in an uncontrolled fashion. What triggers this abnormal division has not been established. There appears to be an involvement of gene mutation. Even though we have been able to identify genes associated with different forms of cancer, it is still unclear why the genes mutate.

Typically, we recognize and label cancers based on what cell type they originated from and their location within the body. There are five basic categories:

1. **Carcinoma** is a growth or tumor that arises from cells lining the inside or outside of any organ. For example, if the cells from the lining of the colon are involved in the cancer, then it is called carcinoma of the colon.

2. **Leukemia** originates in the tissue that produces blood cells and is categorized within blood cancers. These cancers affect the bone marrow, which is the site of blood production.

3. **Lymphoma** originates in the lymphatic system. Lymphoma is part of the immune system and affects lymph nodes and certain parts of the intestines and, sometimes, the brain.

4. **Myeloma** originates in the plasma cells of the bone marrow. Plasma cells are the cells that produce antibodies, which are the body's response to infections. It is a type of blood cancer.

5. **Sarcoma** originates in the supportive tissue of the body, also called connective tissue...bone, muscle, cartilage, etc.

There are many other details about different cancers that are beyond the scope of this book. However, for our purpose, it will suffice to say that Western medicine has made the evaluation of a tumor a science. Once a patient is suspected of having a tumor, he or she is sent to a specialist (called an *Oncologist*) for further work up and treatment. It is important to understand that the suspicion for a tumor would have been initiated in one of three ways:

- The patient complained of symptoms that led to the identification.

- The patient was tested for some other medical condition and the tumor was detected incidentally.

- The patient underwent a regular health-screening test on an annual or biannual basis and the test was positive, even if there were no symptoms, as was the case with the friend I referred to earlier in this chapter.

In most cases, by the time a cancer is detected it is too late for complete recovery. The best way to identify cancer is with screening tests. There are excellent screening tests available in Western medicine. What this means is that we often meet the disease half way down the road and then devise methods to fight it. With regard to the causes of cancers in humans, the Western medicine recognizes the following as being risk factors:

- Family history of cancer (or genetic predisposition)
- Obesity
- Alcohol consumption
- Smoking
- Aging
- Excess exposure to the sun
- Ionizing radiation
- Certain chemicals
- Some viruses and bacteria
- Certain hormones
- Physical inactivity
- Stress

Although we know that these factors are associated with cancer, we do not know how exactly these factors lead to cancer.

For example, how does physical inactivity lead to cancer? Not everyone who is physically inactive gets cancer. I have known several older people who have never been physically active to the degree that's typically recommended, but who lived to be 90 or even 98 years old without developing any cancer. I believe that physical inactivity is an expression of an underlying mindset.

By the same token, I also believe that other diseases that are associated with cancer result from an abnormal coping mechanism for internal conflicts that eventually leads not only to cancer, but also to other associated conditions that precede the development of cancer. Bear with me as I repeat that last statement: I believe that other diseases associated with cancer result from abnormal coping mechanisms for internal conflicts that lead not only to cancer, but also to other associated conditions that often precede the development of cancer. That said, just because you have abnormal coping does not mean you will develop cancer. Several factors conspire to lead to cancer, but I would urge you to be careful of what you "wish for."

Once the diagnosis of cancer is made, the treatment can include chemotherapy, radiation, or surgery based on the type, extent, and location of the cancer. Most cancer treatments have significant side effects and often the treatment is supportive care rather than curative, especially when the cancer is identified at a later stage. If the cancer is not curable, the patient will reach end-stage cancer at which point hospice care is perhaps the best solution.

The Eastern side of the cancer coin

Acupuncture and traditional Chinese medicine recognize several factors as contributors to the development of cancer. These contributors are divided into two categories: internal and external. The internal contributor is our emotions, either excessive expression or suppression. The external factors are work and sexual habits, as well as other habits such as alcohol consumption, smoking, drug use, etc. Regardless of what initiates the development of cancer, Acupuncture proposes a pathway that incriminates an imbalance of the body's energy that could culminate in the disease. A general stagnation of *Qi* (our body's overall energy), reduction in spleen

Qi (through poor dietary habits and taxing the organ that processes food assimilation into the body), and reduction in *Zheng Qi* (energy that deals with warding off diseases) are incriminated in the development of cancer.

Ayurveda proposes a similar mechanism for the development of cancer. As mentioned in previous chapters, Ayurveda proposes three major philosophic regulatory energy systems in the body. They are *Vata, Pitta,* and *Kapha.* These energy systems pass through the entire body and are represented by the nervous system, the venous system, and the arterial system. Cancer is thought to develop when these three system are not functioning synergistically. In other words, when they are not in balance *with each other*—as opposed to each of them, individually, being in imbalance. We know (from Western medicine) that a growing tumor needs a blood supply (via the arterial system) and venous drainage (via the venous system) to survive.

Cancer can also result in significant neuropathic pain, which involves the nervous system. Ayurveda, like Western medicine, recognizes the lining of organs to be the birthplace of cancers and calls it *rohini.* Poor hygiene, unhealthy food, and poor behavior habits are all implicated in the development of cancer just like in Acupuncture and Western medicines. Similar to Western medicine, Ayurveda also divides the tumors as either benign or malignant, and recognizes different forms of malignancies related to the three energy systems, or the combination of those energy systems. **Nevertheless, it is important to recognize that, contrary to Western medicine, both Acupuncture and Ayurveda propose a presence of energy imbalance in the development of cancer.**

Interestingly, from a treatment perspective, Ayurveda proposes surgery as the definitive treatment for cancer. It does propose concoctions prepared in the traditions of an alchemist from a medical treatment perspective, but cautions that the effect will be minimal with regard to rapidly growing tumors unless they are utilized in the early stages of cancer. Likewise, Acupuncture proposes herbal therapy from a medical perspective. Surgery is not strongly mentioned in the Acupuncture tradition.

The major difference in these disciplines is that Eastern medicine proposes an energy imbalance leading to abnormal function of the cells and the development of cancer, and looks for causes that led to the abnormal energy imbalance. Western medicine, however, starts with abnormal cell function or growth and looks for causes that led to that abnormal cell growth. Western medicine totally ignores the energy (the *Qi* or *prana*) as having anything to do with the development of cancer, and in doing so dismisses the connection of the disease to the individual person.

Once again, Western medicine looks for biochemical and structural changes and Eastern medicine looks for energy imbalance. They both differ in this respect. They appear to have diametrically-opposed views on health and disease. But what is notable is both these disciplines recognize STRESS as a cause of disease without any opposition. What is the common factor with regard to stress? I believe it is you and how you cope with stress. Hence my emphasis on the significance of you and who you are—your You Power—as the most important player in your life.

You Power • The third side of the cancer coin

The notion that emotions play a role in the development of cancer has been around for more than 100 years. The personality of a person has been proposed as a factor that can influence the development of cancer. In addition, the suppression of emotions and inadequate coping mechanisms have been proposed as having an influence on the development of cancer[3,4,5]. Several studies have been published in this regard. Additionally, two characteristics—a tendency to react negatively to life events and an outgoing interpersonal attitude—have been implicated in the development of cancer[6,7,8,9]. These two characteristics are described below:

1. **Negative reaction to life:** These individuals tend to be anxious people who are apprehensive and worry a lot. They can be easily frustrated, feel irritable, and get angry with others, and are prone to feel lonely, sad, and rejected. They tend to have difficulty

controlling their impulses, wants, and wishes, but have no problem handling stress.

2. **Outgoing interpersonal attitude:** In contrast to what is described above, these people are affectionate and warm toward others and enjoy being the center of attention. In fact, they may dislike a situation if they are not the center of attention. They have a tendency to please others and seek their approval. The stimulation of thrills or excitement has little appeal to these people and, as a result, they tend not to experience feelings such as joy and happiness.

Most of the recent studies, however, have documented no causative influence of personality as a factor in an individual being prone to cancer. As incomplete as these studies are, this finding is encouraging because, as I have alluded to in most of this book, just because you have a certain personality does not mean you will develop a disease. However, most of these studies fail to recognize the combined results of the interaction among the characteristics that make up the personality. In other words: Most research fails to study the combined contribution of internal and external factors to the development of the disease.

A person's personality alone is an insufficient cause of disease — our personality must combine with certain behaviors or habits (such as smoking) that result from inadequate coping mechanisms for disease to develop. This association has been previously documented by studies[10]. It is clear, I believe, that the personality of a person—the collection of his or her emotional tendencies and resulting behaviors—has an association, if not causation, with regard to the development of cancer. A good discussion of these earlier studies can be found in a paper by German psychologist Dr. Hans Eysenck[11].

What is proposed in that paper is that the combination of personality and poor coping mechanisms leads to adverse behavior, which (through biological mechanisms) results in cancer by altering genetic dispositions. Personality alone, without adverse behavior, may not result in cancer.

In summary, there is no evidence that the personality **causes** cancer, but there is evidence that personality has an **associative relationship** to cancer.

While the research world struggles to either validate or dispute the association theory by studying populations of people where people are grouped in a category, we should recognize that human beings are unique, each with their own individuality. What applies to a group of people may not always apply to any given individual—if that individual was not represented in that group. In other words, categorizing a person within a statistical group is much different than assessing you as an individual. When it comes to your life and your health, do *you* want to be evaluated individually as the unique person you are, or as a component of a category? I think the answer is obvious. Therefore, it is important to know the emotional types that have been linked to cancer so that you can start being mindful of these tendencies that can influence your own health and wellness.

Up to this point we have only discussed personality and emotions from the third side of the coin perspective, the "edge" of the coin from which we have a vantage point overlooking both East and West. An important aspect is to identify the trigger for reactions that are handled poorly by the inadequate coping mechanisms. In my experience, most patients who have cancer tend to have experienced a sense of self-worthlessness, rejection, and of being treated as if they are dispensable. These patients tend to have experienced either physical or emotional abuse, or developed a *sense* of having been abused, even if they weren't. The key, I believe, lies in the way they coped with their feelings.

And the way they coped with these feelings was by hiding them and behaving as if they did not exist. As a result, they fall into the category of people who suppress emotions while feeling a very deep sense of not being wanted and rejected by either loved ones, important people in their lives, relatives and family, or society. It is as though these patients, at the height of these feelings of **worthlessness,** convinced themselves that life is **not worth living** and triggered a process, an action, to accomplish this. The result: the development of cancer. Obviously, once cancer develops, the person is on his or her way to accomplishing that intended result.

What can you do?

Again, I will stress what, by now, should appear to be obvious: Understand that there are three sides to our "medical coin" that need to be considered if you have an established disease. These are Western medicine (one teammate), Eastern medicine (another teammate), and your You Power—captain of your health and your life—and they can influence the outcome of the game.

What if you do not have an established disease? Even in this situation, there are three sides. This is a concept that most of my patients and friends (even fellow physicians) have a hard time understanding. When you do not have an established, "diagnosed" disease, it is important to be aware of what you are at risk of developing. Avail yourself of the tools of technology and have periodic screening tests, like age-appropriate cancer screenings (from our Western medicine teammate). Today, there are even specialists who can perform quite innovative genetic and cancer screening tests. Likewise, obtain screenings for energy imbalances to detect abnormalities early and to get recommendations on natural ways to enhance your health (via Eastern medicine teammates). Regardless of whether you have a diagnosed disease or not, you can still use all three members of your health team.

For example, when I was working in London with my good friend Dr. Ravi Ponniah, we had a very well known person who came to us for wellness visits on a regular basis. We used what is called "Iris analysis" to determine a person's underlying weaknesses that then helps decide a future tendency to develop diseases. The iris is part of your eye and can be examined with the help of a magnifying lens to identify pre-existing weaknesses. This iris analysis is also called *Iridology*. Ravi is one of the best Iridologists that I know. In this patient, we diagnosed a tendency to develop cancer by analyzing the iris. The patient had been diligently undergoing the recommended screening tests yearly, and these test were negative for many years. At some point, her screening tests were stopped because these very screenings are not recommended as patients grow older. A few years later, the patient was diagnosed with cancer and subsequently did not survive the disease. This was an experience that made me realize that weaknesses can be picked up by modalities other than Western medicine even before the disease develops.

In the case of my patient I described earlier in this chapter, Western medicine came into play when she was being investigated for functional decline and weight loss, and subsequently with powerful chemotherapy as a palliative therapy. Even though she was open to and seemed to have an affinity for Eastern medicines, she did not use them because she could not afford it. In her case, her You Power was completely neglected; she did not have the support or support system to address this aspect of her health and wellness. More importantly, no one paid attention to her continued complaints. I had suggested repeatedly that she move out of her daughter's home and live independently, utilizing assistance programs available in her community such as a senior home or assisted living. She refused, and her rationale was that she did not want to hurt or offend the child with whom she was living.

The key message that is illustrated by this patient's story is that if you have very strong feelings, do not ignore and bury them. Do not behave as if everything is fine. You need to address your feelings so that they do not manifest in the form of disease down the road. My friend satisfied the two characteristics (negative reaction to life events and outgoing interpersonal attitude) that I have described in our discussion of You Power.

What can Western medicine offer you?

How would a Western medical practitioner address this situation? You and I know that, once symptoms develop, functional and structural changes have already occurred in the affected organ. In my friend's case, she was offered chemotherapy only as a palliation. She was told that there were no treatments that would cure her cancer, but that chemotherapy could slow down the spread of the disease. She was offered pain medications to control pain. She opted to not take the chemotherapy and allowed the disease to consume her, but she did accept the pain medications.

Medications

Several options are available from a Western medical perspective when it comes to the treatment of cancer. Once the extent of the cancer is determined, the practitioner will describe what type of medications and therapies are advisable. The main focus is to eliminate the cancer from your body. But this is not always possible. Surgery will be recommended if the cancer can be removed. After surgery, your practitioner may recommend chemotherapy to make sure no cancer cells are left behind. Along with chemotherapy, radiation may be recommended as well. Sometimes chemotherapy will be instituted first to shrink a tumor so that it can be surgically removed. In this case, chemotherapy will precede surgery. These options tend to be the mainstay of treatment modalities in Western medicine. Recently, some Western medical facilities have started to use a few alternative and complementary therapies, such as Acupuncture and massage, in their institution as adjuncts.

Diet

As we have seen, Western medicine recommends responses only after the cancer is diagnosed. Dietary recommendations for cancer patients vary. You may be asked to consult with a nutritionist to get appropriate recommendations. The recommendations will be tailored to the type of cancer you have and other complications or complexities. Additionally, cancer patients tend to have weight loss and poor nutrition. Chemotherapy and radiation therapy may result in poor appetite, nausea, and vomiting—all of which lead to poor oral intake of foods and nutrients. Your diet will be addressed and adjusted to take all these factors into account. The type of diet that is recommended may also depend on the stage of cancer that is present.

Although there are lots of claims that certain types of foods and or chemicals play a role in predisposing us to the development of cancer, most of them have not yet made it to the point of being generally acknowledged or accepted. One example of a preventive diet recommendation is a high-fiber diet to prevent colon cancer. More information on dietary recommendations can be found on the National Cancer Institute's website[12]. There is also recent evidence that a diet high in sugar can play a role in cancer development and progression. Ongoing research may one day prove that cancer has a sweet tooth!

Exercise

Physical inactivity is listed as one of the risk factors for the development of cancer. As such, a Western medical practitioner will recommend engaging in regular physical exercise. Physical exercise in general is very important for the overall well-being of the cancer patient. It helps in handling stress and weight issues, and can function as a substitute to help eliminate other risk factors like smoking and excessive alcohol consumption.

Risky behaviors

The recommendation here is straightforward: Avoid them! Alcohol consumption, smoking, all types of radiation, and excessive sunlight are all considered risk factors for the development of cancer. Therefore, it is recommended that you avoid these risk factors to prevent the development of cancer. Obesity is another risk factor, therefore weight loss, as well as weight control and management, will be recommended. As I've stated before, regular exercise to combat the risk of physical inactivity is suggested. Additionally, risky behavior such as sexual promiscuity, which can lead to viral infections that predispose a person to cervical cancer, should be avoided.

Although there have been studies linking personality-trait associations with cancer, no current recommendations exist for the prevention of cancer. However, once you develop cancer, you may be encouraged to seek counseling to learn how to cope with the devastating news of a cancer diagnosis and the rigors of treatment.

What can Eastern medicine offer you?

As with other diseases, there are a myriad of Eastern medical disciplines that you can choose to use as adjuncts to Western medicine to help you continue to address your cancer or enhance your wellness and reduce your chances of developing cancer. Cancer is one of the diseases where Eastern modalities are most often used.

Acupuncture

While Acupuncture does not treat the cancer disease directly, it helps the overall well-being of the person before the disease takes hold or after it has developed. If you find that you are at risk, and prior to the development of cancer, you can use Acupuncture to improve your general well-being and resistance to cancer by enhancing your energetic balance.

Once cancer develops, Acupuncture can be used to address several side effects of the therapy. First of all, it can be used prior to surgery to enhance the chances of a successful outcome with regard to recovery and complications. After the surgery, it can be used successfully for the treatment of post-operative pain. It can also be successfully used with chemotherapy to treat its side effects such as nausea, vomiting, and loss of appetite. Neuropathic pain caused by certain cancers can also be successfully treated with Acupuncture.

Currently, Western medicine will prescribe narcotic pain medications for cancer pain. These medications come with significant side effects such as altered sensorium and constipation. What is the point in alleviating pain if you have altered sensorium so extreme that you cannot even identify members of your family? My friend experienced severe constipation and altered sensorium due to taking narcotic pain medicines. She could not even recognize people she knew well because of the medications. She did not want to eat because she feared the discomfort and dangers of constipation. Imagine a cancer patient who needs nourishment but will not eat for fear of constipation resulting from pain medication.

Acupuncture for pain relief, the reduction of nausea and vomiting, and the enhancement of appetite works well without any major negative side effects.

Massage

Massage is a great adjunct for the treatment of side effects due to therapy for cancer. In addition, it helps with stress reduction and helps patients cope with combating a deadly disease like cancer. It enhances a person's overall well-being and nurtures a positive attitude—both of which are essential in fighting the disease. In a subtle way, these practices remind patients about living and take their minds off the devastating endpoint of death due to cancer. In many cases, it is the patients who approach cancer with a positive attitude who survive. Therefore, *any* modality that will help you achieve and maintain a positive attitude can be used with varying degrees of success.

Caution should be used with regard to the pressure used during massage therapy, if you have bone cancer and fragile bones. This is also the case if you have external cancers on the surface area of the body. Caution is advised when it comes to massage in an affected area.

Homeopathy

Although Homeopathy is not strictly Eastern in origin (since it originated in the West) it is widely practiced in Eastern countries as natural therapy. Homeopathy believes cancer develops in patients who have what they call the *Psoric* miasma. As such, a homeopathic practitioner will select remedies that treat such miasma. Homeopathic practitioners may recommend remedies to prevent the development of cancer if they identify you as having Psoric miasma. This treatment is based on the theory of treating the underlying constitutional make-up of the person. And since Homeopathic remedies tend not to have significant side effects, it is not unreasonable to obtain therapy.

Once you have been diagnosed with cancer, several remedies can be used for the side effects that often result from Western medical therapy modalities. It is important to discuss the use of Homeopathic remedies with your Western doctor. However, while Homeopathic practitioners are not regulated in the United States, many of the remedies they recommend are somewhat regulated. You may find that many physicians are not familiar with Homeopathy and may discourage you from using it. With a little research, you can find Western physicians who use Homeopathy in their practice. You can consult with them to obtain appropriate information to suit your situation and educate your regular Western physician so that you are able to benefit from both Eastern and Western disciplines.

Chiropractic Care

The principles of treatment with Chiropractic therapy are the same as with other diseases. Chiropractic is used to invigorate the nerve supply to the organs. Experienced chiropractors can perform manipulation without much discomfort and can be cautious, given the details related to the severity of your illness. It is important to inform the chiropractor about your cancer, its severity, and (if appropriate) specifics related to its spread. This helps them to adjust the manipulation effort as well as to concentrate on any area that needs special attention. Caution should be used with bone cancers. If your cancer has spread to your bones, this discipline may not be appropriate as your bones may be more fragile. A well-trained Chiropractor will give you the appropriate advice when you tell them details of your condition.

Herbs

Traditional Chinese practitioners, Naturopaths, Chiropractors, and even some Western medical practitioners use herbs as either primary treatment or as adjunct for various illnesses. While herbs are promoted by some practitioners for the prevention of cancer or to enhance your basic constitutional make-up, they can also be recommended for the alleviation of side effects of cancer therapy. Once again, caution should be used with regard to the interactions of herbs with other drugs you may be taking for the treatment of your cancer. It is important that you share information about any use of herbal medications with your Western practitioner and advise your herbal practitioner of the drugs or medications you are taking. The best results can be achieved only when both practitioners—and you—work together to serve your best interest.

Yoga and Meditation

Yoga exercises are excellent for anyone's overall healthy status. There is tremendous benefit to be gained from Yoga when it comes to serious illnesses like cancer. Yoga exercises help invigorate your entire body and facilitate better flow of energy. Yoga balances your mind and strengthens it to help handle the stress of your illness. If you are able to perform most of the poses, you will be able to maintain physical strength and flexibility. Yogic breathing helps to calm your mind and invigorate the lungs. Meditation calms the mind and reduces emotional fluctuations. It assists with better focus, positive attitude, and enhanced ability to handle uncertainties and stressors. Overall, Yoga and meditation strengthen the musculoskeletal system, invigorate the nervous system, and steady the mind. Regular use helps to alleviate some of the psychological effects of having a serious disease like cancer.

Including meditation as a part of your daily ritual will also help you deal with your internal dialogue with clarity and assist with mindful living.

Ayurveda

As I've explained in previous chapters, Ayurveda uses a system of healthy living to promote the health and well-being of a person. This system utilizes various cleansing methods to purify the body of toxins and unwanted substances on a regular basis. As such, it is a very helpful adjunct to help cleanse our bodies of impurities that, in turn, allows optimal function of all our organs.

An Ayurvedic lifestyle and its remedies can be very useful when you attempt to prevent the development of cancer, especially if you think that you are predisposed to develop this disease.

The outlook, however, is different once you have been diagnosed with cancer. An Ayurvedic physician may recommend a diet that is designed to pacify the body's underlying abnormality based on the Ayurvedic evaluation. A specific diet is not harmful as long as it provides the necessary nutrition. Make sure to consult with a nutritionist to confirm the nutritional value of a specific Ayurvedic diet. Additional remedies may also be prescribed.

However, just as with liver disease or kidney disease, the use of Ayurvedic remedies for cancer should be approached with caution. While lifestyle modifications are harmless with existing cancer and may enhance your well-being, oral remedies should be taken with extra caution under the supervision of an experienced practitioner and with full awareness of your Western medicine practitioner.

There is always an aspect of any Eastern modality that can be very useful when used in conjunction with Western medical therapy to enhance your chance of winning the game of health and disease. Make sure to explore all options. On the other hand, it is also important for you to explore the adverse influence of Eastern medications—just as you would the side effects of Western medications—when you have an established disease. Guidance from a practitioner who is well versed in both disciplines is very useful.

As a general rule, most Eastern modalities are useful in acquiring and maintaining health while Western therapy is used to restore health once a disease is diagnosed. Some aspects of most Eastern modalities can be used even if you have an established disease, as long as you do the research and understand how they interact, as well as complement, each other.

There are several other modalities that can be used successfully to cope with cancer. Some of these modalities include aromatherapy, music therapy, spiritual therapy, reflexology, biofeedback, and hypnotherapy. I have included only the most predominant disciplines in this book.

Handling your You Power

As I've stated in previous chapters, your You Power plays a major role in your ability to reap the benefit of whatever tools you use from both modalities. I think that cancer offers the greatest opportunity to understand the influence of the Power of You in the development of human disease. Aggressive research is being conducted in this regard.

Do not forget that there are several Eastern and other adjunct modalities available to enhance your well-being and strengthen your spirit, your vital energy. The strength of your spirit plays a major role in health and disease and how successful you will be in combating a disease.

Internal dialogue or Primal being

In the case of my friend, she felt as if she was not needed. She felt worthless, and disrespected as a human being. She felt as if others did not even realize that she existed. She felt that she was being deprived of food and socialization. Over time, she developed a sense of worthlessness, especially after she had lost her husband. Her life did not have meaning and she questioned the reasons she would want to continue living.

The internal dialogue that she was trying to communicate was that "I have become meaningless to everyone and feel as if I am a burden. What is the point in continuing to live?" These feelings may have been unfounded, but the fact of the matter was they were festering within her. These feelings are a form of energy that resided within her, coloring her entire view of life. This energy, energy that sat within her for years, along with her emotions, may have created the downward spiral of her health. This downward spiral led, ultimately, to her demise.

Your internal dialogue—your innermost thoughts and feelings— is rarely communicated to the outside world, but it has a significant impact on your life. It manifests in our actions, based on our personality. However, if a person does not express his or her actions (as in the case of my friend), no one will ever know what they are feeling.

The solution here is simple, but not always easy. When you have thoughts or feelings from deeply buried secrets or emotional pain—feelings that are part of you and your You Power—explore those feelings. Do not just suppress them or ignore them...or just hope that they go away.

About 15 years ago, I met a patient who was being worked up for a heart transplant. During the process, he admitted that he had cancer a few years back. The cancer had been treated and apparently cured. While questioning him about his psycho-social well-being—the way he handled his emotions and feelings—he respectfully requested that he did not want to discuss his psycho-social history with anyone. His wish was respected. Over time, the trust we developed led him to confide in me that he was abused as a child. Clearly, he had not worked through the trauma of this experience in any meaningful way and it was still buried deep within him. This was his secret, a deep hurt that continued to affect him and his behavior on a daily basis.

This habit of burying our internal dialogues is not beneficial. And over time it will eventually lead to the development of an adverse outcome. That adverse outcome, in my opinion, is an illness. This patient had already experienced cancer. Years later, his heart condition made him a candidate for a transplant. One can't help but wonder what his health picture might have looked like had he faced his "demons" at a younger age and eliminated them from his life once and for all.

The key factor here is to recognize the internal dialogue that goes on within each of us and engage in what I call an *emotional cleanse*. This can be done by seeking the help of a counselor or psychologist. Our emotional health is a critical component of overall health, so I will take a moment to explain an *emotional cleanse*.

Throughout our lives—beginning from early childhood, through our teenage years and as young adults—we grow up experiencing powerful emotions. Some of these emotions arise from experiences that may have been traumatic or unpleasant. The trigger for these emotions can vary based on individual experience, religion, culture, race, etc. Some of the examples of these triggers are abuse (physical, sexual, verbal, or emotional), bullying, peer pressures, major disappointments, abandonment issues, relationship issues or upsets, and so on. These triggers can leave deep scars in our psyche (our You Power) and get buried deep within us—if not dealt with immediately. As time goes by, these deep-seated emotional scars influence and shape our behavior throughout our life. And the longer they remain unaddressed, the longer they will be heavy influencers of our progress, heavy baggage to carry around, affecting every step we take. Unresolved issues stay deep down in us and fester. Those festering memories, hurts, and emotions become an ongoing conflict in our minds, both consciously and unconsciously. This, in turn, can use significant amounts of our vital energy, leaving us feeling drained. In other words, you live your life in an unbalanced state, consciously or unconsciously channeling a lot of energy toward these unresolved conflicts, instead of spending that energy on joyful, positive living.

An emotional cleanse is a process of traveling back to the incident that resulted in a specific buried issue and re-living it...come face-to-face with it, challenge it, and uproot it from your psyche and get rid of it. That is easier said than done. But it *is* doable. And the impact it can have on your life is significant.

You will need the help of an objective counselor to assist you in this. I have done it, and I can assure you that, when you re-live an incident and get it out in the open and let go, it is uplifting and satisfying. An example of this is re-living an event or emotion from your childhood that now, as an adult, can be viewed from a new perspective...one that can change that negative childhood experience forever. Once it is explored, it may seem insignificant or meaningless. The meaninglessness may become evident only when you choose to confront these buried issues. You may ask yourself how a childhood memory, with the hindsight of adulthood, could have caused you such emotional pain for so many years. If you do not address this baggage, the issue will continue to hold you under the same power that it did when you first experienced it.

Most of my patients refuse to seek help from counselors or psychologists, as they consider this a sign of weakness. But, in fact, it is quite the opposite. You need a tremendous amount of courage to face the demons from your past. There is nothing wrong or shameful in trying to find out how well you are coping with a conflict that threatens to shorten your life or to seek out tools that will improve your coping abilities.

This was the case with my friend. She did not face her demon (her feelings of worthlessness) and was not open to the idea of an emotional cleanse. She allowed her deep-seated conflict to take hold of her and perhaps, lost the chance to live longer.

Emotional cleansing can be used in many circumstances. It may be a basic internal conflict that you need to get out in the open. You may have had a disagreement with your boss and find that it is, still, not sitting well within you. An emotional cleanse may shed some light on the issue, or at least allow you to address it in a healthy manner so that it does not continue to fester negatively within you.

Personality or Social being

Personality refers to an individual's characteristic pattern of behavior *driven* by their deeper thoughts and emotions, but modified by their rules of conduct to suit the outside world. In other words, it is the primal self modified to suit the outside world and acceptable behavior in society.

My friend's strong emotional characteristics, along with her stored energy (i.e. negative thoughts and feelings) made her cancer prone. The displaced strong emotions and energy that were stored within her led to her demise. She had no idea about these characteristics or how to identify them—or the fact that this concept was associated with development of cancer. Could it have helped if she knew and took action to address it rather than suppressing it? Perhaps. It's impossible to know for sure. We only know the answer when we take action and observe the outcome. Maybe she could have been more forceful in expressing herself and in discussing her feelings with her children rather than simply using me as her sounding board. I would venture to say that neither her children nor grandchildren knew how she was feeling. By discussing and searching for a solution in which she could have eliminated the feeling of worthlessness, created a purpose in life, and then felt as if life was worth living, may have altered the course of her life.

Chapter Eight

Lungs

The Constrictive Killer

I cannot live life fully.

When you breathe, you take air into your lungs. The lungs then deliver oxygen from the air you breathe to the cells in your body via the blood circulation. Cells need oxygen for nutrition and to work properly. Each day we breathe about 25,000 times.

Our lungs are paired organs situated in the chest—and they are complex organs. The structure of the lungs is more complex in some ways than that of the heart in that the lungs contain several different cells, and each performs specific and complex functions. For example, our heart is a single muscular organ which pumps blood through the entire body. The lungs, on the other hand, have several functions. First of all, our lungs are exposed to the outside world through our nose, where countless pollutants can enter into our bodies. Therefore, our lungs should perform a protective role. The major function of the lungs, as we know from Western medicine, is exchanging the oxygen we breathe in for the carbon dioxide that we breathe out. The oxygen coming in nourishes our body and the carbon dioxide going out is waste product. Through this exchange, the lungs provide the oxygen that is essential for the generation of energy in all our cells and eliminates the waste products. If oxygen is not available, our cells will die.

Lung disease was the third leading cause of death in the United States in 2010, according to The National Heart, Lung and Blood Institute[1]. In 2010, 235,000 deaths were attributed to lung disease in the United States[1]. The economic cost of chronic lung disease in the United States was estimated, in 2009, at $106 billion[1]. It is a major problem worldwide as well. Globally, chronic lung diseases account for one in six deaths[2]. In Europe, it accounts for one in ten deaths[2].

However, on a daily basis, most of us are not even aware of our own breathing unless we feel the sensation of heavy breathing or when we sigh. The function of our lungs is vital to our existence, and yet we are often unaware of its steady function in our body unless abnormal symptoms cause us to think about it. This observation is a prime example of how busy we are on a daily basis, and how little time we allow for mindful breathing.

Several years ago, one of my young patients was being evaluated for a lung transplant due to end-stage lung disease. He was 37 years old and had a less than 50 percent chance of living more than another 10 years. He had been my patient for many years and was on several medications for his lung problems. He had been a smoker and stopped smoking after he developed significant lung disease. He was an outgoing but nervous person who loved gambling and traveling. And although he had stopped smoking, he was a victim of second-hand smoke when he was in casinos.

He was doing reasonably well with the combination of medications that he was taking. However, he was not very happy with one of the medications because he inherently felt that the medication was not helping him. So when a new medication was available on the market, I recommended that the new medication could deliver more benefits and that he should discontinue the medication that he was unhappy with and replace it with the new one. He got very nervous about this. His initial reaction to the suggestion was anxiety. He was conflicted and reacted negatively to the idea of changing his medications. I found this interesting, especially in light of the fact that he was unhappy with the medication I was recommending he discontinue.

We started the new medication in place of the other. During follow-up visits, all the objective tests we performed showed improved results. However, subjectively, he started feeling more symptomatic. He began saying "I am not feeling well" more and more frequently. I conducted several of the objective tests again to see if he was, in fact, clinically declining with the new medications. All the tests showed that he was doing as well as or better than when he was on the old medication. Yet, subjectively, he was feeling worse—in spite of Western medical tests showing the opposite. I decided to explore his symptoms more deeply because I could not document any underlying reason for them.

I found him to be very sensitive to his feelings and aware of even the slightest changes. He would communicate these subtle changes to us, but we could not corroborate his symptoms with any objective findings. These worsening symptoms occurred only episodically. His main complaint during the episodes was that he felt like his chest was constricted and that he was unable to take a full breath of life. Yet, all of the chest X-rays and CT (computed tomography) scans of his chest showed no abnormality. Blood tests were normal. His lung-function tests did not show any worsening.

As a Western medical practitioner, I was stuck. As I have stated before, if a biochemical or structural abnormality cannot be documented, Western medicine cannot progress effectively in treating a problem. At this point, I could have proceeded one of two ways. The first strategy would be to watch him closely and wait for something that is currently undetected to progress and come to the surface so that action can be taken to address it. This is the most frequently used strategy in Western medicine. The second strategy would be to watch him closely and explore deeper—not with the idea of identifying a disease, but by exploring him, as a person.

During one of his visits, we started talking. After explaining to him that we could not find any corroborative, objective finding to explain his symptoms, I asked about stressors in life. After a few minutes of talking, he opened up and unloaded all the stress that he had been handling for the past few months...which coincided, coincidentally, with the start of the new medication. He described how busy he was with multiple responsibilities that he had to handle daily. His eyes welled up and he became quite emotional and told me that he feels as though he could not live his life fully. I asked him if he had discussed these conflicts with anyone. He said "No."

At that point, I had an avenue to treat him as a person. I suggested that he should get objective counseling, not just advice from family, friends, and peers. He said that his insurance might not cover professional counseling. I told him that the worst advice he can get is free advice. When you get free advice from people who already know you, I told him, they already have a bias: they know you. They tend to tell you what they think you want to hear or how they would treat themselves. That advice is not likely to be beneficial for you. It may make you feel better for a short while, but it has no power to change your situation.

The second strategy was to suggest that he use what is known as *Pranayama*, a breathing exercise that is part of Yoga practice. My hope was that this would give him some time alone to reflect, introspectively, about life and his situation. Time when he could achieve some calm and clarity, rather than constantly distracting himself by being so busy. This type of breathing has been shown to be beneficial in patients with lung conditions. But, more importantly, this breathing exercise involves taking deep breaths and holding that breath for a few seconds. This exercise would give him a chance to experience life without the feeling of constriction. Taking a deep breath is the first step in experiencing life—just like what a newborn baby does at the time of birth—as it should be lived. He walked out of the office that day with a positive attitude and feeling much better than when he had come in.

This story illustrates several points that are not optimal in the area of Western medicine, and your You Power. Western medicine, while exceptional and the best tool available to treat disease, cannot progress when no structural or biochemical abnormality can be corroborated related to the symptoms.

My patient, as a person, was an outgoing, open, and emotionally sensitive person—but he was someone who reacted negatively toward life events and who did not have a good handle on dealing with his internal world. For some reason, he kept feeling constricted and limited with regard to his life. And finally, not only was he able to establish the deeper relationship and understanding necessary to become partners in handling his health and disease, he was open to my recommendations of Eastern techniques as adjunct therapy.

The Western side of the lung disease coin

From the Western medical perspective, there are several different lung diseases that permeate the human race. These different diseases are related to different functions and locations of the organ we call the lungs. The extremes of lung illness range from a simple viral infection that affects the lining of the lung (that resolves without treatment in three to five days), to such severe destruction of the lung organ where a lung transplant is the only option for extending survival. Several risk factors are identified in the development of chronic respiratory distress due to various diseases[3]. I have included risk factors for chronic respiratory distress rather than for the individual diseases of the lung. These include:

- Aging
- Hereditary and Congenital abnormalities
- Tobacco use (cigarettes, pipe tobacco, and cigars)
- Indoor and outdoor air pollution
- Allergens

- Occupational agents such as asbestos and coal
- Unhealthy diet and physical inactivity
- Excess weight and obesity
- Diabetes
- High blood pressure
- Other diseases such as heart disease, stroke, cancer, diabetes, allergies, and rheumatologic diseases
- Infections

Western medicine asserts that if these risk factors exist in a person's life, they will lead to the development of lung diseases in susceptible individuals and may ultimately result in lung failure. Not everyone who is exposed to the risk factors for lung disease develops the disease, which leaves gaps in our current understanding. It is the same for all other organ diseases as well. Some of the diseases that are identified in Western medicine, where advanced therapies are available, include (but are not limited to) the following:

- Infections from viruses, parasites, and bacteria, including tuberculosis.
- *Emphysema*, a condition that manifests as an inability to completely expel the air we inhale. The most common cause is smoking and another common cause is asthma.
- *Cystic fibrosis*, an inherited condition that afflicts children.
- *Interstitial lung diseases* that result from pollutants or an association with other chronic diseases known as *connective tissue diseases*.
- Lung cancers
- *Pulmonary hypertension*, a condition where the pressure in the lungs is too high, resulting in too much stress on the heart and subsequent heart failure.

As you can see, while Western medicine has made significant strides in treating these diseases, we have not been able to prevent their development or recurrence. We also identify susceptible individuals only by identifying an association between risk factors and the development of symptoms, well after the disease manifests and not before. From my point of view, this is not satisfactory.

Additionally, just as I have described with regard to my patient, Western medicine can only be effective as long as a pathology—a disease—can be identified in the body. If you have symptoms but no additional biochemical or structural changes can be documented, then the management of such symptoms becomes very challenging to a Western practitioner. On this point I can speak from experience: We often get stuck not knowing how to proceed...with only waiting and watching as our course of action. Most of the guideline-based recommendations do not tell us what to do in these situations.

The Eastern side of the lung disease coin

In Acupuncture tradition, the lungs are understood and described by several functions. The most important function governs the respiration and the energy (Qi). The lungs are the connection between the external, heavenly clean Qi, and the internal body. When the lung energy is balanced and functions properly, all physiological activity in the body is well maintained. Imbalance of the lung's energy can result in abnormal physiological activity in any organ. The factors that affect and can cause imbalances in the lung's energy include the following:

- Emotions such as **sadness, grief, and worry**
- Excessive consumption of raw and uncooked food
- Excessive consumption of dairy products
- External climatic factors such as cold, heat, and wind, as well as dryness and dampness

- Inefficient work habits such as **excessive mental activities, long work hours**, and being hunched over a desk or computer for prolonged periods of time
- Lounging and laziness that leads to physical inactivity

When the lung's energy is affected, the resulting imbalance over a long period of time can lead to chronic lung diseases and ultimately the failure of the organ. As you can see, looking at lung symptoms from this perspective gives additional insight into a person (*not the disease*) and helps to manage them. In my patient's case, I was able to identify at least a few issues (in bold in the preceding list of causative factors) that he was not aware of, but which I could influence by making him aware. Besides, the interventions I recommended (counseling and Yogic breathing) would have no side effects. In the future, he could be encouraged to explore other Eastern medical therapies as adjuncts that could help him. It is a win-win situation for all. Such is the power of combining Western and Eastern medicine...or what I like to call playing with your two strongest team members.

Ayurveda also proposes an energetic disequilibrium in keeping with its underlying philosophy. Lung disease is explained as resulting from abnormal balance of the energy axis called *Kapha*. Just as with Acupuncture, an accumulation of phlegm is at the root of lung injury in Ayurveda. Phlegm is the final product of abnormal lung function in Western medicine. In Acupuncture, phlegm is said to result from abnormal functions of the spleen, but in Ayurveda this abnormal function is attributed to the stomach organ. Interestingly, in Acupuncture, the organs spleen and stomach are coupled organs. This means that they function together like husband and wife or Yin and Yang. In fact, in Acupuncture, spleen is the Yin organ and the stomach is the paired Yang organ.

I think you'll agree that it is easy to see the similarities in seemingly different philosophies. Causative factors similar to Acupuncture are described in Ayurveda for development of the energy imbalance, which in turn leads to organ dysfunction in susceptible persons. These include:

- A diet with too much fat, fried food, sugar, meats, dairy products, and nuts

- Too much sleep during the daytime and physical inactivity

You can readily see the similarities in both traditions that propose the foundation of energetic imbalances leading to structural abnormalities—as opposed to Western medicine where energetic considerations are absent. You can also realize that diet and physical activity are a common thread as causative factors in all three aspects (Western medicine, Acupuncture, and Ayurveda). Interestingly, attention to our diet and physical activity are the first things to fall by the wayside under emotional stress as we opt for the comfort of physical *inactivity* and comfort foods.

You Power • The third side of the lung coin

My observations of my interactions with patients with chronic lung disease include seeing some of the end stage patients. Intimate work with patients who have chronic diseases such as emphysema and pulmonary hypertension have allowed me both an appreciation and a sense of these patients as people, rather than just someone with a disease.

Involvement in disease management programs allows continuity and long-term follow-up. As such, one begins to appreciate patterns that are unique to people and thus start to understand individual characteristics. Patients with lung abnormalities tend to have the following underlying personal characteristics:

- An inability to experience life fully due to a sense of unworthiness, shyness, and social anxiety—or a sense of not wanting to experience life to the fullest.

- A deep, undercurrent manifestation of sadness, pessimism, a flat affect, and an inability to discuss this openly. Flat affect or blunted affect means not showing emotions or lacking facial expressions that reflect their emotions. They tend to speak in a monotonous voice. One of the most common diseases that is characterized by flat affect is depression.

- An inability to be organized.

These characteristics are my own observations. There have not been a lot of studies that looked at the correlation between personality traits and lung disease. In studies that did look at these aspects, patients with chronic lung diseases tended to score high on anticipatory worry[4], pessimism[5] and fear of uncertainty, and scored low on self-directedness[6] and resourcefulness[6].

From the social being or personality perspective, people who develop end-stage lung disease where a lung transplant is needed, had the predominance of two distinct characteristics[7]. These characteristics are:

1. **Prone to stress and worry:** These individuals tend to be anxious people who are apprehensive and worry a lot. They can get easily frustrated, feel irritable, and get angry with others. They are prone to feel lonely, sad, and rejected. While they tend to have difficulty controlling their impulses and wants and wishes, they have no problem handling normal, day-to-day stress.

2. **Inventive and curious:** These individuals are open to experience. They are responsive to beauty they find in poetry, music, art, and nature. They are very responsive to their feelings and emotions. They take part in new activities with ease and have a high need for variety in life—hence the manifestation of not living life fully if variety is not present in their life. They are very imaginative.

The United States Centers for Disease Control (CDC) reports that the jobs with most smokers include miners, construction workers, workers in foodservice and hotel industry, and workers in transportation. Many of these workers might characterize their jobs as monotonous.

My patient was prone to stress and worry, but he was also inventive and curious. He was very responsive to his feelings and emotions and was able to detect subtle changes in them. He was feeling lonely, frustrated, and irritable. As a result, he experienced the symptoms more intensely even though no abnormality could be confirmed by objective means.

In most cases, when patients have an abnormal feeling or symptom but investigations do not reveal a biochemical or structural abnormality, the culprit tends to be an imbalance in the energy of that person. Most diseases start as an energy imbalance and then progress to a stage where they can be diagnosed as a disease. The good news is that if you pick up this energy imbalance and address it early on, you have a better chance of either preventing the progression to a disease state or retarding the process. There is only one team member that can help you—apart from you yourself and your role as captain—and that team member is Eastern medicine. But, more importantly, you as the captain of your team can help yourself…if you pay attention to your You Power. And a large part of the Power of You is related to your internal dialogue and personality.

What can you do?

As with all diseases, it's important to understand that there are always three sides that need to be considered. They are your teammates from Western medicine, Eastern medicine, and You Power—with YOU as captain of your health team. In the case of my patient, the Western medicine provided treatment to its fullest extent. However, when it came to symptoms that were not backed up by test results, Western medicine had nothing more to offer except watchful waiting. Eastern medicine on the other hand was able to help the patient during this watchful waiting period. Eastern medicine is able to support and enhance the You Power of any patient. With Eastern medicine modalities, the patient as a person, instead of just a disease, is addressed and treated. Personally, I do not see why this kind of hybrid, multi-faceted practice is not adopted universally. This combination therapy satisfies the 30/30/30 Rule we discussed earlier in this book.

While many practitioners of medicine may not be familiar with these Eastern concepts or may be limited in their ability to practice and provide such complete care, there is nothing wrong with you educating yourself in understanding how you want to be treated. This is You Power at its most powerful.

What can Western medicine offer you?

What Western medicine can offer for a particular disease is well known. We see TV commercials that advertise new medications that are on the market and encourage you to discuss these courses of treatment with your medical care provider. What we know now is that Western medicine, while one of the best medicines available to treat disease, can only do so much.

Medications

Medications are usually directed at treating a disease. Case in point: The appropriate therapy I prescribed for my patient based upon his condition. In fact, as new and suitable medications became available we added them to his regimen. Additionally, medications may be prescribed to treat other diseases that may be underlying causes for a lung problem. For example, a condition called *scleroderma* can affect the lungs. Scleroderma is a condition that affects the skin and makes it tough and less elastic. In addition, your lungs can also become stiff, and that condition is called *fibrosis*. Damaged lung tissue is replaced by scar tissue and cannot perform its function properly. In Western medicine, it may seem to be a strange association, but in Acupuncture the sensory organ *skin* is associated with lungs. This association was discovered thousands of years ago, and it is no surprise to an Acupuncture physician that both organs are affected.

So, as a result of associations like these, you may be prescribed medications to treat lung fibrosis as well as other medications to treat the scleroderma. Additionally, you may be prescribed oxygen, if needed, and other medications called *bronchodilators*. These bronchodilators dilate and expand airway tubes to make it easy to breathe. If an infection, such as pneumonia, is the cause of the lung problem, then you may be prescribed an antibiotic.

Diet

There are no specific diets recommended for end-stage lung disease, per se. However, most allergic reactions manifest via your lungs. Allergies can cause shortness of breath due to the constriction of your airways in response to chemicals released during an allergic reaction. This can be life threatening if treatment is not instituted immediately. You may have noticed TV commercials for EpiPen®. It is an emergency medication delivered via an injection pen that is carried by allergy-prone people at all times. In the event of a food or other allergy, the medication can immediately be administered by injection into the muscles—which can save your life before emergency medical personnel arrive at the scene. A peanut allergy in children is one of the scenarios where an EpiPen is very useful, and there are many others. The injection can be used in an emergency for any allergic reactions. As a side note: Extreme caution must be used with the administration of this medication. Always get instructions from your medical provider as to when and how to use this emergency medication.

If you suffer from allergies, your Western practitioner may restrict your diet to avoid the foods to which you are allergic. Some people are allergic to nuts, others to fruits, and still others are allergic to seafood and shellfish. The same is true for allergies to medications.

The medication allergies are not limited just to those prescribed by Western medical practitioners. You might find yourself allergic to herbs and other remedies that may be prescribed as part of the Eastern medical therapy as well. Therefore, avoid any foods, medications, supplements, and herbs, if you are allergic to them.

One other interesting observation is that allergic reactions manifest not only via the lungs, but also as skin reactions like a rash or eczema. Once again, this validates the observation in Acupuncture philosophies that our lungs and the sensory organ skin are paired. I have seen patients who have asthma and when their asthma resolves, they develop eczema or other kinds of skin rashes. On the other hand, when patients' skin rash or eczema is successfully treated, they often develop shortness of breath.

Exercise

Regular moderate exercise is one of the best ways to maintain your overall health. Exercise plays a major role in lung disease. The main function of the lungs is to exchange oxygen and carbon dioxide between the body and the environment. The lungs are able to do this through our breathing. Breathing involves the expansion of the chest so that the lungs can fill with air, then as the chest returns to a normal state after expansion, the air is expelled. The good news is that this movement of the chest and lungs can be done in two ways. First, is via the brain triggering this activity without getting a conscious command from us to do so. In other words, even if you forgot to breathe, your chest will move and you will breathe. The second is you can willfully increase or decrease or even hold your breathing by commanding your brain to trigger that action.

This ability to consciously control your breathing is often used in exercises after someone has had chest surgery. In this case, a breathing apparatus is given to the patient and he or she is asked to breathe into it so that the lungs can be fully expanded and exercised. This simple exercise speeds recovery.

Regular exercise makes you breathe faster in response to the pace of the exercise and thereby strengthens the muscles between your ribs that are important for chest expansion. Exercise also expands the diaphragm. The diaphragm is comprised of two muscles that sit at the bottom of your chest cavity (between the abdomen and the chest) that, by contracting and relaxing, cause the lungs to expand and collapse. These muscles play a major role in our breathing. In fact, aerobic exercise is one of the best exercises for your lungs and to strengthen the respiratory muscles.

Behavior and lifestyle modifications

If it seems like I am repeating myself, you are right. I am. As Western medicine focuses on disease, you will find that all of the tools it offers are geared towards a particular disease. In the case of behavior modifications, you will be advised the following:

- Stop smoking, if you are smoker
- Lose weight, if you are obese
- Eat low-fat, low-cholesterol food
- Avoid allergy-causing foods
- Exercise regularly
- Do not smoke or snort recreational drugs
- Take your medications regularly
- Avoid noxious gas, fumes, and pollutants
- If you have seasonal allergies, use caution during those seasons

With these recommendations, you are left on your own with periodic follow-up appointments with your doctor to make sure that you are progressing on the right track. If you are not, then it may become a lifelong struggle between Western medicine and the disease process.

What can Eastern medicine offer you?

There are several types of Eastern medical disciplines that a person can choose to use either alone or in combination as adjuncts to Western medicine. These can help you address an ongoing disease process, or simply maintain a healthy state.

Acupuncture

When I was an instructor at the University of Alternative and Complementary Medicines in Sri Lanka, we treated all kinds of medical illnesses. One day, a patient who was being treated for asthma had an acute asthmatic attack. The clinic where we practiced Acupuncture was located in one section of a major Western medical hospital. Although there was a hospital available to care for the acute asthma attack, the professor decided to treat the patient with Acupuncture. (And of course, if you are having an asthma attack, seek appropriate care--do not just show up at an Acupuncturist's office.) This Acupuncture treatment was appropriate in this patient's situation because the onset occurred while the patient was with us in a medical setting. A simple needle inserted and stimulated in the lower part of the neck—in the center where the two collarbones meet—successfully resolved the acute attack of asthma. As a 4th year medical student, that was very impressive to me.

You may recall that, earlier in this book, I shared the fact that my motivation for entering this university was to see how much of a "quack" this professor was. I can tell you that after watching the effect that Acupuncture had on this patient's acute asthma attack, everything changed for me. When I saw the results that an

Acupuncturist achieved with simple needles inserted into specific points in the body, my views on medicine and the treatment of disease changed forever.

Needless to say, Acupuncture can be very effective in energy balancing with regard to the lungs and can be used alone for minor illnesses or as an adjunct to Western medical therapies for major problems.

In the case of my patient with lung disease, systematic treatment with Acupuncture could not only influence his lung energy, but also help him with anxiety-related consequences of the disease. Acupuncture has been studied in chronic lung disease patients and has been shown to be beneficial[8,9]. The lung channel and its associated channels that belong to the large intestine are both located on our arms. Your acupuncture practitioner may place needles along those channels in one or both of your arms. On the other hand, the Acupuncture practitioner may place needles elsewhere on your body, based on the traditional diagnosis, which may point to an imbalance in another organ system as an underlying cause of your lung problem.

Massage

Massage is one of the best therapeutic interventions when it comes to lung conditions. The reason is simple: Most of a massage therapist's time is spent on the back of the thorax where most of the muscles that support our breathing are located. Relieving tightness and knots and releasing toxins from these areas by massage is an excellent intervention.

Massage therapists can also manually stimulate Acupuncture points on the arms along the lung channel or on the back of the thorax where strong Acupuncture points that influence the lungs are located.

I recommended massage therapy for my patient after he started counseling and the Yogic breathing exercises. It is important to add Eastern therapies in a sequential fashion, weighing their chance of benefit to the patient against any side effects. As far as we know, counseling, Yogic breathing, Acupuncture, and massage do not have any measurable side effects that should concern patients. Additionally, these therapies had no interaction with the Western medicines that I had been prescribing for him. I do not see any reason why every patient cannot enjoy and benefit from playing with both Eastern and Western team members.

Homeopathy

Homeopathy can be used successfully as an adjunct to other treatments. However, most frequently, Homeopathy and other Eastern modalities are used only after Western medicine has given up on the condition of a patient. This is unfortunate because, by that time, it may be too late to see any meaningful recovery or change in the condition of the patient.

Let's use my patient as an example. I used alternative therapy only when I did not have a Western-medicine remedy for his complaints. In fact, only when I got stuck did I decide to delve into his You Power in search of an answer. This is *not*, in my opinion, how it should be done. All forms of therapy should be entertained for every possible benefit to the patient right from the beginning. An underlying principle in the mind of a medical practitioner is that the best interest of the patient should drive his or her care.

Today, there are homeopathic remedies that are being used for the treatment of chronic lung diseases, such as a condition called *interstitial lung fibrosis*. There are no effective therapies for this condition in Western medicine, although a lot of research is currently being done. Because of that fact, increasing numbers of patients are seeking alternative forms of therapy. Keep in mind that, just like Acupuncture or Ayurveda, Homeopathy is not designed to treat a specific disease. It treats the underlying constitutional make-up of the person. A Homeopathic practitioner may prescribe additional remedies to relieve symptoms but there should be a primary remedy that is specific to your constitutional make-up or what is called *miasma*. Just like other oral therapies, I would caution that you discuss the use of any Homeopathic remedy with both the Western and Eastern medical practitioners before you engage in using them to treat lung disease.

Chiropractic Care

Chiropractic manipulation relieves the compression and stress on the nerves by other structures in the body through manipulative adjustment of the vertebral column and adjustments of other joints. Osteopathy is also useful in this regard. By enhancing the vitality of the nerves that supply the lungs and the respiratory muscles, chiropractic adjustment from time to time can positively enhance the results of other therapies that you are using for the treatment of chronic lung disease.

Herbs and supplements

Traditional Chinese practitioners, naturopaths, chiropractors, and even some Western medical practitioners use herbs for the treatment of chronic lung diseases. In Western medical research, for example, a garlic-based substance has been found to have beneficial effects in the treatment of interstitial lung disease, a condition where the lungs have more scar tissue than normal tissue[10]. Herbs that are prescribed as part of Traditional Chinese Medicine are usually used in response to a specific energetic diagnosis to treat the patient rather than a specific disease. So, for example, five different people with the same diagnosis of interstitial lung fibrosis may be given five different remedies. As always, it is important for you to discuss the involvement of herbal therapy with both your Western and Eastern medical practitioners prior to using these therapies to identify side effects and any interactions with other drugs that you may be taking.

Yoga and meditation

The benefits of Yoga for patients with chronic lung disease are numerous. We discussed how a Yogic breathing exercise can be very useful for patients with chronic lung diseases and how I used that therapy for one of my patients with this disease. Another aspect of Yogic breathing is worth mentioning. Controlled breathing and slowing down the frequency of breathing is fundamental to Yogic practice. Every Yoga pose is associated with its own breathing technique. An understanding of this is essential if we are to reap the full benefits of Yoga, especially in the body-mind union aspect of Yoga. Let me explain this further.

When you are fearful, angry, or extremely upset...what happens to your breathing? If you observe people experiencing these emotions, you will find that the rate of their breathing increases—and they don't even know it. This is a normal reaction to emotions triggered by our mind via specific areas of the brain. Therefore, it is clear that there is traffic from our brain telling our lungs to breathe faster when under the influence of emotions. In Yoga exercises and pranayama (Yogic breathing), you do precisely the opposite. You consciously control the rate of breathing and train your brain to slow down your breathing. This results in a reciprocal influence on your brain. In this case, there is traffic from your body to the brain and mind—an attempt at a conscious union of body and mind. This influence, when maintained over a long period of time with Yoga practice, allows you to acquire an ability to react calmly and objectively to emotional triggers. People who practice Yoga have a serenity about them that can even calm other people who come into their space.

As a Yoga instructor, I get upset when Yoga exercises are practiced as a form of physical exercise without giving the body-mind aspect any consideration. For most people, it is a form of physical exercise. That distorted concept cannot be further from the truth. The most important aspect of the Yoga exercise is this coupling of the movement of the body with proper breathing, while being intensely aware of both.

The lungs are exercised with any Yogic pose that you use because proper breathing technique is embedded in the performance of each pose in Yoga. As a result, no matter what pose you have incorporated into your routine, it will exercise your lungs. However, there are several poses that have specific influences on the lungs. These poses are too numerous to list in this book. Still, whether you are performing a series of exercises while standing, sitting down, lying down, or in an inverted position, you will find poses that will exercise the lungs and the chest.

Yoga has been found to improve respiratory parameters when practiced consistently three times a week in patients who have chronic lung disease[11]. These findings indicate the increased interest in using modalities like Yoga in the treatment of chronic lung diseases as an adjunct therapy. My recommendation is to practice Yoga daily.

In the patient I described earlier in this chapter, the next step would have been to introduce not only massage therapy, but also daily Yoga practice designed to help the chest and lungs to improve respiratory parameters. These parameters can then be easily measured with follow-up visits as an outpatient. Again, there are no potential side effects with Yoga exercises, as long as appropriate poses are designed by a certified Yoga instructor. Caution should be used if you have other medical conditions in addition to lung problems. It is important that you share all your medical issues with your Yoga therapist before commencing a series of Yoga poses.

Ayurveda

Ayurveda is a system of traditional Indian healthy living. It involves cleansing practices as well as Yoga exercises, proper eating, and natural oral remedies. The Yoga exercise portion of the Ayurveda is described above. When it comes to cleansing, the use of a *Neti pot* (a nasal irrigation system) to cleanse your nasal passages bears significance with regard to your breathing. This practice cleans the nasal passages and improves their vitality, thereby preventing conditions like nasal blockages due to allergic reaction or sinus infections. Most Ear, Nose, and Throat (ENT) surgeons recommend this practice after nasal surgery for chronic sinus problems.

Nasal irrigation helps prevent allergies and sinus problems by clearing the sinuses and nasal passages of mucus, dirt, and allergens. There are tiny, hair-like structures (called *cilia*) that are present in our nasal passages and sinuses. These structures move back and forth, propelling mucus, dirt, and other allergens either backwards towards the throat (to be swallowed) or forward to the front of the nose (to be expelled when we blow our nose). It is thought that the irrigation of these linings with saline improves the movement of the cilia and can prevent allergic reactions and sinus problems.

Additionally, there are specific Ayurvedic remedies that may be prescribed by a traditional Ayurvedic practitioner for the treatment of chronic lung conditions. Just as with any oral medications, caution should be used when taking Ayurvedic remedies along with medications prescribed by Western medical practitioners. There is potential for these Ayurvedic remedies to interact with Western medications and result in either a serious side effect or reduce the beneficial effect of the Western medicine. Therefore, I can't stress this point strongly enough: It is important to inform all of your practitioners about all the medications you are using or planning to use before starting any new therapy.

Handling your You Power

You Power not only plays a major role in your ability to reap the benefits of whatever tools you use from both modalities, but is also influential in the progression of disease over time. If not maintained at an optimal level, the Power of You can result in a *decline* in your condition—even with the best treatment.

A 45-year-old patient of mine with chronic lung disease was receiving treatment for his condition for many years. Over the years, he had difficulty managing his psychosocial stressors. One day, he was admitted to the Emergency Room with acute respiratory distress and was placed on a breathing machine to help him breathe. He was admitted to the Intensive Care Unit for further treatment. Over the next few days, his condition continued to deteriorate and subsequently he died in the hospital.

Further history obtained from his wife revealed that he had stopped one of the medications that had been prescribed for him and had occasionally missed taking other medications. This is termed *non-compliance* in medicine. In other words, he was not adhering to medical recommendations related to his treatment and prescriptions. Many of my patients exhibit this behavior and at times it results in loss of life.

I discussed a similar situation in Chapter 5 and this patient's story is no different from the kidney patient who stopped his dialysis and subsequently died as a direct result of that action. This behavior is associated with the personality of the patient (his or her social self), but the reason or the trigger for the behavior comes from the internal dialogue (the primal self of the person).

Internal dialogue or Primal being

In the case of the first patient I described in this chapter, it was obvious that he was going through a tough time handling the stressors in his daily life. He may have had too much on his plate or the disease and its limitation may have been too stressful for him. Or it may have been a combination of both. Nevertheless, the internal mechanisms he was using to cope with these stressors were producing symptoms. His complaints improved when he started counseling and began practicing Yogic breathing. He subsequently took up Yoga exercise as part of his daily routine.

In my opinion, in patients with lung diseases, an internal dialogue of "I cannot live life fully" dominates their existence. These patients may not even be aware of this internal dialogue. I have also seen this in people who are smokers. I frequently ask my patients who smoke how they inhale the smoke. I pose the following question: "When you pull smoke from your cigarette, do you take a half breath or a full, deep breath?" Most of my patients tell me that they take an incomplete breath. Some of them even say that they just take a few small breaths of the smoke and then discard the cigarette. Obviously, it appears that there are several ways of inhaling smoke, but the general tendency is to take an incomplete breath. It is because of the inability to take a full breath, not tied to a physical problem, but because of a mental inhibition. This inhibition probably comes from an internal conflict or a dialogue.

Let's suppose you go on a well-deserved vacation to a cabin in the country along a nice river or lake or to a beachfront cottage. The very first time you enter the cottage and open the windows, what do you do? You take a nice deep breath.

Most of us do this even when we simply open the windows in our own home. This is taking in the breath of life. This action is not a conscious one, but a spontaneous reaction that is part of our programming. This reaction is impaired in patients who develop lung diseases. Later on, if the disease progresses, they may develop a physical limitation that truly limits their ability to take in life fully. This feeling—when it comes from the mental inhibition or from the physical impairment—is not a pleasant feeling. It is therefore important to get rid of this feeling at the earliest possible stages rather than continue to smoke.

Have you ever experienced an inability to breathe when you get very anxious? Sadness, grief, and subsequent anxiety are in the make-up of people who develop chronic lung diseases. Additionally, when we are profoundly sad or grieving, we find ourselves not taking proper breaths. The key is to search for (and find!) the internal dialogue that is leading to these emotions and eliminate it or deal with it.

Personality or Social being

Personality refers to an individual's characteristic pattern of behavior *driven* by their deeper thoughts and emotions. This is modified by their rules of conduct to suit the outside world. In other words, it is the primal self modified to suit the outside world and society in order to be accepted.

The characteristics of the first patient I've described in this chapter confirm the personality tendency of reacting negatively to life events and being very sensitive to emotions and feelings. If we want to conquer our internal dialogue and its derivative behavior, we need to first understand how we most often behave, in a general sense. This can be done by undergoing a personality test. Once you understand your rules of engagement through understanding your personality, you can then determine how the internal dialogue portion of your You Power is manifesting itself through your behavior. You may simply find out that you reach for a cigarette whenever you are confronted with a particular internal dialogue. Understanding this will aid in changing your behavior pattern.

For example, if you find yourself smoking, reactively, whenever you are anxious, the key is to first find out why that emotion (in this case, anxiety) prompts you to pick up the cigarette. The next step is to figure out what triggered that particular emotion. Was it your work environment, interactions with family members, performing some action like driving, or just being alone? Once you determine the triggers, it is easy to then learn (through counseling) to adapt a different way of coping with the trigger and the resulting emotion.

In the case of the first patient example I've used in this chapter, you may have noticed that the patient developed symptoms when he became overwhelmed by several stressors in his life. He felt as though he was being prevented from living life to the fullest by the overwhelming responsibilities he carried. Because he was sensitive to his feelings, he reported physical symptoms of suffocation as he communicated them to us. He could, on the other hand, have chosen another way of behaving (like smoking) to address these feelings of suffocation.

The second patient had a different coping style. He stopped his medication in response to some trigger. And that action led to the loss of his life.

It is therefore important to understand your style of function and coping methods, or what we call *social behavior,* to help you prevent a downward spiral that may have serious consequences.

Chapter Nine

The Power of You

Be – Do – Have

I control my outcomes.

At one point or another, we are all victims of our reality—real or perceived. It is the same when it comes to health and disease. Shifting from victim to victor—someone who sees more than the visible truth and uses that knowledge to his or her benefit—will enable you to emerge as a person who can achieve what you aspire to in life.

Throughout this book I have described three players who make up your health team, partners that partner with you in taking charge of your health and fighting disease. These players are Western medicine, Eastern medicine, and you as the captain of the team. When it comes to the concept of *you,* I have used the terms You Power and the Power of You.

I have explained Western medicine and Eastern medicine in detail in Chapter One, but have not yet explained You Power in detail. More importantly, I have suggested that *who you are*—the being that you present in your primal and social life—plays a significant role in health, disease, and how they play out in your life. This chapter delves into You Power... the Power of You and the importance of the **Be–Do–Have** principle.

The elephant and the blindfolded doctors

There are many versions of this parable, and it is a story that illustrates the risks of believing that the totality of anything is represented by any one of its parts. I think you'll see how dangerous this limited thinking can be.

As the original story goes... six blind men were asked to describe an elephant. Each of the blind men felt a different part of the elephant and reported his findings. Each man's inspection was limited to a single part of the elephant and from those isolated identifications each claimed to know what the subject of their analysis looked like.

I like this parable because it can easily be applied to health care. In our case, let us replace the six blind men with blindfolded doctors and use the elephant to symbolize a patient [Figure 1]. Anyone who has obtained multiple opinions—from six "blindfolded" (figuratively speaking) physicians—related to an illness, disease, or a condition will attest to the truth it reveals: It's hard to find six physicians who agree on a single diagnosis, the single best course of treatment or a wellness program. It's just like the six blindfolded doctors trying to describe an elephant using only their sense of touch—and focusing on only one part of the animal. They miss the whole picture.

The doctors in this story offer a variety of descriptions for the elephant—and maintain that their subjective description is the correct one. Each of them is convinced that the limited area of the elephant to which they have access is representative of the entire elephant. More importantly, I think, is that they are confident that their limited exposure and experience is sufficient to describe *the whole* of the animal and to dispute the others' exposure and experience.

Their findings?

- The doctor who felt the trunk describes that the elephant is like a snake.

- The second doctor who felt the tusks describes that the elephant is like a spear.

- The third doctor who felt the ears describes that the elephant is like a fan.

- The fourth that felt the body describes that the elephant is like a wall.

- The fifth that felt the legs describe the elephant is like a tree trunk.

- The sixth doctor who felt the tail describes that the elephant is like a rope.

They are all right—and they are all wrong!

While each man's subjective experience related to a specific part is true, the totality of truth or the conclusions that are drawn are far from accurate. The story of these "blind" men and the elephant illustrates not only the current mindset of health care practitioners of all kinds, but also our individual thought processes, as human beings, related to health and disease. Today most all health practitioners do the same when it comes to health and medicine—they function from an understanding of one part of a situation as opposed to an understanding of its totality.

Figure 1: The concept of six blindfolded doctors attempting to describe the totality (of an elephant) through exposure to only a part of it.   Source: blogspot.com

In my experience, all of us do this type of isolated inspection (and "diagnosis") on a daily basis in many areas of our lives. And it is no different when it comes to our personal concept or understanding of health. This is because the parts often appear greater than the whole.

Let me put this into a real-world perspective. I often see patients who take one issue and fixate on it. Then they relate all of their problems to that particular issue. For example, I hear things like *I am always getting stomachaches*. Or *I'm sure I have an allergy to gluten. This week I'm constipated, and I'm sure it's from the gluten allergy I diagnosed myself with last week*. I think you can see the point I'm trying to make here.

In this example, the patient is quick to mentally justify his or her ill health, rather than look within themselves and work to acknowledge the real cause. The actual cause could be poor diet, excess weight, stress, lack of exercise, unhappiness...the list could go on and on and might include things like what they were doing at the time the aches began. This list of activities or circumstances could include being around a specific person, performing a certain task, or feeling emotional turmoil.

This is why totality is so important, as is getting in-tune with You.

I've found that when someone gets ill, the illness prevails and, subjectively, all that person thinks about is the illness...and what its consequences could be.

In Western medicine, if the disease is heart-related, we focus on the cardiovascular system; if it is in the lungs then the focus is on the lungs. This example describes several medical specialties, but only *one* aspect of medical practice: Western medicine. What about Naturopathy, Homeopathy, Acupuncture, Osteopathy, Chiropractic therapy, spiritual therapy, herbal therapy, and nutritional supplements? There is a group of people (practitioners and patients) who claim that only Naturopathy is the answer to disease. Others claim that Acupuncture and traditional Chinese medicine are the answer. Yet another sector of both practitioners and patients claim that Ayurvedic medicine or Homeopathy is the best course. And a biomedical practitioner, of course, would claim that Western medicine is the answer.

From a patient perspective, I have known several people who refuse to see a biomedical practitioner—a Western-medicine doctor—even for regular health maintenance screenings and tests. Likewise, there are others who refuse to use other modalities, such as chiropractic manipulation, Acupuncture, or nutritional therapy, even when they are fully aware that biomedicine alone cannot help them. In their subjective experience, they are all right...yet, at the same time, they are also all wrong. It all comes down to a **lack of totality.**

Today, thousands of self-help books advise, "Do this and don't do that." Or "Eat this, rather than that." And "Practice this— but not that!" The media bombards us with health programs, and Special Reports and commercials that tell us what we need to do to be healthy. Magazines portray attractive and toned bodies and suggest various nutritional, physical, and herbal solutions that claim to help us be the best we can be.

Worst of all, perhaps, are the drug companies that advertise their newest discoveries in mainstream media and ask you to "talk with your doctor"—just before rattling off a laundry list of possible side effects that include "thoughts of suicide" and death! Biomedical practitioners and alternative medical practitioners alike will tell you that *what they do* is best for you. But, in fact, many of them oppose the other practices. This one-or-the-other attitude couldn't be farther from the truth when it comes to how to approach complete health and wellness. None of us—not the Western or the Eastern medical practitioners—is right in a collective sense. **We are all like the blind men trying to describe a complete elephant with only the knowledge of one aspect or one piece of the totality.**

I am not suggesting that health practitioners give you bad advice. I am merely pointing out that, in most cases, they are addressing only parts of the problem, parts that lie within their specialty or expertise. And, with that myopic vision, often ignore the totality. It is up to each of us to focus on (and figure out!) the totality. And that, sadly, is where we have little or no help.

Although each of the multitude of health 'recommendations' may be sound—in and of itself—it's no wonder that we seldom see the results we want or expect. More often than not we are addressing only isolated parts of the body, and not the whole, integrated being. I have observed this consistently in patients. They get recommendations from me, related to the Western medical point of view, and from their Naturopathic doctor and follow these recommendations to the letter. Yet, despite these efforts, they do not get better.

In other words: No one can tell you what—in totality—is best for you. The reason for this is two-fold. First, no single practitioner understands the totality of health. And secondly, no one practitioner can understand the totality of *you*. They can guide you, but you and you alone to the best of your ability need to determine the ultimate path that is best for you.

So...the million-dollar question: How do we do that? The process starts by developing a simple, working understanding of ourselves. If I compiled a list of all the recommendations that are supposed to be good for us and gave it to you, you would never be able to do them all in your lifetime. So how do we choose what recommendations fit each of us best?

How did patients who are successful in maintaining good health and fighting disease do it? **They do it by understanding themselves.**

It comes down to how we handle information in our lives. My perspective is that what you *do* is less important than *who you are*. Why? Because who you are—what you are *being*—drives what you do. If the *being* part of your life is aligned with what you want to *do* then the doing leads to what you want to *have*. Hence the process described as **Be–Do–Have** is the key to success in all aspects of our lives.

As I described in all eight of the previous chapters on diseases, it is the *intention* (the internal dialogue and the primal being*) behind the doing* that matters most. Intention is you, and what you *do* (as a social being) is a derivative of that intention. Understanding the context for this concept and fully adopting the *doing* into what and who you are, makes you *you*, the totality of who you are.

Hence my recommendation: **It is not what you must do, but who you must *be*, to achieve an effective and productive outcome in addressing health and wellness. Said another way: *Doing* is partial and *being* is total.**

One difficulty you may face is that *being* requires an understanding of how we operate as human beings. And understanding how we operate requires knowledge of all aspects of our total being. There are several ways to look at a human being. When it comes to understanding ourselves, we are often like the blind men with the elephant! This was my problem—until my heart attack. When I faced the potential of cardiac arrest I came face-to-face with the unknown.

It was that day that I realized I had been playing the game with the right teammates—utilizing both Western and Eastern medicines. But I was only doing what was recommended by the two medical practices. Within myself, the primal and social beings were separated and in conflict. Even though I exercised, meditated and practiced Yoga, obtained Acupuncture treatments, and ate right, my internal dialogues and the behavior driven by those internal dialogues were not addressed. My *be*-ing was not optimal. It was no surprise that, even as an expert in both Western and Eastern medicine, I was unable to fully reap the benefits of both. The same has been true for most of my patients, and I believe it will be for you as well.

Over the years I have questioned how and why I failed to experience and enjoy good health—despite having all the right information and doing all the right things. I was a doctor, after all. I knew what to do and why I should do it. And I was conscientious in my pursuit of a healthy lifestyle. On October 11th 2006, I realized why. On that day, at 44 years of age, I experienced a heart attack because my *being* was not optimal. I asked myself: *I am an expert when it comes to health and disease, how can I not have an optimal being?*

I realized that being an expert in Eastern and Western medicine has nothing to do with optimal being. Optimal being requires understanding one's internal self. My problem was that I did not have a structure that I could use consistently to understand myself. I later realized that this was also the case with all my patients.

Since then, I've come to realize that a simple, fundamental structure is needed to identify and understand ourselves, as humans. From that realization came the development of a basic operational structure that is easy to understand and can be used over and over again—not only related to health, but in every aspect of our lives. The rest of this chapter is devoted to an introduction of this basic operational structure, as I understand it, based on Eastern and Western philosophies, observation of thousands of patients, and their interactions with every aspect of their total being.

Human Interaction: The H-I Triangle

Ever since I was introduced to Yoga at the age of 17, I have been curious about who I truly am. My continued training in Yoga and Buddhist meditation further fueled that curiosity. I was taught that a human being is more than the physical self.

However, my observation of others—especially several hundred patients who were experiencing varying degrees of stress in life-and-death situations—gave me an opportunity to develop a deeper understanding of the four levels at which humans function: physical, mental, emotional, and spiritual. And when I was lying in the Emergency Room bed following my own heart attack and watching the abnormal beats of my own heart on the heart monitor—what I knew, as a doctor, to be a predecessor to sudden death—my mind transcended to a level previously unknown to me. At that moment, all other levels that I had known and functioned within up to that point—the physical, mental, emotional, and spiritual—evaporated and the only thing that remained was this "UNKNOWN" state.

Although I knew that there are actions that could be performed to resuscitate a person in the event of sudden cardiac arrest, the outcome of those measures is never guaranteed. I have defibrillated several patients who were experiencing cardiac arrest; some of them survived and some did not. It is a sobering reminder that although we can take action, the outcome is never guaranteed. That is the unknown.

In fact, no one can ever guarantee the outcome of any action. At that point I understood that I was on my own in dealing with the unknown.

The interesting aspect of this level is that, when it appears at the conscious level, there is a sense of calm that we seldom experience. For me, on that day in 2006, this fact came into sharp focus...and, with a startling clarity, the missing pieces fell into place. The puzzle of what has the most influence over our health and disease was finally solved.

As a physician, I had never realized that **no matter what the action or how strongly we can guarantee that action,** *the outcome of the action is always unknown* **until the outcome actually manifests itself.** It took my experience as a patient, in a life-and-death situation, to realize this fundamental truth.

This was my realization that day, nearly a decade ago, as I lay in the ER. It is the same dilemma all of my patients face when they have to make a decision about major interventions regarding their treatment. My patients are always asked to make life-altering decision without the guarantee of a favorable outcome. They are given percentages on possible outcomes, both good and bad. And, at that point, they are dealing with the unknown level of life experience. The same is true when you decide how to invest your money. There is no guarantee on what the actual outcome will be. You weigh the options, consider the percentages, and take a gamble—expecting (and hoping) that the outcome will be favorable.

We, as humans, interact not only with the outside world, but also within ourselves. Most often we think of ourselves as one person. However, when it comes to our interactions—either within ourselves or with the outside world—we function from *several* perspectives (levels or planes) of our self.

We perceive ourselves (and want others to perceive us) from the level at which we originate most of our thoughts, the thoughts that result in our daily actions. Close observation of my patients and myself (through Yogic practices) has resulted in identifying five different levels from which a person appears to function.

There is...	the physical you
	the emotional you
	the mental or intellectual you
	the spiritual you
And finally, there is...	
	the unknown part of you

And while it may seem, at first glance, that these five levels of function represent a complete picture, they are not the complete picture of the *total you*. In additional to the five levels of function, there are two types of *being*. **No matter the level from which we operate, we are being one of two selves, or beings, at the conscious level:** A **Social being,** that is manifested when we interact with the world around us, and a **Primal being**, when we interact within ourselves. Underlying these two selves or beings are our social and primal **instincts.**

I have created a diagram to help us visualize how these components relate to one another. Our understanding of this H-I Triangle, pictured on the following page, starts with the *foundation* for the five different levels of function and the two types of being. That foundation is our genetic make-up or what we inherited that predisposes us to (and strongly influences) a specific outcome of an action. These eight components make up the working model of the total You.

The H-I Triangle

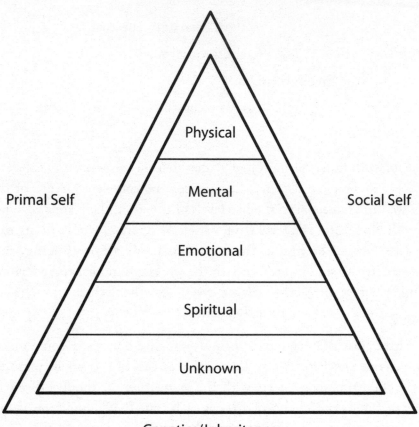

Figure 2: The H-I (Human-Interaction) Triangle. Inside the triangle are the five levels or planes of our day-to-day function. The words *levels* and *planes* are used interchangeably in reference to the H-I Triangle. The boundaries represent Genetics (bottom) and the two types of our being: Primal and Social (the two sides).

The H-I triangle is a diagram of my assessment of the overall components that comprise our existence and functions as humans. When we look at a person, within the context of this triangle, much of their behavior begins to make sense in the broader sense. This clarity and understanding comes from observing people in situations with and without stress, as opposed to psychological insights. The H-I Triangle diagram helps us to understand and assign origins to our inner drives (internal dialogue) and to the modifiers of these drives for actions (personality) and view them more clearly. It is a simple illustration of a person...of you and me.

Let me explain the organization and structure of the Triangle. As detailed in the diagram on the facing page, there are five fundamental levels from which our drive for action manifests. These five levels are depicted in the five interior sections the Triangle. When we want to perform a social action prompted by an internal dialogue, or simply to justify something within ourselves, we turn to one of these five levels and choose which level we want to use. For example, in response to a stressful event or a conflict within us...

- Some of us will go for a run or exercise to deal with it – physical
- Some of us will rationalize the thoughts and feelings to explain it – mental
- Some of us will express it emotionally and act out – emotional
- Some of us will turn to prayer and religion to deal with it – spiritual
- Some of us will transfer the weight onto hope and just keep going – unknown

The level at which you choose to engage at any given moment is determined by the predominant intelligence that drives the action. In fact, every action you perform on a daily basis can be associated with one of the five levels in this triangle.

The physical: You are driven by your physical intelligence.

The emotional: You are driven by your emotional intelligence.

The mental: You are driven by your mental intelligence.

The spiritual: You are driven by your spiritual intelligence.

The unknown: You are driven by the universal intelligence.

With the exception of the universal intelligence, all other intelligences are partially inherited and partially acquired. Universal intelligence, on the other hand, does not belong to us. We are, rather, a part of it. And, therefore, we share it with every other living being as well as non-living matter. (Yes, even non-living matter is an energetic, although inert, manifestation.)

With this understanding, embracing your You Power should be a little easier. I use the H-I Triangle not only to understand and be mindful of what goes on within myself, but to understand my patients who come from many different races, cultures, religions, and backgrounds. The H-I triangle transcends race, culture, religion, and ethnicity. In using this method, I have found myself able to accept a person for who he or she is, without judgment, and suggest behavior modifications that will enhance their You Power.

I believe that You Power is the most important, but frequently ignored, player in the game of health and disease. And an essential component in gaining greater control of your health.

Closing Thoughts

The "second opinions" described in this book are an attempt to give you—readers and my fellow humans—a bird's eye view of the interactions among health, disease, Western medicine, and Eastern medicine, as well as the playing field on which health interactions occur. My hope is that the information contained in this book will shift the power on this playing field to your advantage and make you a winner. And winning means greater control over your health and well-being.

The precise outcome of any activity in life always includes an element of *chance*, an aspect I call The UNKNOWN. This aspect is constantly present in our life whether we acknowledge it or not. Winning in health and disease depends on how well we increase the influence of our *effort* and decrease the influence of *chance* in this game. And the influence of *chance* can only be reduced by educating ourselves on the resources and options that will enable us to increase the *effort* we put into staying healthy and fighting disease—and knowing how, when, and where to utilize those resources.

In the opening chapters of this book, in an attempt to understand the interaction between *effort* and *chance*, I proposed the 30:30:30:10 Rule. The players that contribute to the respective percentages of effort in this game—Western medicine, Eastern medicine, and your You Power—should all be very familiar to you by now. The ultimate question is whether or not you will *choose* to involve all three players, versus merely two players or only a single player, to increase the odds of success for your effort. If you play with Western medicine alone, the proportions shift to 30 percent Western medicine *effort* and 70 percent *chance*. The same is true if your team plays with only Eastern medicine. If you involve two players in any of the combination—Western and Eastern medicine, or Western medicine and your You Power, or Eastern medicine and You Power—the balance shifts to 60 percent effort and 40 percent chance. Changing the odds is something each of us can control and our odds of winning at the health game can increase significantly.

We have seen examples of the dynamic nature of the states of health and ill health—this dance between *effort* and *chance*—in many of the patient stories I've used as illustrations in this book.

I encourage you, and challenge you, to take this a step farther. If you choose to involve all three players then your strategy will look like this: 90 percent effort and 10 percent chance. I will take those odds any day!

Finally, if you choose to embrace the role as an active captain of your health team by strengthening and *engaging* your You Power, the odds of winning get even better.

A question posed early in this book was whether Western medicine and Eastern medicine, in combination, could be a game-changer in the quest for health and wellness and the fight against disease. It's quite likely that, after reading this book, you now see this question as a moot point. A new and more relevant question, I believe, is: What is the best strategy for using these modalities in combination throughout our lives as we navigate the continuum of health and wellness, disease, and death?

Western medicine understands disease by looking at *biochemical* and *structural* changes. Eastern medicine understands disease by *energy imbalances* and *energetic changes*. Energetic changes occur before biochemical changes occur—which is why awareness of changes in energy can, truly, mean the difference between life and death. How often do we hear that "early detection" and treatment of disease increases the odds of beating it? This is yet another perspective on the many ways Eastern and Western medicines complement each other and offer us humans the best of both worlds.

The progression from health to disease follows a path that Figure 1 illustrates:

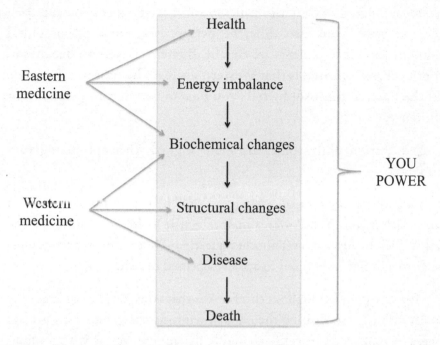

Figure 1: The sequence involved in the development of disease and how different players influence its progression.

An understanding of the progression depicted above allows us to determine exactly where to position the players involved in the game of health and disease. The captain, you armed with your You Power, will be involved through the entire progression and therefore have an opportunity to influence the outcome at any of the levels or the stages that the diagram details.

My intention is that this simple diagram makes the point that there is one element, one factor or variable, which can stop the progression of disease and control the entire process. That factor is you—and your You Power.

Yet, as difficult as I find this to fathom, the influence of our You Power—our power to be mindful of our bodies and our minds, our complete selves—is not the norm (let alone the optimal goal) in health care today. Because Western medicine and Eastern medicine approach a disease state from two different perspectives, their philosophical recommendations to patients are equally different. **Based on decades of experience, my opinion is that Western philosophy tells us *what to do* and the Eastern philosophy tells you *how to be*. That is a significant difference.**

And Eastern philosophies are more aligned with optimizing your You Power.

Both your *doing* and your *being* can only be successful in impacting your health if your You Power is maintained at its highest, most optimal level. Which brings us to yet another question: What type of person must you *be* to *do* what is required to achieve optimal health?

My suggestion throughout this book is that your You Power holds the utmost influence in shifting the odds of winning the game of health and disease in your favor. This life-changing dynamic leaves us with a simple sequence of Be–Do–Have.

> Being = You Power
>
> Doing = Action and a commitment to being healthy
>
> Having = Health

To live a healthy, disease-free life is what all of us strive for. Good health allows us to enjoy life to the fullest and experience all that it has to offer. And wealth, without health, can be worth little...as so many, with means, would attest as they struggle with or are limited by illness and disease.

Life is an amazing journey and our minds and our bodies are nothing short of miraculous in their ability to function, reproduce, excel to incredible heights, fight disease, and even heal themselves. Our minds not only contribute to living mindfully—fully aware of our bodies and the world around us—but to the discipline and focus and commitment that **will bring out our most powerful selves, our You Power at its strongest.**

If we are open to seeing every side of the health and wellness coin, embracing every opportunity to use all that the world of medicine can offer and harnessing the incredible power that's within us, I have no doubt that you can bring the full force of your You Power to address every aspect of your health and wellness. We can emerge as victors, not victims, on the playing field of health and wellness, and empower ourselves in ways that can tip the scales, the balance between *effort* and *chance,* in ways that can mean a life that personifies *complete well being* and is rich in every way.

Healthcare... or Wealthcare

by Robert Kiyosaki

We all know the rich are getting richer. And the gap between the rich and everyone else grows ever wider.

The same is true for health. The rich grow healthier, while the health of the poor and middle class declines.

The October 2, 2015 issue of *The Week* magazine stated, *"The gap in life expectancy between rich and the poor is growing. An upper income 50-year-old man is now expected to live until 89. A lower-income man of that age has a life expectancy of 76. For women, the corresponding life expectancies are 92 and 78."*

Obviously, there are many reasons for this gap in life expectancy among rich, middle class, and poor. One reason is food. For example, there is a large construction site near my office. Every day, a "roach coach," a mobile lunch truck, pulls up at 11:00 am. Peeking over the shoulders of the workers, I was shocked at both the selection and their food choices: potato chips, corn chips, soft drinks, and candy bars. The plate lunches were fatty protein smothered in sauces, starches, sugars, and fats. No fresh vegetables or fruits anywhere. Although I am sure the food is tasty, I would not feed my dog food from the "roach coach."

Now you may say it's the fault of the "roach coach." But "roach coach owners"—like other purveyors of fast food—only provide what the customer wants. If customers wanted carrots and bananas the roach coach would sell carrots and bananas.

Another reason for the gap in health and longevity is because our medical system is an Emergency Room system. Many people only see a doctor in the event of an emergency.

A very big reason for this is money. The poor and middle class have less and less money to invest in their health.

For example, I can afford to fly from Phoenix to New York for health checkups with Radha. I can also afford to fly to London, for iridology checkups with Ravi, one of Radha's teachers. I have also flown to Costa Rica for a medical procedure, performed by an American doctor, but not available in the United States.

In Scottsdale, Arizona, I pay regular visits to an ND, a Naturopathic Doctor. His waiting room is like a professional sports locker room. Every time I visit his office, I want to carry my autograph book! Sitting next to me are healthy, young, professional football, baseball, and basketball stars I see on television. These young millionaire athletes visit the ND, **as well as their MD, because their health is their wealth.** If they are not **at peak physical health, they lose their multi-million dollar jobs.** They go to this ND because he can perform procedures medical doctors do not perform, procedures insurance companies do not cover, procedures the average person has never heard of, and procedures the average person cannot afford.

The reason Dr. Gopalan's book is included in the Rich Dad family of books is because our health, wealth, and happiness are all related.

One of the reasons why the gap between the rich and everyone else widens is because we have no financial education in our schools. Today, governments of the world are printing money, causing to prices to go up for essential items such as food and and healthcare, making life more expensive for the poor and middle class.

Without financial education, people have little knowledge of the crisis the world economy faces. Today, millions of people are working longer—

sometimes working two and three jobs—and earning more, which means they're paying higher taxes. And yet these hard-working people grow poorer and less healthy.

One reason why healthcare is so expensive is because *health care* has become *wealth care*. It is not just the doctors who are getting rich. Our healthcare has been taken over by insurance companies, pharmaceutical companies, accountants, and trial lawyers.

In the same October 2, 2015 issue of *The Week* magazine I saw an article titled, Pharma: Outcry follows massive drug-price hike. The article states that Turing Pharmaceuticals CEO Martin Shkreli became the face of price gouging this week after his company abruptly raised the price of a 62-year old drug from $13.50 a pill to $750. You would think the company would have covered their research and development costs after 62 years. This is one blatant, but not exceptional, example of *health care* becoming *wealth care*.

And, in my opinion, it's absolutely disgusting.

The *This Week* article also reported that Congress is likely to continue to resist any proposals to lower drug prices, given how influential pharmaceutical companies are in the political process. The industry doled out nearly $22 million in campaign contributions in the 2014 elections, rewarding friends and punishing enemies, and spend another $229 million on lobbying.

I'll say it again: It's disgusting.

Recently I was in the hospital for "observation." I was shocked to find, on my itemized list of expenses, a $10 charge for an aspirin, $6 for the paper cup the aspirin was delivered in, and $12 for the nurse to hand me the paper cup with the aspirin in it. That was just the start. My total bill for an overnight stay was $34,000. Thankfully I only had to pay $7,000, since my insurance company covered the rest. I wonder what my bill might have been, had I not had insurance.

Recently, another medical doctor friend of mine said, "I am getting out of medicine because I do not like what I see coming." His fear is that insurance companies will take over hospitals. He said, "Once insurance companies control the hospitals, they will turn self-employed, private-practice physicians into employees, working for a medical system based around a large hospital." In other words, he is afraid he will soon be working for hospital CEOs and CFOs who will tell doctors what they can and cannot do. In other words: accountants and attorneys may soon be "playing doctor."

Another medical doctor friend gave me a bit of disturbing information. He is an ICU (Intensive Care Unit) physician who said, "Fifty percent of patients who are treated in an ICU, are forced to declare bankruptcy." In other words, you might be a person who is young and healthy—someone who eats healthy, exercises, and has no bad habits—yet for some reason meets with a catastrophic event, requiring care in the ICU. When in ICU, many medical bills are not covered by insurance, often wiping out healthy people, financially.

And another medical doctor friend confided in me, saying, "I do not accept Medicare or Medicaid patients. I can't afford to treat them. As a group, these patients tend not to take care of themselves, tend not to follow my instructions, and tend to sue their doctor, blaming the doctor for their problems. Rather than get better, they tend to get worse."

We at Rich Dad support Dr. Gopalan's work because we do not believe money alone will solve our personal challenges of health, wealth, and happiness.

For example, a recent article in *TIME* magazine, the August 31, 2015 issue, states, "It takes more than money to fix broken schools." The article describes the failure of Mark Zuckerberg's $100-million donation to Newark, N.J. schools to "turn Newark into a symbol of educational excellence for the whole nation."

The article goes on to state, "Five years later, most of Zuckerberg's $100 million has been spent, and Newark is no one's model for education excellence. In fact, student achievement in the troubled district has gone down, not up, on the state's standardized tests." This is what happens when we turn the education of our children over to the government. I fear the same will be true of health care.

Even if you are not rich, by following the lessons in Dr. Gopalan's book you can afford to give yourself the best healthcare in the world. It does not cost much for you to sit quietly and tune into *you*. It is important for you to be proactive about your physical, mental, emotional, and spiritual health—as well as your financial health. Your medical doctor needs all the help he or she can get to keep you healthy.

The Rich Dad Company supports Dr. Gopalan's work because we believe our health, wealth, and happiness are our personal responsibilities and not the responsibility of the government, teachers, hospitals, or doctors.

Afterword

Something, or someone, compelled you to pick up this book. Curiosity or concern, quite likely, moved you to read it. But now what?

In *Second Opinion*, I have proposed some interesting, even controversial, thoughts and insights. Whether or not you choose to embrace them is your decision.

I will leave you with two parting thoughts as I close this book. The first is this: What if?

What if combining Eastern and Western medicine practices could make a difference in your health and wellness? What if taking the time to explore your You Power and how it could, quite literally, mean the difference between life and death? What do you have to lose by taking a path that allows you to put all the resources at your disposal to work for you? Is there a downside? And, more importantly, what might you gain?

And the second thought... another question: What now?

What will you do with this new information, this expanded perspective on the power of combining the very best that both Eastern and Western medicine have to offer? How will you strengthen and use your You Power? Will you learn more and apply what you learn? Will you make changes in your lifestyle, in your diet, in your activity levels? In living a more mindful life? Because, as the saying goes: *If nothing changes, nothing changes.*

What will you do with the information I've shared in this book? It's a question only you can answer.

That choice is up to you. And your life may depend upon it.

A Wish...a Goal...or a Plan?

A goal without a plan is just a wish.

I have always believed in the saying "Give a man a fish and you feed him for a day; Teach a man to fish and you feed him for a lifetime." I implement this principle when I teach medical students, residents, and fellows in my practice. Rather than giving them the information that's needed, I challenge myself to stimulate their thinking and let them find the answer for themselves. My reason behind writing this book is to bring knowledge regarding health, disease, and our You Power into the hands of the consumer in the form of a second opinion, different points of view presented to stimulate your thinking. As a result, I have not focused on telling readers what to do. Rather, I have focused on describing the context in which to perform their process of *doing*.

This book has supported the premise that, when it comes to health, **It is not what you do, it is who you must *be*.**

And while I emphasize *being* as the most important determinant of outcome, I do recognize that there are activities that we can perform that reciprocally influence our being. So, for those of you who are hungry for what needs to be *done* in the world of heath and disease, I have shared some (but not all) of the activities that can positively affect your You Power and the role you can play in driving positive health outcomes. The following pages will give you a glimpse of what I would like to suggest to my patients—and, now, my readers.

Each of these routines and health practices affects different levels of your being, which are also levels within the H-I Triangle and, as discussed in Chapter 9, a key to unlocking the Power of You. When you combine all of these levels, you influence the entire H-I Triangle —and thus your entire being. Remember, health results from balance. And balance of a person relates to all five levels of the H-I Triangle. Therefore, regular, pro-active routines that enhance all levels of our function as human beings should be incorporated into our lifestyle to enjoy healthy living to the fullest extent possible.

On the following pages I am suggesting routines that I regularly incorporate into my life to balance the five levels.

Daily and Weekly Health Care Routines

1. Long walks… holding hands with someone you love.

Seldom does a person take long, leisurely walks. Even among people who take daily walks, they are very often purpose-driven in nature. In other words, these walks are often done as part of an exercise routine, work itself or in travel to work, or to walk the dog. While these walks give us physical benefits that may lead to better health, they may not benefit you from the perspective of boosting your You Power. The type of long walk that would benefit your You Power is a walk that has no purpose at all—other than just being with yourself and enjoying whatever comes your way. The focus is to experience life as it comes, without expectation or **judgment, and allowing yourself to embrace the** unknown. It is a **walk that is unhurried.**

With an unhurried walk, every walk is as if you are doing it for the first time. It is like meditating, because meditation also has no purpose and is full of unknowns. When you engage in an activity that has no purpose and from which the results are unknown, it becomes an exhilarating experience—a *true* experience. Such true experiences have the positive psychological benefits by boosting your spirit...as well as the obvious physical benefits that come from physical activity.

The benefits are even better if the walk is associated with the positive experience of love and joy...like walking with someone you love and expressing the emotions of love, joy, and happiness. The benefits of walks like this are numerous and have been shown to reduce the perception of stress, improve a person's sense of well-being, improve longevity, promote weight loss, reduce appetite—as well as reduce the risk of heart disease, diabetes, and high blood pressure, increase bone density, and strengthen bone health.

And last, but certainly not least, this simple exercise can enhance and improve your relationships. Perhaps this is why Hippocrates said, "Walking is man's best friend."

2. Sleep when you're tired.

Lack of sleep has been associated with several aspects of our day-to-day functions and productivity. For example, it has been documented that the lack of sleep affects us in the areas of mood, performance, health, and overall well-being. I can personally attest to this. How do I know this is true? Because, I have experienced *each* of these effects. The worst part (but, perhaps, a necessary part) of medical training is being on call for extended periods of time that results in sleepless nights on a fairly regular basis.

When it comes to our moods, lack of sleep can cause irritability, anxiety, lack of motivation, and symptoms of depression. More importantly, sleep deprivation affects our positive emotions first. In other words, if you are sleep deprived, you may say that you are happy, but you do not *feel* happy, internally. There is a disconnect between what we actually feel and what we communicate. Remember, positive emotions boost your You Power. Losing positive emotions means losing a bit of that power.

With regard to performance, the ill effects of sleep deprivation are numerous. They include the inability to focus and concentrate, attention deficits, lack of energy, fatigue, restlessness, poor decision-making, distractibility, forgetfulness, and delayed reaction times.

When it comes to health, sleep deprivation has been found to be associated with high blood pressure, heart attack, diabetes and obesity—four of the diseases that have been discussed in this book.

Feeling tired is our body's way of telling us that we are sleep deprived. When your body is telling you it's tired, don't drink coffee or an energy drink—make sure you get the sleep that you deserve. If you feel you need too much sleep, then it is time to seek medical assistance. The amount of sleep we need varies from person to person. As a general guide, adults need seven to eight hours of sleep a night to feel invigorated. Teens need about nine hours, and younger children need nine hours or more.

3. Eat a nutrient-rich, balanced diet (and fast for 24 hours each week)

Diet has a lot to do with our physical being and energy levels as well as our emotions, moods, and mental acuity. I did not fully understand the effect of diet on my You Power until I performed a dietary cleanse recommended by my naturopath. After that cleanse, I was able to mindfully add different dietary habits into my daily consumption and witnessed changes in my energy, mood, and mental acuity. This has helped me to create a personal diet plan that best suits me.

Having a well-balanced, nutrient-rich diet that best fits you will aid in overall wellness. Certain foods, drinks, additives (or *lack* of certain nutrients) can negatively affect you. Learn how to read nutritional labels, so that you can make wise food choices. There is no one dietary recommendation that fits everyone. There are however, many nutrients that will benefit most all people. For example, foods that are rich in Omega 3s, such as wild salmon, eggs, flax, nuts, and spinach, act as natural anti-inflammatories and can help lower cholesterol levels. Human beings do not produce Vitamin C, so it must be ingested by eating dark green, leafy vegetables, peppers, citrus fruits, and berries. Vitamin C is a massive antioxidant that offers immune protection. Co Enzyme Q10 helps produce cellular energy, treats a multitude of diseases including heart disease and immune dysfunction, and is found in fatty fish, meat, fruit, and seeds. I recommend heightening your awareness related to food labels, consumption of processed foods, and chemicals, as well as misleading diet and nutrition information. Processed foods and chemicals can lead to inflammation, discomfort, and dysfunction in our body. Consider working with a nutritional specialist who can tailor diet recommendations to your individual needs. And be mindful of subtle intolerances or mood changes based upon your food choices.

Lastly, it is very important to detox your body with a nutritional detoxification cleanse. A nutritional cleanse is a must for anyone who wants to embark on a healthy lifestyle. Once you perform a cleanse it is important to continue to cleanse yourself periodically. Personally, I do nutritional detoxification twice a year.

Another important habit is to incorporate fasting into your weekly dietary regimen. I recommend fasting one day each week, so that over the course of a year you will have the benefit of 52 days of fasting—without even realizing it. Every Friday is a day of fasting in my world. I only drink water and herbal tea from dinner on Thursday evening until dinner on Friday. Consider this: Your stomach and bowels work non-stop due to the frequency of daily eating habits. And I know many people who eat—even when they don't feel hungry. Given the popular dietary recommendation of eating small, healthy snacks every two to three hours throughout the day, the chance of feeling hunger is greatly diminished. Another benefit of weekly, 24-hour fasting is that it helps to teach us how to eat in a mindful way and differentiate between the trigger of true hunger and emotional eating. The ability to do this has a tremendous impact on your You Power. I suggest that you consider fasting once a week as a "reset button" for your digestive system.

One final thought on this subject: Most people are afraid of feeling hungry. In fact, feeling hunger has several benefits when experienced in a controlled fashion. Fasting actually increases longevity, speeds up metabolism, improves insulin sensitivity, improves hunger, helps lose weight, improves brain function, improves immune system function, and helps with self-knowledge and self-enlightenment. All of these are associated with positive health benefits.

4. Practice Yoga and exercise regularly

By this time, you are probably well versed in the benefits of Yoga that I have described in this book. As you now know, Yoga exercise is meant to promote mind-body union. Mind-body union means alignment of your *doing* (with the body) with your *being* (mind). Throughout this book, we have seen how our You Power can help us reap the best results from anything we do and support the principle of Be–Do–Have. Without question, Yoga positively influences your You Power. And Tai Chi has similar benefits.

Exercise and Yoga have been shown to increase the production of oxytocin, a hormone involved in human bonding and love. These activities also promote increased levels of serotonin, a hormone that is associated with happiness. Studies of the brains of long-term practitioners of Yoga have shown more mass in certain areas of the brain associated with the feeling of contentment.

Finally, Yoga and meditation have been shown to influence conditions such as heart disease, insomnia (difficulty sleeping), arthritis, asthma, multiple sclerosis, infertility, post-traumatic stress disorder (PTSD) and chronic back pain.

5. Salt Bath and Neti Pot

The skin is considered the largest organ in our body, yet it is often ignored. Skin, while functioning as a barrier to invading pathogens, can absorb nutrients as well as other chemicals, allowing them to enter our system. Our skin is also an organ of excretion, enabling us to rid the body of toxins.

An Epsom and sea salt bath (containing two cups of Epsom salt to one cup of sea salt) two to three times a week is an excellent way of nourishing and cleansing your skin. Additionally, these salt baths help remove toxins from our body, as well as small amounts of chemicals and heavy metals. If repeated on a regular basis, this cleansing method can be very effective. Many people choose to add therapeutic oils to the bath for aromatherapy benefits and to nourish the skin. The use of Epsom salt also nourishes our body with much-needed magnesium, as it is rich in both magnesium and sulfate. The health benefits of magnesium and sulfate are numerous, as they trigger several chemical reactions within our body, and contribute to nervous system health.

We live in a world filled with pollution and inhale polluted air each day. This means that toxic particles enter our respiratory system on a regular basis. While we do not have a way of cleansing the air passages beyond our throat, we can actively cleanse our nasal passages and sinuses. This is achieved by using a Neti Pot to clear our air passages and help with respiratory illness such as asthma, allergies, and sinus infections.

6. Be humble, and do something selfless for another human

I have repeatedly emphasized the fact that positive emotions are the most powerful influencers of our health and wellness. They elicit joy, happiness, and contentment. Selfless giving also elicits these emotions, which reach our core being and bring that being to our consciousness during daily life.

These acts do not have to be elaborate. Actions as simple as holding a door open for someone or giving positive feedback elevate the mood of both the giver and the receiver. My favorite action is to donate the food that I deprive myself of on my fasting Fridays, or the money that I would spend, to someone who could use a good meal. Giving while enjoying abundance may make us feel good about ourselves, but I believe that giving while depriving ourselves is an even more positive and powerful experience and results in satisfaction and contentment at a deeper level of our being. Tremendous power can be acquired by engaging our core being on a daily basis.

7. Meditation…beyond silence to stillness

The benefits of meditation—the act of reaching mental stillness and beyond—are numerous and positively influence mood, health, relationships, and mindfulness. Meditation leads to a lower perception of stress, improved mental acuity and focus, enhanced sense of contentment and happiness, neutrality of emotions, and improved creativity. With daily practice, we can develop the ability to access the universal energy and reach a state where accomplishments can be realized without much effort. In other words, you are able to affect your reality at a quantum level.

Researchers conducted a study in which a group of people was subjected to mindfulness meditation, with guidance, for an eight-week period. Magnetic resonance imaging (commonly referred to as an MRI) of the brains of those people revealed increased grey matter in the area of the brain that is concerned with learning, memory, regulation of emotions, perspectives, and a sense of self. In only eight weeks…

I believe that emotions and our ability (or inability) to cope with emotions lead to significant imbalances and may have a lot to do with the development of disease. Therefore, developing the ability to manage our emotions and achieving better coping mechanisms for dealing with them can lead to better handling of our internal dialogue which, in turn, influences how we behave. Our behavior over the long term leads each of us to our individual destiny.

8. Prayer…asking for what we need

Prayer influences our spirituality. We can pray for guidance or strength, or with prayers of petition, asking for what we need or for the special intention of others. We can also pray with gratitude, offering thanks for what we have and have been given. Spirituality in medicine is not a new concept, as people have relied on prayer for health, and as a means of overcoming disease, since ancient times.

Prayer helps enhance our self-control, helps us forgive others more easily, increases our ability to trust, reduces stress, and serves to make us (generally and overall…) nicer people.

Interestingly, prayer when used for the benefit of another appears to have more physical and emotional benefits than prayer for material gain. When you pray, you descend down to the core levels of being where the spiritual and unknown levels of our being exit. Prayer, meditation, and selfless acts of kindness are of some of the most powerful ways to balance those deeper levels within your being, as referenced in the H-I Triangle.

You can perform these activities on your own, without the help of trained professionals. But, you do need to dedicate time to perform them on a regular basis. For so many of us, time is a scarce commodity—given all the time commitments in our busy lives—so planning and budgeting time for health and wellness often gets put on the back burner. I succumbed to the same prioritization problem before my heart attack. For those who have a little or no time to invest in their health and well-being, the following actions may offer some benefits. They do, however, cost money. And since we all know that time is money... we can choose to make this investment in one commodity or another. In my opinion, optimal health benefits come from actions that I have described above. The actions that I describe below can provide significant supportive benefits for those of us who have very busy lives.

Monthly, Quarterly and Annual Routines
for Health Maintenance, Youthfulness and Longevity

1. Guidance from a Complementary Medicine Practitioner

Complementary medicine offers natural and alternative treatment methods from a variety of health care practices, treatments that complement Western medicine. These practices are used for health maintenance, longevity, and symptom treatment. I have come across many patients who implement complementary medicine into their life when Western medicine is not helping or offering answers to their ailments. Complementary medicine often involves advanced diagnostic testing, in addition to conventional testing methods. There are many alternative treatment modalities aimed at treating the root cause of the problem. And there are different variations of complementary practitioners, so it is important to find one that has medical training and experience in this specialty, and who also follows safe-practice standards. More importantly, the practitioner you choose should have the ability embrace other practices of medicines.

2. Vitamin Drips

Most patients I see are vitamin deficient and they do not even know it. When I began checking the vitamin panel of my patients, I was astonished to find the degree to which these deficiencies existed. The deficiencies related primarily to vitamins B, C, and D. Almost all of my patients who come to me for heart transplant procedures are deficient in vitamin D. We get our daily dose of vitamins from our diet. If our diet does not contain adequate amounts of these vitamins, over time we will become deficient in those vitamins that can lead to abnormal chemical reactions in our body.

Medicine is advancing rapidly and research is beginning to show the health benefits in the replacement of various vitamins. Custom, high-quality IV vitamin infusions are used for a multitude of symptoms, lifestyle enhancements, and to maximize health maintenance. These IV infusions are typically packed with a variety of vitamins and minerals and have many benefits including reenergizing your cells, improving your immune system and brain function, decreasing stress, aiding in weight loss, detoxification, smoking cessation, and many more. Pre-infusion lab testing should be conducted to determine what your body is deficient in, allowing your custom infusion to maximize your internal wellness.

3. Heavy Metal Detox

Heavy metals—including lead, mercury, aluminum, cadmium, nickel, titanium, gadolinium, and uranium—find their way into our bodies. These substances are found in food, water, wine, lotion, perfume, deodorant, cigarette smoke, imaging procedures, dental fillings, and artificial light sources…to name just a few. We are exposed to significant amounts of heavy metals on a daily basis. Over time, heavy-metal toxicity can lead to manifestation of illness and exacerbate chronic and autoimmune diseases, as these metals accumulate in our organs over the years. Intravenous chelation is recommended as one of the best ways to detoxify our bodies of heavy metals. This treatment consists of one to two infusion bags of chelating agents at each visit. These agents leach the toxins from your organs and facilitate their excretion through your urine.

The important point to remember here is that the presence of these heavy metals in our bodies sneaks up on us…unless the levels are actively checked. For example, many people may experience depression as a result of mercury poisoning but may explain it away to life stress, diet, or lack of exercise without realizing that it could be as simple as an accumulation of heavy metal. Most of these metals have cardiovascular, nervous system, and emotional repercussions if they are present at toxic levels in our body.

4. Prolotherapy or Stem Cell Therapy

This regenerative therapy is often used to treat pain, arthritis and injuries to muscles, ligaments, and cartilage. With stem cell treatment, or what is also called *platelet rich plasma*, blood is withdrawn from the body and spun in a machine to separate the cells and agitate them. With other forms of Prolotherapy, a synthetic or natural irritant solution is used. The cells are then re-injected into the body at the site of injury or pain.. These cells cause local irritation that result in other, inflammatory cells to travel to that area. This starts a brand new healing process.

Imagine a broken or rusted metal beam in your house. If you choose not to replace it, you have two ways to fix it. One way is to place a splint and join them together. The other is to use heat to weld the two ends of the metal beam together with a patch of the same iron material. Prolotherapy is like the welding process. The broken beam is the injured or diseased joint or bone in your body. The fire that irritates and melts the iron is the synthetic irritant (or your own stem cells) that will serve as irritant and provide fresh material for repair. The process of melting and cooling is akin to the inflammatory process that results from an irritant injected into a joint that promotes better healing and repair of the affected area with your own newly introduced stem cells.

5. Acupuncture and Osteopathic/Chiropractic Adjustment

The health benefits of Acupuncture, Chiropractic or osteopathic adjustment have been described in great detail throughout this book and in conjunction with the eight deadly diseases. You may recall that Acupuncture works by balancing our body's vital energy while chiropractic and osteopathic adjustments work to improve musculoskeletal and nervous system health. I use these techniques as a way of maintaining my health and wellness. Monthly Acupuncture and Chiropractic or Osteopathic adjustments every three to five months are great ways to energize and balance your energy. Consider it a boost—or a "re-boot"—to yourself from time to time while living a busy and stressful life in a toxic environment.

6. Hormone Balancing

There are many hormones in our bodies that play key roles in several biochemical reactions, also known as *the hormone cascade.* They can affect your mood, memory, stress levels, weight, sleep, sex drive, bone strength, and organs including the heart, brain, thyroid, and adrenal glands. Optimizing your hormone levels can lead to increased immunity, sense of well-being, longevity, and retardation of the aging process (or anti-aging). There are many specialized tests that can be run, and monitored if treatment is initiated. (These tests are much more in-depth and advanced than the conventional tests and treatments a Western practitioner may routinely recommend and carry out). Further, if treatment is initiated, bio-identical hormones can be prescribed. These are natural forms of hormones delivered via pills, creams, or injections. They are specially made to fit your chemical makeup.

7. Emotional Cleansing

In my opinion, just as nutritional cleansing is important prior to embarking on restorative and health maintenance activities, emotional cleansing is equally important. This aspect has a very close relationship to your You Power. The emotional baggage that we carry drags us down and prevents us from realizing our optimal health. It is important to start with a clean slate by "erasing" or getting rid of all the negative emotional baggage and replacing it with positive emotions. Remember: positivity begets positivity.

There are several ways to accomplish emotional cleansing. We can use a psychological counselor, biofeedback mechanisms, hypnosis, cognitive therapy, behavioral therapy, life coaches, or similar methods. There are also simple daily activities that can help maintain emotional balance once a person has achieved a degree of cleanse. These are meditation, prayer, and regular exercise. Meditation can actually help with emotional cleansing and can have a significant impact over time with daily practice. In fact, meditation allows us to meet the underlying emotional conflicts and deep-down, internal dialogues at a level at which they have limited power and thus we are able to handle and eliminate them effectively.

8. Massage and Reflexology

The health benefits of massage and reflexology have also been described in detail throughout this book. I would like to emphasize that they are part of my health and wellness practice. I also believe that there is no downside to incorporating them into anyone's health and wellness routine. I use these methods periodically (massage every two weeks and reflexology every six months) as a stress-relief technique and to keep my body's energy at a balanced state.

Remember, the more you focus on balance within yourself, the better degree of balance you will achieve. Energy balance is like water in a well. The more water you take out of the well, the more water will replenish it. Energy balance in humans is similar and is unique to each one of us.

Energy spent on the creation of positive energy results in more positive energy. You will appreciate the benefits only when you *feel* the benefits of performing these activities—activities that reciprocally energize your You Power—that, I believe, are the single most important factor in determining the outcome of health and disease.

Not All Health Care Providers Are Created Equal

Thoughts and Observations from Dr. Gopalan

- Each health care provider is different. This applies to both Eastern and Western medical professionals. Health care is an art, not a science. Therefore, you will find providers with many different opinions, judgments, levels of expertise, integrity, and care.

- Get a Second Opinion.
  Make sure you are aligned with your own health care decisions

- Don't take advice from just anyone…i.e. media, advertisements, friends, or co-workers.
  As Robert Kiyosaki has said, "Free advice is the worst advice."

- Find health care providers that are aligned with your health and wellness vision—preferably someone who is an advocate of both Eastern and Western modalities.

- When looking for a source for personality testing, emotional or dietary cleanse, nutrition, a referral, health care, or wellness seek assistance from a professional in these realms, or a professional who can direct you to someone that can assist you..

- Build an honest and trusting relationship with your providers.

- Be an influence in your own health and wellness outcomes. Remember, you are the captain of your team and can influence the outcome of the game. Your You Power is *powerful…* use it!

Most important of all is your relationship with your doctors and practitioners…as well as all the relationships in your life that positively create love, trust, and respect. Each of these relationships is essential if we are to take control of our health and our lives. If you are to avail yourself of all that Eastern and Western medicine have to offer and leverage your You Power in ways that can enhance all facets of your self, you can lead a healthy, balanced, productive, rich, and meaningful life.

About the Author

Radha Gopalan, MD

Born in northern Sri Lanka, Dr. Radha Gopalan started his medical education at North Colombo Medical College in 1985. When civil unrest put his studies on hold, he seized the opportunity to become an acupuncturist at the International University for Complementary Medicines. While already well versed in Eastern and Western philosophies of medicine, in 1990, Dr. Gopalan transferred to St. Georges University to complete his medical degree.

By 1993, Dr. Gopalan's interest in Eastern philosophy took him to London, where he worked as an acupuncturist with the acclaimed Dr. Ravi Ponniah. Again, East met West as he observed the integration of Acupuncture, Homeopathy, Osteopathy and herbs in the treatment of patients. After mastering the art of complementary medicine, Dr. Gopalan returned to the United States for further post-graduate training in-Internal Medicine.

Dr. Gopalan received additional fellowship training in Cardiology, Heart Rhythm Disorders, and Heart Transplant, and is board certified. Additionally, he is board certified in Medical Acupuncture, and is a certified instructor and an avid practitioner of Yoga and meditation. After working in Scottsdale, Arizona for several years, he now lives and practices in New York City.

Glossary

A

Acupuncture
A system of medical philosophy with its origins in ancient Traditional Chinese Medicine and based on the theory of the five elements (fire, water, metal, earth and wood) of which we are believed to be made and the theory of energy balance between two opposing forces of energy called Yin and Yang.

Acupuncture Channels
The pathways related to specific organ systems in the body and along which energy flows. In Acupuncture, these pathways are said to be located between muscles in a plane that Western medicine calls "connective tissue."

Acupuncture points
These are points on the surface of the skin that are numbered and located along the Acupuncture channels pertaining to an organ. These points are stimulated with Acupuncture needles to influence the energy flow along the channel. These points are said to have low electrical resistance compared with other areas on the surface of the body.

affect
A psychological term denoting expression of emotions or feeling. Affect can be expressed through facial expressions (like surprise) or with hand gestures, tone of voice, or other means such as crying or laughing.

autonomic nervous system
A part of the nervous system that regulates involuntary functions including heart beat, functions of the stomach or intestines, and blood pressure. This part of the nervous system is not under our voluntary control therefore we cannot influence this nervous system. A "fight or flight" response is another example of the function of autonomic nervous system.

arteries
Blood vessel pathways that travel from the heart to the cells of the body delivering oxygenated blood

atrial fibrillation
An abnormal rhythm of the heart. This rhythm results from the top chambers of the heart called *atria*. In this condition, the atria exhibits an irregular, uncoordinated, and rapid beating and as a result the atria appear to be quivering instead of contracting and relaxing in a rhythmic fashion that is typical of normal heart rhythm.

autoimmune disease
Autoimmune diseases are conditions that result from our body attacking itself. The body normally produces killer cells and other products called "antibodies" to destroy bacteria and viruses that invade our bodies. These killer cells and antibodies attack unwanted bacteria and viruses and kill them to protect us from infection. In the case of autoimmune disease, our body produces these antibodies and killer cells against the cells of our own body through a mistaken identity.

Ayurveda
This is a traditional ancient Indian medical system and is an Eastern medical philosophy. The Ayurvedic medical system believes that we are made up of five elements—air, water, earth, fire and ether. These elements combine to make up three predominant energy axes in us called Vata (air and ether), Pitta (water and fire), and Kapha (water and earth). In the Ayurvedic medical system, fundamental abnormalities of health and ill health are explained related to these three energy axes called Vata, Pitta, and Kapha.

B

blood clot
A blood clot is exactly that: clotted blood. It consists of a collection of blood cells, clotting factors, and many other substances from the blood. A blood clot can completely block a blood vessel if it is large enough.

blood urea nitrogen or BUN
A chemical substance that is measured in the blood as part of evaluating the functions of the kidneys. When functioning normally, the cells in our body produce waste products that contain nitrogen. These waste products are transported to the kidneys for elimination by the blood. In cases of abnormal kidney function, the level of this blood urea nitrogen (BUN) is elevated, indicating abnormal kidney function. An elevated BUN can also result from dehydration.

blood vessels
The body's system for blood transport consisting of vessels called arteries and veins that carry blood throughout the body.

biofeedback
A technique used to measure or electronically monitor bodily functions that are usually not under our conscious control. Through biofeedback, a person learns to manipulate involuntary bodily functions such as heart rate and brain function to improve their health.

biomedicine
Modern medicine practiced in the Western countries of the world and also called *Western medicine* with components of chemical, biological, physical, psychosocial, and genetic aspects. The word biomedicine is used interchangeably with Western medicine in this book. This is the medical practice that is widely used in hospitals and urgent care and emergency medical centers.

Body Mass Index / BMI
The measurement of body fat for men and women based on height and weight.

bronchodilators
These are substances, used in Western medicine, that have the capacity to dilate the breathing passages in the lungs. These medications are normally prescribed to patients with asthma or COPD (Chronic Obstructive Pulmonary Disorder), a chronic, inflammatory lung disease that obstructs airflow from the lungs.

C

cancer
Diseases that are characterized by uncontrolled proliferation (or replication) of abnormal or disease-ridden cells from any part of the body.

carcinoma
A carcinoma is a growth or tumor that arises from cells that line the inside or outside of any organ. For example, if the cells from the lining of the colon are involved in the cancer then it is called carcinoma of the colon.

chemotherapy
Medications made of special chemicals used to destroy cancer cells.

Chiropractic
A complementary medical system that diagnoses misalignments of joints and provides adjustment to correct these misalignments. These adjustments invigorate and enhance health of the nervous system.

cilia
Tiny hair-like structures in our nasal passages and sinuses. These structures help move mucus either backward toward the throat to be swallowed or toward the front of the nose to be expelled.

constitutional make-up
The term constitutional make-up is used in Homeopathic medicine and is similar to the three-energy axis of Ayurveda and the Yin and Yang of Acupuncture. Homeopathy explains the development of disease and our response to disease based on three types of constitutional make-up categories. This constitutional make-up is also called *miasma*. The three constitutional make-up categories, as described by Samuel Hahnemann—who is considered by many to be the father of Homeopathy—are Psora, Sycosis, and Syphilis. A fourth miasma has since been added called Tubercular miasma.

coronary artery disease
Disease of the blood vessels that supply the heart, called coronary arteries. This disease is most frequently caused by deposits of cholesterol plaques in the coronary arteries that result in narrowing of those arteries.

coronary angiography
The injection of dye into the blood vessels of the heart (the blood vessels that supply the heart...called coronary arteries) followed by an X-ray of the heart area to determine if there are blockages of those blood vessels. This procedure is done when a person suffers a heart attack or has chest pain and is performed to diagnose a condition called *coronary artery disease*.

cortisol
A hormone produced by the adrenal glands in our body. Cortisol is considered to be a stress hormone as its levels tend to increase when a person is under stress.

creatinine
A compound that is formed in muscles, and is a waste product of living muscle cells. It is measured in the blood and is an indicator of kidney function.

CT scan or CAT scan
Known as computed automated tomography (CAT), this diagnostic tool uses X-ray beams to generate a series of cross-sectional, multi-angle images of an internal organ to provide a detailed image for assessment and diagnostic purposes. It provides more information than an X-ray alone.

cystic fibrosis
A serious, life-threatening disease that causes abnormal production of sweat and mucus. This excess production of mucus affects the lungs and can result in lung failure. Diagnosis of this condition occurs during infancy.

D

diabetes
A name given to a disease that is characterized by the abnormal handling of glucose in the body. There are two main types of diabetes: Type I and Type II.

diaphragm
The diaphragm is a respiratory muscle actually comprised of two muscles (right and left) that sit at the bottom of the chest cavity (between the abdomen and chest). These muscles, as they contract and relax, cause the lungs to expand and collapse as we breathe.

diuretic
A medication that is commonly known as a "water pill" taken to increases urine production and excretion. Diuretics are usually prescribed for patients with heart failure or kidney failure. These must be used with caution and with medical supervision.

E

emphysema
A condition in which the lungs are unable to completely expel the air that is inhaled, resulting in air being trapped in the lungs. The most common cause is smoking and other common cause is asthma. This condition is also called COPD, or Chronic Obstructive Pulmonary Disorder, a chronic, inflammatory lung disease that obstructs airflow from the lungs.

essential hypertension
A high blood pressure condition, typically diagnosed in older patients, when no other cause can be identified.

F

fibrosis
Excess formation of fibrous, connective tissue as a means of reparative body functions, damage, or autoimmune processes. A scar in or on our body consists of a lot of fibrous tissue.

G

gastric bypass surgery
Gastric bypass surgery is also called bariatric surgery. It is a surgical procedure involving two steps. The first step is to decrease the size of the stomach by dividing it into a small pouch and a larger pouch. The small pouch is where food will be taken in, with the goal of eating less to experience a "full stomach." The second step is to connect the small intestine to the small pouch (bypassing the larger pouch) so that food from the small pouch can then be digested and absorbed.

Glycemic Index
The Glycemic Index is a numerical Index that ranks carbohydrates based on their rate of glycemic response (i.e. their conversion to glucose within the human body). The Index uses a scale of 0 to 100, with higher values given to foods that cause the most rapid rise in blood sugar. High-glycemic foods raise blood glucose levels quickly and low-glycemic foods are those foods that help stabilize blood glucose levels.

H

heart
A muscular organ that functions as a pump and pumps clean and oxygenated blood into the arteries of the body and receives blood carrying waste products, via the veins. (Also see: **arteries** and **veins**).

Herbologist
A specialist in the field of herbal plants and in the study of herbs.

Homeopathy
Homeopathic medicine is a philosophy based on the idea that the body has the inherent ability to heal itself. It originated in the 1700s and Samuel Hahnemann, a prominent physician in Europe at the time, is considered to be the father of Homeopathy. Hahnemann believed that factors that cause symptoms serve as the remedy when those same factors—or substances—are administered to the patient in very small doses. That is why the philosophy of Homeopathy is often described as "like cures like." This philosophy is somewhat similar to the modern principle behind inoculation and vaccination therapies.

Homeopathic remedies
Oral medicines dispensed by Homeopathic practitioners. These remedies have been regulated in the United States since 1938 and are generally considered safe.

hypertension
High blood pressure. Different guidelines offer different ranges for high blood pressure, but the most commonly and currently practiced measure is higher than 140/90 mm Hg.

I

interstitial lung diseases
A condition in which the lungs have more scar tissue than normal tissue as a result of pollutants or an association with other chronic diseases known as *connective tissue diseases.*

iridology
A discipline, also called "iris analysis," that analyses the iris portion of your eye to diagnose inherent weaknesses in your body. Once identification is made, a practitioner is able to better direct therapeutic interventions to treat those imbalances.

ischemic stroke
A stroke resulting from blockage of an artery that carries blood to the brain. The blockage can either be due to a blood clot, air bubbles, or cholesterol plaques. The most common cause of strokes is blood vessels becoming blocked by cholesterol plaque or a blood clot. The other type of stroke is called *hemorrhagic stroke,* in which a stroke results from a ruptured blood vessel that triggers bleeding inside the brain.

J

jing
This energy is also called *original energy,* and in Chinese it is called *Yuan Qi.* Original energy encompasses the entire energy that a person is born with.

K

Kapha
The ancient Indian Ayurvedic medical system believes that we are made up of five elements (air, water, earth, water and ether). These elements combine to make up three predominant energy axes in us called Vata (air and ether), Pitta (water and fire) and Kapha (water and earth). Therefore in Ayurvedic medical system fundamental abnormalities of health and ill health is explained related to these three energy axis called Vata, Pitta, and Kapha. Kapha is the governor of all structures and lubrication in our body. It is said to govern formation of all the tissues in our body; blood, fat, fluids, marrow, muscles, bone, and reproductive tissues.

kidneys
A pair of organs that filters the blood, dispose of waste, balances fluid levels and minerals in our body via the production of urine. These organs are located in the abdomen.

L

leukemia
Originates in the tissue that produces blood cells and is categorized within blood cancers. These cancers affect the bone marrow, which is the site of blood production.

liver
An organ that is like a factory and acts as a detoxification system, as well as metabolizes, stores, and converts different substances, hormones, vitamins, and blood cells.

liposuction
A procedure considered cosmetic surgery where unwanted fat tissue is surgically removed from any part of the body.

lungs
These are paired organs that are responsible for the exchange of air between the environment and our blood. Air, rich with oxygen, enters through the nose and into the lungs and the blood in the lungs when we breathe in. Likewise, air carrying carbon dioxide enters the lungs from the blood vessels and is eliminated through the nose when we breathe out.

lymphoma
A disease that originates in the lymphatic system. Lymphoma is part of the immune system and affects lymph nodes and certain parts of the intestines and, sometimes, the brain.

M

meditation
A calming and restorative practice to unite your conscious being with your unconscious being. It is a process of training your mind to acknowledge the contents of your mind without identifying with those contents.

metastasis
Metastasis is a medical term used to denote the spread of a cancer from its origin point to other areas of the body. When cancer spreads, it is said to have *metastasized*.

miasma
See **constitutional make-up**.

morbid obesity
An high amount of body fat, more than the body requires. This condition is usually diagnosed by calculating a person's Body Mass Index or BMI. A BMI of more than 40 denotes obesity.

myeloma
This type of blood cancer originates in the plasma cells of the bone marrow. Plasma cells are the cells that produce antibodies, which are the body's response in fighting infections.

N

Neti pot™
A Neti Pot™ is a specially designed container used to deliver water or any other special solution to clean nasal passages of excess mucus, debris, and pollen. It is also used to irrigate the sinus passages for the same purpose.

O

obesity
An increased amount of body fat, more than the body requires. Usually diagnosed by calculating what is called Body Mass Index or BMI. A BMI of 30 to 39 denotes obesity.

osteopathy
A type of non-invasive medical practice that focuses on healing through stretching, movement, manipulation, and strengthening of the joints and muscles.

P

palliative
Palliative care in medicine refers to eliminating the pain and stress of serious illness without treating the underlying disease itself. It makes the process of dealing with very serious illness or end of life less painful.

personality
Personality is an individual's characteristic pattern of behavior driven by their deeper thought and emotions. It is expressed by individuals in their unique way of thinking, feeling, or behaving.

Pitta
The ancient Indian Ayurvedic medical system believes that we are made up of five elements (air, water, earth, water and ether). These elements combine to make up three predominant energy axes in us called Vata (air and ether), Pitta (water and fire) and Kapha (water and earth). Therefore in Ayurvedic medical system fundamental abnormalities of health and ill health is explained related to these three energy axis called Vata, Pitta, and Kapha. Pitta is said to govern metabolism and transformation in the body, including heat. Therefore, functions like digesting food, processing sensory perceptions, and discriminating between right and wrong are all related to Pitta.

Prana
Prana is an Indian Ayurvedic term denoting the total sum of energy of the universe, and is similar to Qi in Traditional Chinese medicine. Prana can also be used to mean the entire energy of a person, since a person is considered to be a part of the universe.

Pranayama
A breathing exercise that is part of Yoga practice. There are several types of breathing exercises that are part of Pranayama in which a student can train his or her breathing in a controlled and systematic fashion.

prehypertension
A precursor to high blood pressure: 120/80 mm Hg –139/89 mm Hg.

Psoric miasma
One of the three types of constitutional make-up that underlie Homeopathic medical principles. The other two miasma are Sycosis and Syphillis. (Also see **Homeopathy** and **constitutional make-up**.)

pulmonary hypertension
A condition in which the pressure in the lungs is too high, which can result in too much stress on the heart and lead to heart failure.

Q

Qi
Qi is a Chinese term, pronounced *Chi,*...that means energy. It is used to denote energy under different circumstances. For example, Universal Qi means the sum total of the entire energy of the universe. When it relates to a person, it can mean the entire energy of that person. In Acupuncture, when describing energy pertaining to organ systems, it can be called the heart Qi, kidney Qi, lung Qi, etc.

R

radiation
Waves of high energy which can be used as a means to either shrink cancer cells or kill them. Radiation can also be used to create an X-ray image of organs to detect abnormalities.

S

sarcoma
This condition originates in the supportive tissue of the body, also called connective tissue... bone, muscle, cartilage, etc.

secondary hypertension
High blood pressure that is caused by another pathological dysfunction. For example: kidney dysfunction.

sensorium
The term sensorium is used to denote all of our collective sensory faculties—the part of the mind or brain concerned with the reception and interpretation of all sensory stimuli. For example, when one's sensorium is diminished, that person's ability to touch, smell, hear, see, and taste are all abnormally decreased.

scleroderma
A condition that affects the skin and makes it become tough and less elastic. It develops when our body "attacks itself," a process called *autoimmune disease*. This is a disease that affects many organ systems including lungs, when the lungs can develop more scar tissue than normal tissue.

stroke
A stroke is a brain attack. Similar to a heart attack, a person suffers a stroke when the blood supply to the brain is abruptly cut off. (Also see **ischemic stroke**).

T

Tai Chi
A discipline that involves slow, choreographed movements coordinated with breathing and mindfulness. It is considered to be meditation in movement. It originated as a form of martial arts and has now evolved as a means of alleviating stress and promoting overall wellness.

thrombectomy
Removal of a blood clot through surgical procedures. These surgical procedures can be performed with catheters inserted through the blood vessels or by open surgical methods.

tumor
Also called a *mass*, a tumor is an abnormal proliferation of cells that results in a growth, or an excess of tissue. A tumor can develop from abnormal proliferation of either normal cells (called *benign tumor*) or abnormal cells (called *cancer*).

V

Vata
The ancient Indian Ayurvedic medical system believes that we are made up of five elements (air, water, earth, fire and ether). These elements combine to make up three predominant energy axes in us called Vata (air and ether), Pitta (water and fire) and Kapha (water and earth). Therefore in Ayurvedic medical system fundamental abnormalities of health and ill health is explained related to these three energy axis called Vata, Pitta and Kapha. The Vata is said to govern the movement of body and mind. Therefore, it is said to control flow of blood, elimination of waste products, and even the constant movement of our thought processes. Since it controls movement, it is the leader of the three-energy axes—as Pitta and Kapha cannot move without Vata.

veins
Blood vessel pathways that take the de-oxygenated blood from the cells in the body back to the heart

W

white coat syndrome
A physical response that is related to the anxiety and stress of being at a doctor's office in which patients tend to exhibit higher blood pressure levels than normal.

Y

Yin / Yang
A Chinese philosophy that has its origins in duality and the balance of opposites. For example, female is Yin and male is Yang, the sun is Yang and the moon is Yin, outside is Yang and inside is Yin... and day is Yang and night is Yin.

Yoga
An ancient Indian system that combines physical, mental, and spiritual practices as a lifestyle program. The entire yoga system has eight limbs. One of the limbs is physical exercise, called *Hatha Yoga*, which entails a series of breathing and body positions to unite the mind, body, and spirit.

Z

Zheng Qi
One of the six types of Qi (energy) that are described in the traditional Chinese medicine. The Zheng Qi is concerned with protecting ourselves from external pathogens. This type of Qi is described when contrasting the strength of the pathogen with the strength of our own vital energy. In this circumstance, the portion of vital energy that opposes and fights the strength of the external pathogen is called the Zheng Qi.

End Notes and Citations

Chapter One: Heart

1. Murphy SL, Xu JQ, Kochanek KD. Deaths: Final data for 2010. *Natl Vital Stat Rep.* 2013;61(4)

2. Go AS, Mozaffarian D, Roger VL, Benjamin EJ, Berry JD, Blaha MJ, et al. Heart disease and stroke statistics—2014 update: a report from the American Heart Association. *Circulation.* 2014 ;128.

3. Heart and Stroke Foundation. Canada. Statistics Canada – 2012

4. British Heart Foundation. Coronary Heart Disease Statistics – 2012

5. Australian Bureau of Statistics National Health Survey Report – 2014

6. From Guanzi, a Daoist classic, prior to 200 B.C.

7. Li Ting. A Primer of Medicine (Yixue Rumen), 1575.

8. Li Yuheng. Unfolding the Mat with Enlightening Words (Tuipeng Wuyu) Ming dynasty, 1570.

9. Ilan S. Wittstein, M.D., David R. Thiemann, M.D., Joao A.C. Lima, M.D., Kenneth L. Baughman, M.D., Steven P. Schulman, M.D., Gary Gerstenblith, M.D., Katherine C. Wu, M.D., Jeffrey J. Rade, M.D., Trinity J. Bivalacqua, M.D., Ph.D., and Hunter C. Champion, M.D., Ph.D. Neurohumoral Features of Myocardial Stunning Due to Sudden Emotional Stress. N Engl J Med 2005; 352:539-48.

10. The Foundations of Chinese Medicine. Giovanni Marciocia 2005. Churchill Livingstone.

11. Wujastyk D. *The Roots of Ayurveda*. New Delhi. Penguin Books. 1998.

Chapter Two: Liver

1. http://www.liverfoundation.org/patients/organdonor/about/

2. The OPTN Web site offers a wealth of information about transplantation (http://optn.transplant.hrsa.gov).

3. S Kechagias, Å Ernersson, O Dahlqvist, P Lundberg, T Lindström, F H Nystrom, for the Fast Food Study Group. Fast-food-based hyper-alimentation can induce rapid and profound elevation of serum alanine aminotransferase in healthy subjects. *Gut* 2008;**57**:5 649-654 Published Online First: 14 February 2008 doi:10.1136/gut.2007.

Chapter Three: High Blood Pressure | Hypertension

1. Mozzafarian D, Benjamin EJ, Go AS, et al. Heart Disease and Stroke Statistics – 2015 Update: a report from the American Heart Association. *Circulation*. 2015; e29-322.

2. Nwankwo T, Yoon SS, Burt V, Gu Q. Hypertension among adults in the US: National Health and Nutrition Examination Survey, 2011-2012. NCHS Data Brief, No. 133. Hyattsville, MD: National Center for Health Statistics, Centers for Disease Control and Prevention, U.S. Dept of Health and Human Services, 2013.

3. Sanz J, García-Vera MP, Espinosa R, Fortún M, Magán I, Segura J. Psychological factors associated with poor hypertension control: differences in personality and stress between patients with controlled and uncontrolled hypertension. *Psychol Rep*. 2010 Dec; 107(3):923-38.

4. Eman M. Alissa and Gordon A. Ferns, "Heavy Metal Poisoning and Cardiovascular Disease," Journal of Toxicology, vol. 2011, Article ID 870125, 21 pages, 2011.

5. Groppelli A, Giorgi DM, Omboni S, Parati G, Mancia G. Persistent blood pressure increase induced by heavy smoking. J Hypertens. 1992;10(5):495.

6. Bowman TS, Gaziano JM, Buring JE, Sesso HD. A prospective study of cigarette smoking and risk of incident hypertension in women. J Am Coll Cardiol. 2007; 50(21):2085.

7. Jatoi NA, Jerrard-Dunne P, Feely J, Mahmud A. Impact of smoking and smoking cessation on arterial stiffness and aortic wave reflection in hypertension. Hypertension. 2007; 49(5):981.

8. Robert D Brook, Lawrence J Appel, Melvyn Rubenfire, Gbenga Ogedegbe et al. Beyond Medications and diet: alternative Approach to Lowering blood Pressure: A Scientific Statement From the American Heart ssociation. *Hypertension.* 2013; 61:1360-1383; originally published online April 22, 2013.

9. Nahida Tabassum and Feroz Ahmad. Role of natural herbs in the treatment of hypertension. Pharmacogn Rev. 2011 Jan-Jun; 5(9): 30–40.

Chapter Four: Stroke

1. World Health Organization. http://www.who.int/mediacentre/factsheets/fs310/en/index3.html

2. CDC, NCHS. Underlying Cause of Death 1999-2013 on CDC WONDER Online Database, released 2015. Data are from the Multiple Cause of Death Files, 1999-2013, as compiled from data provided by the 57 vital statistics jurisdictions through the Vital Statistics Cooperative Program.

3. American Stroke Association. http://www.strokeassociation.org/STROKEORG/AboutStroke/Impact-of-Stroke-Stroke-statistics_UCM_310728_Article.jsp

4. Stroke Association, UK. https://www.stroke.org.uk/sites/default/files/stroke_statistics_2015.pdf

5. Stroke and Heart Foundation, Canada. http://www.heartandstroke.com/site/c.ikIQLcMWJtE/b.3483991/k.34A8/Statistics.htm

6. Jokela, M., Pulkki-Råback, L., Elovainio, M., & Kivimäki, M. (2014). Personality traits as risk factors for stroke and coronary heart disease mortality: pooled analysis of three cohort studies. *Journal of behavioral medicine, 37*(5), 881-889.

7. Russ Erickson, MD. American Academy of Medical Acupuncture. Acupuncture in Stroke Treatment. http://www.medicalacupuncture.org/ForPatients/ArticlesByPhysiciansAboutAcupuncture/AcupunctureinStrokeTreatment.aspx

Chapter Five: Kidney

1. U.S. Renal Data System, USRDS 2014 Annual Data Report: Atlas of End-Stage Renal Disease in the United States, National Institutes of Health, National Institute of Diabetes and Digestive and Kidney Diseases, Bethesda, MD, 2014.

2. https://www.kidney.org/news/newsroom/factsheets/FastFacts

3. http://www.cdc.gov/bloodpressure/

4. Coresh et al. JAMA. 2007. 298: 2038-2047.

5. http://www.usrds.org/2014 Annual Report

6. http://optn.transplant.hrsa.gov/data/ as of October 28, 2014

7. Manish V. Patel, S.N. Gipta and Nimesh G. Patel. Effects of Ayurvedic treatment on 100 patients of chronic renal failure (other than diabetic nephropathy). *Ayu* 2011 Oct-Dec; 32(4): 483-486

8. Y. Sun; T. J. Gan; J. W. Dubose; A. S. Habib. Acupuncture and Related Techniques for Postoperative pain: a Systematic Review of Randomized Controlled Trials. Br J Anaesth. 2008;101(2):151-160

9. https://www.kidney.org/atoz/content/herbalsupp

Chapter Six: Obesity / Diabetes

1. WHO fact sheet, January 2015 http://www.who.int/mediacentre/factsheets/fs311/en/

2. American Diabetes Association. http://www.diabetes.org/diabetes-basics/statistics/

3. American Medical Association (AMA) 2013 annual meeting. http://www.ama-assn.org/ama/pub/news/news/2013/2013-06-18-new-ama-policies-annual-meeting.page

4. American Heart Association (AHA). http://www.heart.org/HEARTORG/Conditions/Diabetes/UnderstandYourRiskforDiabetes/Understand-Your-Risk-for-Diabetes_UCM_002034_Article.jsp

5. National Institute of Diabetes and Digestive and Kidney Diseases. http://www. niddk.nih.gov/health-information/health-topics/diagnostic-tests/a1c-test- diabetes/Pages/index.aspx

6. Yoko Yokoyama, Neal D. Barnard, Susan M. Levin, Mitsuhiro Watanabe. Vegetarian diets and glycemic control in diabetes: a systematic review and meta-analysis. Cardiovasc Diagn Ther 2014; 4(5):373-382

7. Gloria Y. Yeh, Ted J. Kaptchuk, David M. Eisenberg, Russel S. Phillips. Systematic Review of Herbs and Dietary Supplements for Glycemic control in diabetes. Diabetes Care 2003; 26:1277-1294

Chapter Seven: Cancer

1. National Cancer Institute

2. The World Health Organization

3. Eysenck, H. J. (1981). Personality and cancer: Some comments on a paper by H. Berndt. *Archiv fuer Greschwuelstforschung*, 51, 442-443.

4. Eysenck, H. J. (1983). Stress, disease and personality: 'the inoculation effect'. In C.L. Coper (Ed). *Stress Research* (pp. 121-146). New York: Wiley.

5. Eysenck, H. J. (1985). Personality, cancer and cardiovascular disease: A causal analysis. *Personality and individual differences*, 9, 453-464.

6. Kissen DM, Eysenck HJ. Personality in male lung cancer patients. J Psychosom Res 1962; 6:123–7.

7. Coppen A, Metcalfe M. Cancer and extraversion. BMJ 1963; 2:18–9.

8. Morris T, Greer S, Pettingale KW, Watson M. Patterns of expressing anger and their psychological correlates in women with breast cancer. J Psychosom Res 1981; 25:111–7.

9. Kissen DM, Brown RI, Kissen M. A further report on personality and psychosocial factors in lung cancer. Ann N Y Acad Sci 1969; 164:535–45.

10. Grossarth-Maticek, R., Eysenck, H. J., & Vetter, H. (1988). Personality type, smoking habit and their interaction as predictors of cancer and coronary heart disease. *Personality and individual differences*, 9, 479-495.

11. Eysenck, H. J. Cancer, personality and stress: prediction and prevention. *Adv. Behav. Res. Ther.* Vol. 16, pp 167-215. 1994.

12. http://www.cancer.gov/about-cancer/treatment/side-effects/appetite-loss/nutrition-pdq

Chapter Eight: Lungs

1. National Heart, Lung and Blood Institute. Prevalence of Common Cardiovascular and Lung Diseases, U.S., 2007. http://www.nhlbi.nih.gov/about/documents/factbook/2012/chapter4#4_5

2. European Lung *White Book.* http://www.erswhitebook.org/chapters/the-burden-of-lung-disease/

3. WHO International Publication. Risk Factors for Chronic Respiratory Distress. http://www.who.int/gard/publications/Risk%20factors.pdf

4. Hynninen KM, Breitve MH, Wiborg AB, et al. Psychological charasteristics of patients with chronic obstructive pulmonary disease: a review. J Psychosom Res 2005; 59:429-43

5. Kubzansky LD, Wright RJ, Cohen S et al. Breathing easy: a prospective study of optimism and pulmonary function in the normative aging study. Ann Behav Med 2002; 24:345-53.

6. Hasan Kahraman, Fatma Ozlem Orhan, Mustafa Haki Sucalkli et al. Treatment and character profiles of male COPD patients. J Thorac Dis 2013; 5(4):406-413.

7. Lutz Goetzmann, Eberhard Scheuer, Rahel Naef et al. Personality, illness perceptions, and lung function (FEV1) in 50 patients after lung transplantation. GMS Psychosoc Med. 2005;2:Doc06. Article available at http://www..egms.de/en/p5m/2005-2/p5m000015.5html

8. Suzuki M, Namura K, Ohno Y, et al. The effect of acupuncture in the treatment of chronic obstructive pulmonary disease. *JAltern Complement Med.* 2008;14:1097-1105

9. Suzuki M, Muro S, Ando Y, et al. A randomized, placebo-controlled trial of acupuncture in patients with chronic obstructive pulmonary disease (COPD): the COPD-acupuncture trial (CAT). *Arch Intern Med.* 2012; 172:878-886.

10. Yanhua Wang, Rong Gao, Bo Wei, Xiaoyu Chai, et al. Diallyl disulfide inhibits proliferation and transdifferentiation of lung fibroblasts through induction of cyclooxygenase and synthesis of prostaglandin E2. Molecular and Cellular Biochemistry. 2014; 393(1):77-87

11. Fulambarker A, Farooki B, Kheir, F Copur AS , Srinivasan L, Schultz S. Effect of yoga in chronic obstructive pulmonary disease. Am J Ther. 2012 Mar; 19(2):96-100

Notes

Healthy Human

Mission

*Healthy Human is dedicated to providing education
to harmonize Eastern and Western medicine with the
power of "you" to promote health and well-being*

Philosophy

A Human is a complete being. Medicine is incomplete.
The secret of achieving optimal human health is
through combining all medicines with the
infinite power of an individual.

Health Education
Healthy Human
www.healthyhuman.us

Treatment Center
Cura Personalis
www.curapersonalis.us

Research and Education Non-Profit Organization
American Academy of Global Medicines
www.aagm.us

*"Health of a person is not defined by the presence or
absence of disease. It is rather defined by the ability of
any given individual to get back to the balanced and
optimal level from derangement and maintain that
balance at all levels that constitutes a human being."*

— Radha Gopalan MD, FACC, DABMA

Notes

Cura Personalis
~care of the whole person~

Complementary Medicine
Ultimate Anti-Aging and Regenerative Wellness

An exclusive practice that focuses on combining
Eastern and Western philosophies
with complementary medicine,
and enhancement of You…

- **Lifestyle Enhancement** – antioxidant therapy, anti-aging techniques, internal purification, IV vitamins and nutrients, heavy metal detoxification, custom nutrition, hormone and genetic optimization, stress management, sleep optimization, energy enrichment, brain health.

- **Symptom/Disease Treatment** – We work to find the root cause of the problem through advanced diagnostic testing and innovative, evidence-based treatments.

- **Custom therapies** – IV nutrient infusions, IV chelation, Bio-Identical hormones, Custom compounded medications and vitamins.

- **Energy Medicine** – Medical Acupuncture, Iris Analysis, Massage Therapy

Nicole Srednicki, FNP-C, MSN, ABAAHP
Georgetown University, Magnum Cum Laude, board certified Family Nurse Practitioner. Also, board certified from the American Academy of Anti-Aging and Regenerative Medicine.

WWW.CURAPERSONALIS.US

Curapersonalis25@gmail.com
Scottsdale, Arizona and New York City
480-699-4242

Notes

New Books from Dr. Gopalan

FALL 2016

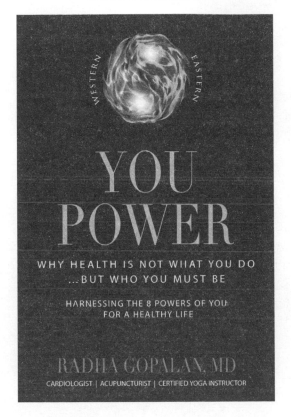

SPRING 2017

The Illusion of Health

Notes